Money Games

Money Games

*The Inside Story of How
American Dealmakers Saved
Korea's Most Iconic Bank*

Weijian Shan

WILEY

Published by John Wiley & Sons, Inc., Hoboken, New Jersey.

Published simultaneously in Canada.

For general information on our other products and services or for technical support, please
contact our Customer Care Department within the United States at (800) 762–2974,
outside the United States at (317) 572–3993, or fax (317) 572–4002.

Wiley publishes in a variety of print and electronic formats and by print-on-demand.
Some material included with standard print versions of this book may not be included in
e-books or in print-on-demand. If this book refers to media such as a CD or DVD that
is not included in the version you purchased, you may download this material at http://
booksupport.wiley.com. For more information about Wiley products, visit www.wiley.com.

Library of Congress Cataloging-in-Publication Data:

Names: Shan, Weijian, 1953- author.
Title: Money games : the inside story of how American dealmakers saved
    Korea's most iconic bank / Weijian Shan.
Description: Hoboken, New Jersey : Wiley, [2021] | Includes index.
Identifiers: LCCN 2020026499 (print) | LCCN 2020026500 (ebook) | ISBN
    9781119736981 (cloth) | ISBN 9781119737001 (adobe pdf) | ISBN
    9781119736998 (epub)
Subjects: LCSH: Cheil Ŭnhaeng. | Bank mergers—Korea (South) | Financial
    crises—Asia.
Classification: LCC HG1722 .S588 2021 (print) | LCC HG1722 (ebook) | DDC
    332.1095195—dc23
LC record available at https://lccn.loc.gov/2020026499
LC ebook record available at https://lccn.loc.gov/2020026500

Cover Design: Wiley
Cover Image: © People Images/Getty Images

Printed in the United States of America.

SKY10020936_090420

To all our limited partners

Contents

Foreword

In 1998, during the Asian Financial Crisis, the central banks in many Asian countries melted down and could not protect their nations' currencies or their commercial banks, and thus needed bailouts from the International Monetary Fund (IMF). As a condition of these bailouts, the IMF often required the governments of recipient countries to sell off assets, particularly failed commercial banks. Korea was no exception. In fact, it was the poster child for this paradigm. Among the assets the Korean government attempted to sell was Korea First Bank (KFB). KFB had historically been the largest commercial bank in Korea, but by this time had shrunk to the fourth largest. Still, under the right ownership and management, KFB could be a very profitable asset. Accordingly, Korean government officials and their investment bankers went around the world in the hope of finding a strategic investor to turn around KFB. They didn't have much luck. Part of the problem was that the few Western financial institutions interested in KFB wanted to buy the whole bank, and only after a bailout had left all the bad loans with the Korean government. This would leave the "good" bank for the foreign investors. The Koreans, however, were keen to keep a significant ownership stake so that if the bank was indeed turned around, the Korean government would have something to show for all the financial support it had given KFB by keeping the bad loans. Into this fray came Weijian Shan and his team at Newbridge Capital, the Asian affiliate of our private equity firm TPG. TPG had pioneered the good bank/bad bank model in the United States some years earlier and we thought that this model could work for the Korean government and the failed banks. *Money Games* is the story of a major takeover: the origin of the deal, the incredibly difficult negotiation between the Newbridge team and the Korean government, and the subsequent transformation of the most iconic bank in Korea, the first to be fully controlled by a foreign investor. The two sides negotiated for more than a year through a series of understandings and misunderstandings, which ultimately led to the injection of needed capital by Newbridge in KFB for a majority stake with full control of the bank. It was through an arduous process that Newbridge finally took over control of KFB. Shan, our teammates, and I held secret meetings outside of Korea because we worried our phones might be tapped. (Mr. Kim Chee was the nickname I was supposedly given by the Korean negotiating team after they had heard me complaining about kimchi, the spicy Korean cabbage, on a tapped phone.) Strong personalities and divergent cultures clashed, often resulting in colorful manifestations of different negotiating styles and tactics.

It turns out that while negotiating sessions were grinding on, Shan was taking notes and writing detailed memos. These give *Money Games* a strong backbone, making it a truly riveting read. Not only does it shed much light on the Asian Financial Crisis of 1998, but it also serves as an interesting primer for anyone who is curious about how private equity works and how private equity investors make deals and create value. The bank was ultimately restructured by Newbridge, which brought in new management, and returned to profitability, particularly in the housing mortgage business, which KFB had more or less invented for Korea. Shan's account of this fascinating story sets forth some lessons for us all, whether we are private equity veterans or curious outsiders hoping to better understand this secretive world. I hope you enjoy the journey.

—David Bonderman
Chairman and Founding Partner, TPG
April 9, 2020

Acknowledgments

This book is the inside story of how Newbridge Capital, a U.S.-based private equity firm, acquired and turned around Korea's most iconic bank. Almost everyone in high- and middle-income countries is a beneficiary of private equity investing. The sovereign wealth funds that manage money on behalf of their countries' citizens; the pension funds that provide for government and corporate employees; the endowments that fund schools and universities; not to mention the banks, insurers, and other financial institutions that look after the savings of millions of retail clients: All are active investors in private equity for the benefit of their constituencies. I am grateful to all our investors who have entrusted us with their money over the years, first at Newbridge Capital, then at TPG, and now at PAG.

Almost every private equity deal is accomplished by the coordinated efforts of a large team, involving the dealmakers who source and underwrite the deal; the operational specialists who monitor the company's performance and work closely with its management; the management team itself; and a myriad of financial, legal, accounting, and consulting advisors. Some of these individuals appear in this book, but many do not, and those who deserve recognition are too numerous to name. I thank all my colleagues who worked on the Korea First Bank transaction in their different capacities. This deal would not have been successful without their collective effort. Robert A. Cohen served as CEO of KFB (2001–2005). I thank him for leading the rebuilding of the bank and for his memoir *Turning Around a Bank in Korea* (2008), which fills some information gaps in chapter 15 of this book.

David Bonderman, founder and chairman of TPG, has been my mentor and inspiration ever since I began my investment career more than 20 years ago. I owe him a great debt of gratitude for guiding me professionally and for penning the foreword for this book.

Mark Clifford, Jill Baker, Tim Morrison, and Christina Verigan helped edit my manuscript at different stages of the writing process. I am thankful to them for their painstaking and meticulous work.

I thank Bill Falloon, executive director at Wiley, for his support and help with the publication of this book as well as my first book, *Out of the Gobi: My Story of China and America* (2019).

Rachel Kwok provided the best secretarial support any author could hope for, allowing me to concentrate on writing.

In the years that I was working on the Korea First Bank transaction, and again as I was writing this book, my wife, Bin Shi Shan, our son, Bo Shan, and our daughter, LeeAnn Shan, often had to endure a distracted and sometimes absent husband and father. I owe them greatly for all I have been able to accomplish, including the publication of this book.

Weijian Shan
June 10, 2020
Hong Kong

Author's Note

It can be difficult to decide how to write Korean names in English. Typically, Korean family names come first, followed by given names (as in President Park Chung-hee or President Kim Dae-jung). When dealing with foreigners, however, many Koreans reverse the order of their family and given names to follow Western convention.

Koreans may also abbreviate given names to make them easier for foreigners to remember or pronounce. For example, some people occasionally refer to President Kim Dae-jung as DJ Kim (or simply DJ) when speaking to foreigners. Some people, especially those who have lived in Western countries, adopt Western first names, which they place before their surnames (e.g., David Kim, Steve Choe, or Peter Jeong).

In this book, for the convenience of the reader, I consistently use the Western way to write Korean names, placing the given name first. For example, President Park Chung-hee becomes President Chung-hee Park and President Kim Dae-jung becomes President Dae-jung Kim or DJ Kim. There are exceptions, however; in cases where I quote from archived memos and letters, the original reference, which may follow Korean convention, remains intact.

South Korea's currency is the *won*, which is sometimes presented as *KRW* (Korean won). During the period of this book, 1997 to 2004, the won's exchange rate against the U.S. dollar fluctuated widely. In December 1996, the average won–dollar exchange rate was 842, meaning it took 842 won to buy one U.S. dollar. By February 1998 the won's value had dropped 48 percent. By December 1998 the won had regained some of its value, reaching 1,213 won per dollar. For the purposes of simplicity, I use the exchange rate at the particular moment in the story to approximate the dollar equivalent.

All dollar amounts represent U.S. dollars, unless otherwise indicated.

Preface

Big Money Legends

It was a brisk autumn day in 1900, and Andrew Carnegie, 66 years old, was enjoying winning a game of golf against 39-year-old Charles M. Schwab, the president of Carnegie Steel Company. Carnegie was, at that point, one of America's most prominent businessmen. Carnegie Steel, the company he had founded, had revolutionized industrial steel production and had become the largest steel company in the world. Unbeknownst to Carnegie, Schwab had been working on a plan with John Pierpont Morgan, America's most powerful financier. Schwab's mission was to talk Carnegie into selling his company to Morgan. It was widely known that winning a game of golf always eased the Scottish-born industrialist's temperament—and so Schwab played to lose. After the game, Schwab raised the idea with Carnegie, who seemed receptive.

The next day, Carnegie handed Schwab a piece of paper scrawled with numbers adding up to $480 million, a colossal amount in 1900 (approximately $14.5 billion in U.S. dollars today). It was the price

Carnegie was willing to accept for the sale of Carnegie Steel. Schwab took the paper to Morgan.

Morgan glanced at the figures and said, simply, "I accept it."

On a handshake, Morgan acquired Carnegie Steel for $480 million. Around the same time, Morgan consolidated several other steel companies to create U.S. Steel in March 1901. Capitalized at $1.4 billion ($42 billion in 2019 dollars), it was the first billion-dollar corporation in the world.

Carnegie's cut from the sale of his steel company was about $225 million ($6.7 billion in 2019 dollars). The deal, as Morgan observed wryly while congratulating him, made Carnegie the richest man in the world.

For generations, financiers, historians, and the general public have loved telling this tidy little story, amazed at how easy such big-money games seemed to be for the rich and powerful. Such games—the private buying and selling of companies and institutions—are now called *private equity*, and Morgan was probably the first notable private equity deal-maker in history, many decades before the practice became an industry and acquired its own name.

But the real story is unlikely to be so simple.

Where, for example, did Morgan get the money to finance the deal? The largest source, providing $225 million out of the $480 million required, came in the form of an IOU: a 50-year bond, bearing a 5 percent interest rate. In other words, Morgan borrowed almost half of the purchase price from Carnegie himself.

It is plausible that when he accepted Carnegie's price, Morgan was confident he could raise the vast amount of capital he required, if not from Carnegie then from other sources. It's plausible, but doubtful. The amount he borrowed from Carnegie represented too large a percentage of the price tag for the deal to work without it. The amount of capital required was more than 2 percent of U.S. GDP at the time; the same proportion would be equivalent to $426 billion today. Even the great Morgan could not have known for sure if he could raise that sum, or at what cost, or how long it would take, without testing the market first.

In any case, securing Carnegie's acceptance of an IOU, to be paid over a period of half a century, was a critical part of the transaction—and certainly required much negotiation and documentation before the handshake.

In the end, how much was borrowed? How much equity capital was raised? Did some of the shareholders of Carnegie Steel swap their shares for the shares of U.S. Steel? Did Morgan put in any of his personal money? What were the exact sources and uses of Morgan's funds? And, eventually, what was the outcome for Morgan's brainchild, U.S. Steel? How much money did Morgan and his investors ultimately get out of it?

Presumably there were records, locked away somewhere in the House of Morgan. But there is no way to know if these records have survived; the details of the transaction remain hidden from the public eye. The point is that Morgan cannot have agreed to such a big deal without specifying certain conditions, including, for example, his ability to raise the required capital. It is entirely possible that the deal would have fallen apart if Carnegie balked at the idea of lending money to Morgan.

There is no way that a deal of this size and complexity could be done in the same manner as one buys vegetables in a grocery store, even if published accounts make it seem so straightforward.

Private equity is the art of using other people's money (usually) to make investments in private markets (usually), as opposed to buying up stock of a company on a public exchange. It is the job and the fiduciary duty of a private equity dealmaker to generate good returns on capital for his or her investors. The dealmaker does not always win. And that is key: No private equity story is complete without knowing if the deal eventually makes or loses money.

In view of the tough times U.S. Steel went through in the years after its creation, it is possible that those who had entrusted their capital with Morgan ultimately lost money. The moment of dealmaking between Carnegie, Schwab, and Morgan occupies a shining spot in the annals of American business. However, the ultimate outcome of the first mega-buyout deal in history remains buried.

★ ★ ★

In the past three decades, private equity, or PE, has roared into public view, starting with the takeover of RJR Nabisco by Kohlberg

Kravis Roberts & Co. (KKR) in 1988. The transaction was valued at $25 billion, the largest ever at that time, which awed even Wall Street.

PE fascinates the public because of the enormous amounts of money it moves around and the high stakes of the game it plays. The control of iconic corporate giants can be wrested away, and such deals can make an indelible impact on prominent industries. Then there are the larger-than-life dealmakers, who are often handsomely rewarded for their work to the tune of hundreds of millions of dollars. In the United States, there are more than twice as many PE-owned private companies as there are public ones.

Despite PE's solid presence, there is a dearth of literature about the inner workings of the industry. A few big buyouts have been written about in books, in most cases by journalists who try to piece together from the outside how the deal was made. While they are all fascinating, I am not aware of any book that tells the full story of a big deal, from beginning to end, including if the investors eventually made or lost money.

This is understandable because it usually takes years for a buyout deal to complete its cycle from the initial investment to the final exit. No business reporters could wait that long to tell the full story. In the case of RJR Nabisco, it took KKR 15 years to get out—long after the deal had been written up in a bestseller *Barbarians at the Gate* by the *Wall Street Journal* reporters Bryan Burrough and John Helyar. As it turned out, the firm had invested $3.5 billion of equity capital in RJR (the rest of the $25 billion was borrowed) and eventually lost $730 million, according to news reports, making the deal a rather dismal failure. KKR's investors would have been better off leaving their money in a savings account.

Much of PE's history is chronicled through accounts which were written too soon as they usually include only the deal-making part of the investment but not how the investment subsequently performed for the investors. *Saving the Sun*, by the *Financial Times* editor Gillian Tett, was also published only three years after the acquisition of Japan's Long-Term Credit Bank. Some of the investors were able to get out early with sizable gains; others remained invested nearly 20 years later and may have suffered losses. *Dethroning the King*, by the *Financial Times* reporter Julie MacIntosh, is another book recounting events that are far from over: the takeover of the venerated beer giant Anheuser-Busch, orchestrated by the Brazil-based PE firm 3G. For these dealmakers and many others, the jury remains out if these will turn out to be good or bad investments.

★ ★ ★

"Any idiot can buy a company," Henry Kravis of KKR likes to say. "It's what you do with it once it's acquired that matters."

To PE investors, the making of a deal, no matter how big, complex, or high profile, is only the beginning. The deal's success or failure can be ascertained only once the investor fully exits from the investment. In the years between the purchase and exit, teams of PE professionals expend great amounts of energy and resources to create value with the acquired company, to transform and to grow it. To exit from a big investment is often as complicated a deal as the initial acquisition—if not more so.

Any mistake in this deal cycle can lead to disaster and financial losses, erasing whatever satisfaction or glory the closing of the transaction brought years prior—and possibly ending the careers of the dealmakers themselves. Seasoned PE investors know that every deal is like walking on thin ice with a heavy load on their shoulders. They must take great care with every step to avoid plunging into failure. They can celebrate only after reaching the far shore, when they deliver their load to their investors.

Private equity is shrouded in mystery, in part because no PE dealmaker, to my knowledge, has written a complete insider's account of a major PE buyout deal from beginning to end.

This book tells the inside story of a profoundly impactful buyout deal, including the various twists and turns, successes and setbacks, that the American private equity firm at the center of it all encountered. Just as integral as the investors is the setting of the story: Korea in the immediate aftermath of the 1997–1998 Asian Financial Crisis. The country, whose modern history has been intertwined with that of the United States, was plagued by a beleaguered banking system and widespread economic instability.

The depth and severity of Korea's economic crash had come as a surprise to many. Starting in mid-1997, many of the world's most flourishing economies seemed to collapse almost overnight in rapid succession. Thailand, Malaysia, and Indonesia were the first countries to be hit, with Korea close behind. Curiously, there did not seem to be any particular reason why a crisis that appeared to originate with a collapse of the Thai currency should travel so far north, or why it appeared to mutate into a more virulent strain once it got there.

There was no shortage of potential culprits. Some joined Malaysia's then-prime minister, Mahathir Mohamad, in blaming foreign speculators for placing opportunistic bets against Asian currencies. Some pointed to the massive correction that ensued once the government was forced to devalue Korea's currency, the won. But many agree that one of the main reasons that the crisis cut so deeply in Korea was because systemic risk pervaded its financial system.

Nationalized under its authoritarian president Chung-hee Park in the 1960s and nominally privatized in the 1980s, Korea's banks had never fully thrown off the yoke of government control. These banks, regulators, politicians, and Korea's massive industrial conglomerates, known as *chaebol*, existed in a cozy symbiosis. As part of its decades-long effort to cultivate a prosperous nation following the privations of the Korean War, the government chose the industries and companies to bestow favors on. The banks would extend credit to these companies, which would churn out the steel, ships, and semiconductors that under-girded the Korean economic miracle. Implicit in this arrangement was the idea that the government would come to the aid of banks or enter-prises that ran into financial trouble.

The financial crisis brought the entire system crashing down. Many of Korea's largest *chaebol* went bankrupt or were forced to restructure. Two of the country's largest banks failed and were nationalized. After the International Monetary Fund stepped in with a massive $58 billion rescue package, it mandated that these banks be sold to foreign investors, for the purpose of overhauling their shaky lending practices. It was an opportunity to bring some much-needed transparency and structure to Korea's banking system, and it was felt—among the Korean government and global institutions at large—that foreign investors would bring in a credit culture to prevent such risky loans from being made again.

Private equity is not only a source of capital; it is also a vehicle for new ideas and new ways of doing things. Throughout my experiences as a PE investor in Korea, I was conscious of the fact that we were playing an important role in helping a struggling country achieve necessary changes. Similar reforms were occurring across Asia, by choice or necessity. The government-directed economic policies that had served some countries so well during Asia's decades of rapid growth had brought about structural weaknesses that became visible only when the economic earthquake struck, and fixing them was one of the greatest challenges the region faced as it entered the 21st century.

Structural reforms are always painful, especially if necessitated by a crisis and partially imposed as conditions for foreign help. At the time, Korea's economic calamity and the onerous restrictions of the IMF bailout were seen as the humiliation of a proud country on a global stage. The reform agenda was championed by a new president, Dae-jung Kim, who had spent his entire life fighting to bring democracy to the country and who had come to the office only in February 1998, almost at the height of the unprecedented economic crisis. Not everyone in the bureaucracy agreed with his reform agenda, and xenophobia also stood in the way of allowing foreign investors to control the country's venerated financial institutions.

Time and again in our negotiations, we had to deal with the two opposing forces, pro- and anti-reform, which made the deal process exceedingly difficult and uncertain. However, all the government officials we dealt with were fighting for what they considered to be the best interest of their country and people. They were men of high integrity and selfless dedication to their country. (They were all men, as Korea remained a Confucian and male-dominated society at the time.) This book tells the story of the takeover of a national bank, and also provides an inside look, in real time and behind closed doors, at how a government grappled with the greatest crisis it had faced since the end of the Korean War.

—Weijan Shan
Hong Kong
February 2020

Chapter 1

Money Talks—My Path to Private Equity

A couple of years ago I had lunch with some senior executives of Jardine Matheson Holdings on the 48th floor of Jardine House in Hong Kong. Jardines, as it is known, is a British conglomerate founded in Hong Kong with a history dating back more than 180 years. It has interests in everything from aviation and hotels to retail and real estate. The firm's spacious private dining room was decorated with bright and cheerful Chinese paintings and had a breathtaking view of Victoria Harbour.

As my gracious host walked me to the elevator lobby after lunch, I noticed a giant oil painting, darkened with age. It was a portrait of an Indian man wearing a tall black headdress and a long-sleeved robe, cinched at the waist, that appeared to be made of cream-colored silk. He had a dramatic mustache, an enormous potbelly, and eyes that were both keen and kind. He was sitting on a cushioned chair, surrounded by scrolls. He held one in front of himself as if he had just finished reading it. On his chest he wore a large gold medal, signifying some kind of honor. Behind him sitting tall on a pedestal was a giant potbellied brass vase whose exterior bore some barely recognizable letters, which I made out to be *CARITAS*, a Latin word from which *charity* in English was derived. I was instantly curious about this man, who looked anything but English, and his prominent place in the head office of a distinctly British company.

"Who's he?" I asked my host.

"His name was Jeejeebhoy, the man who grew opium for us in India, which we shipped and sold to China," my host replied nonchalantly. It was as if he were talking about someone engaged in selling vegetables.

I later learned that Jamsetjee Jeejeebhoy, a Bombay native, had amassed a fortune in the British opium trade to China. His "distinguished services" to the British Empire were recognized with a knighthood in 1842 and by a baronetcy conferred upon him by Queen Victoria in 1858, the first ever granted to an Indian.

I was a little surprised by my host's forthrightness. Jardines' historical role in the drug trade was common knowledge, but I thought they'd be more circumspect about it.

"Ah," I said, "I thought it was an awkward subject to bring up."

"Nothing awkward," my host reassured me. "We say Her Majesty's government made us do it. But we aren't drug dealers anymore," he added with a twinkle in his eyes.

We both laughed. Jeejeebhoy's story hints at Hong Kong's inception as a British colony. Jardine Matheson was one of the original foreign *hongs*, or trading houses, established in southern China, that engaged in trading goods like tea and cotton among Britain's far-flung colonies. It also had a major interest in smuggling opium into China. Eventually, the Chinese government began seizing and destroying this illegal cargo, so Jardines' principals lobbied the British government to send in gunboats. In the ensuing Opium War (1839–1842), Britain's military forces overpowered the Chinese and forced China to sign the Treaty of Nanking by which, as part of the settlement, China ceded the island of Hong Kong to Britain.

Western commerce in the region grew, the opium trade continued, and Britain continued to tighten its grip on the area around Hong Kong. In 1860, Britain annexed the Kowloon Peninsula, directly across Victoria Harbour, the body of water that gave Hong Kong its name. Roughly translated, *hong kong* means *fragrant harbor*, but by the mid-19th century, the British had named the harbor for their queen and established it as a center of international trade. In 1898, Britain secured a 99-year lease for the New Territories, a mountainous, mostly rural swath of land surrounding Kowloon that connected it to the mainland of China.

Jardines grew with the colony. The skyscraper I was dining in had been the tallest building in Hong Kong when it was completed in 1972, a testament to the *hong*'s enduring legacy and recognizable for its unique porthole windows. Locals called it the "building of a thousand orifices," as a BBC documentary on the British Empire delicately put it. "Doubtless, somewhere in the foundation lies buried the conscience of its founders," deadpanned the narrator.

Hong Kong was still a British colony when my family and I arrived from the United States in 1993. Under British rule, Hong Kong had prospered, attaining a living standard among the highest in the world by the early 1990s.

Located at the southern tip of China, with a land area of about the same size as the city of Los Angeles, it was a laissez-faire market economy, among the freest in the world. As an economic gateway to mainland China, Hong Kong was the regional headquarters to many multinational companies and international financial institutions. From Hong Kong, a business traveler could cover almost all of Asia: Beijing, Shanghai, Tokyo, Seoul, Taipei, Bangkok, and Singapore were all less than a four-hour flight away. English was widely spoken, and families of foreign expatriates could live comfortably there. Despite our Chinese background and Hong Kong being a Chinese city, my family and I considered ourselves outsiders. We did not speak or understand the local Cantonese dialect.

Before moving to Hong Kong, for six years we lived in the United States, in Philadelphia, where I was a professor at the Wharton School at the University of Pennsylvania. The life of an academic at an Ivy League university was comfortable, although it became a little dreary after a few years. American business schools are not exactly ivory towers. Their professors frequently maintain strong ties to the business world, and Wharton had particularly close interactions with Wall Street. While I never felt too removed from the real world of business and finance, I longed for a taste of real *action*. It seemed a bit ironic that I had been teaching business for so long without having actually done any.

By the early 1990s, China's growth had captured Wall Street's imagination—and I followed developments there with keen interest. At the time my research and teaching were focused largely on the management of multinational corporations and on the biotechnology industry, which had nothing specifically to do with China or Asia. Even so, I had grown up in China during its tumultuous years, so I had an intrinsic connection to the country. (My memoir, *Out of the Gobi: My Story of China and America,* chronicles my experiences during this turbulent period.) Eventually, I found my way to the United States, where I received a PhD in business administration at the University of California, Berkeley before becoming a professor at Wharton.

Because of my roots I had followed the developments in China with keen interest and I visited the country from time to time. At Wharton, I founded *China Economic Review,* an academic journal dedicated to researching China's rapidly changing economy and role in the global business landscape. My credentials as a professor at a top business school, combined with my knowledge of the country, were inevitably attractive to some firms with ambitions in the Chinese market. When opportunity knocked on my door, I was ready.

In 1992, I was approached by several major companies involved in management consulting or investment banking. Eventually I decided that the latter, which mainly helps businesses raise capital, was more interesting, and I began to explore related opportunities. In emerging markets, companies grow fast. Businesses tend to be more willing to pay for access to capital than for just knowledge and advice. Money talks, I thought, and at an investment bank, I figured my job would be easier than at a consulting firm.

I was recruited by a tall, shrewd banker named Tad Beczak, then the president of JP Morgan Securities Asia. He took me to a restaurant in New York City for lunch in early 1993. I had expected him to tell me how wonderful it would be to work for his bank. To my surprise, he looked at me across the table with his penetrating eyes and told me, "It's going to be hard." However, he suggested, I might have what it took to succeed.

I found Beczak to be down-to-earth and straightforward, quite different from the stereotype of a Wall Street banker. He had a good knowledge of the Chinese market, especially its challenges and pitfalls. I took an immediate liking to him—and the prospect of doing something new, even something difficult, excited me.

I was offered a job as vice president in JP Morgan's Hong Kong office, with an additional title: Chief Representative for China. At industrial firms, vice presidents are big shots, but investment banks mint them by the dozen. Knowing this, I did not like the title. Even though I had zero experience in banking, I thought my credentials as a business professor ought to count for something. Eventually I accepted the offer, understanding that I needed to prove myself before getting a more senior position.

My major responsibility at JP Morgan was to get clients, typically large companies, to hire us to raise capital for them by underwriting their initial public offerings (IPOs) in overseas markets, or to provide other financial and advisory services. Underwriting IPOs is extremely lucrative for investment banks. Typically, we charged a fee representing a percentage of the capital raised. If the client raised $1 billion, our 5 percent fee would be $50 million (the actual percentage varied). However, qualified IPO candidates were hard to come by in China, and obtaining the mandate to underwrite their stock offerings was a fiercely competitive business.

When I arrived in Hong Kong in 1993, China was still a poor and developing country. In that year, its gross domestic product (GDP) was only $440 billion, one-sixteenth of that of the United States (about $6.8 trillion) and one-tenth of that of Japan (about $4.4 trillion). China's per capita GDP was only $377, a tiny fraction of that of the United States (more than $26,000) and of Japan ($38,000).

At this early stage of China's economic development, any business of decent size was state-owned. Factories were organized like an extension of the government and reported to certain ministries, such as Ministry of Textiles or Ministry of Machinery. They each functioned like a department of the government. As such, they had to be restructured as joint stock companies before they could be offered to overseas investors. There were only a few IPO candidates, all of which were carefully selected by the Chinese securities regulator. From 1992 to 1994, just 31 companies received approval from the regulator to go public on overseas stock exchanges. Each year there were more foreign banks chasing IPOs than there were IPO candidates.

I soon realized, somewhat to my dismay, that not only was I new to the game, but my employer was as well. JP Morgan had a long history, dating back to 1871. But the House of Morgan had been broken up in the 1930s by the Glass-Steagall Act, split into Morgan Stanley, an investment bank, and JP Morgan, a commercial bank. This set of laws, passed in an attempt to eliminate conditions that had helped cause the bank failures of the Great Depression, restricted a commercial bank to collecting deposits and making loans. It was not until 1989, four years before I joined, that the law was relaxed to permit the likes of JP Morgan to get into investment banking business, albeit in a limited way. In 1993, the bank was still building its investment banking business, and its underwriting capabilities were weaker than those of established houses, such as Morgan Stanley and Goldman Sachs. Those competitors were known as *bulge-bracket banks* because they were listed first, in bold type sizes, on the covers of stock offering documents.

JP Morgan's lack of a track record made it doubly hard for us to market ourselves to clients and compete with our bulge-bracket peers. To add to our difficulties, our pool of potential clients was smaller because JP Morgan was able to underwrite stock offerings only in the U.S. market, but not in Hong Kong, where most Chinese IPO candidates chose to go public. The saving grace was that none of our potential clients knew much about overseas capital markets or foreign investment banks. They were reliant on us to walk them through the process, and we made sure to make ourselves look as good as possible while doing so. As a former professor, I could be quite convincing, helped by the investment bank rankings, or league tables, prepared by my colleagues, who often placed JP Morgan at or close to the top.

Only later did I learn that every investment bank rejiggers these league tables to make itself look better. For example, if a league table showed we were in the top three in underwriting U.S. IPOs for Korean companies, it might mean that out of 100 Korean companies that had gone public in a five-year period, only three chose the U.S. market for their IPO, and in that year the bank was able to do one. To an unsophisticated client, though, being in the top three would seem quite impressive.

However, our competitors had their own league tables, and often a track record of underwriting Chinese IPOs, something we lacked. I found myself unsuited for the job because I could not honestly tell a client we were better qualified than our peers when I did not believe that was the case. I could only try to win their trust by going the extra mile, visiting with them so frequently that I am sure I came across like a type of human superglue. But still, it was an uphill battle, and one that was often too hard to win.

One of the IPO mandates I won was from Dongfeng Motor Company (DFMC), one of the three largest automobile manufacturers in the country. It was located in the middle of nowhere, deep in the mountains, accessible only by a slow train or a narrow dirt road, which zigzagged past steep walls of jutted rocks on one side and deep ravines on the other. The road was so bumpy it felt as if all my bones had been shaken loose after the four-hour ride. It was also so dangerous that a couple of times I saw the smoldering remains of vehicles that had plunged off the road into the ravine. My colleagues and I took this road more than 20 times in 1994 alone. Each time I felt lucky to have made it out in one piece.

DFMC had been built in the 1960s at a time of high tensions between China and the Soviet Union. Its remote location was due to an effort to hide China's industrial assets in remote areas in case of Soviet invasion. Shiyan of Hubei Province, where DFMC was located, was a factory town with its own kindergartens, schools, shops, fire departments, hotels, hospitals, water supply, sewage system, waste disposal, and even funeral homes. Most of these social services were offered to employees and their families for free or for a token price. The original purpose of the factory was not to make a profit but to produce whatever output it was designed for without much regard to economics. It would be my job to prepare it to sell shares to savvy investors around the world.

DFMC's managers and engineers knew a lot about making trucks, but international capital markets were completely foreign to them. In one meeting they told me a story that revealed just how limited their exposure to the rest of the world was. DFMC was negotiating a joint venture with the French automaker Citroën, so the senior management team was invited to France for a visit. Citroën's chairman hosted a dinner for his guests at his home. His wife brought out her best silverware and prepared the finest French cuisine. As her Chinese guests sat down, all of them unfolded their napkins and began wiping their forks and knives in unison. The hostess was stunned: Was her silverware not clean enough? She felt so humiliated that she burst into tears. The Chinese guests were shocked to see their hostess so upset but were completely puzzled as to what had triggered her reaction.

The DFMC managers had all come from Shiyan, the backwater factory town, where sanitary conditions were poor to say the least. Conscious of hygiene, they always wiped their chopsticks and bowls with their handkerchiefs before eating. Normally they would have some boiling water ready to rinse with as well. At the home of the Citroën chairman, they followed their pre-dinner habit. At least they had not asked for a bowl of boiling water to complete their sterilization or they would have killed the joint venture right then and there. In short, DFMC needed help, both with its IPO and its knowledge of customs abroad.

JP Morgan won the mandate to take DFMC public in the United States, but we faced the daunting and complicated task of restructuring the company into a shape recognizable and acceptable to overseas investors. A new joint stock company had to be established. And then decisions had to be made as to what assets to put into it and what to keep out. Needless to say, the new entity had to be profitable, which would mean excluding the factory town's not-for-profit social services and making many workers redundant. It was immediately clear that making the new entity profitable might bankrupt the town. How would the social services be financed? Who would pay for laid-off workers? How should the new entity pay for medical care and retirement benefits for the retained workers and their families, and at what prices? These were questions we would need to answer.

Accounting records were another problem. Most of the documents we needed—typical financial statements and business records— had never been created. Others existed, but only in forms that would be incomprehensible to the market. Pro forma financial accounts going back at least three years had to be created, sometimes nearly from scratch. This required a massive amount of work by accountants, lawyers, and bankers, and the process was both time consuming and resource intensive.

At that time, JP Morgan's client banking operations were country-specific, so its bankers were paid if the mandates they obtained were executed. However, the execution was mostly in the hands of product groups, which were paid for selling securities in the capital markets for clients, regardless of their countries of origin. Naturally, the product groups did not want to execute difficult mandates if they didn't have to. Labor-intensive Chinese deals, while a high priority for client bankers, were usually a low priority for product groups. The product bankers would rather execute straightforward deals from traditional market economies such as South Korea or Indonesia, whose businesses were already organized to issue securities in the public market without much work.

I came to the realization that the only way for the bank to develop its Chinese market was to have China-dedicated product teams. Maybe the business volume did not justify it at the time, but if we could start executing more Chinese business, the need for a specialized team would grow. The business volume would never be there without the initial investment. Maybe it was too early. Maybe the bank would not be competitive until it could present itself as a bulge-bracket bank. In any case, it seemed that JP Morgan never figured out how to tackle China. It shut down its Hong Kong capital markets business in the wake of the Asian Financial Crisis of 1997–1998, a year or so after I had left.

The Chinese market was definitely difficult. Quality clients were few and the competition for them was cutthroat. The process of obtaining mandates was opaque, often based not on a team's capabilities and effort but based on connections—or shady quid pro quo. I felt the work was 20 percent financial engineering and 80 percent political engineering. It was frustrating that some hard-fought mandates could not be executed, or were executed so slowly that we missed market windows for IPOs. That was what happened to Dongfeng's IPO, though the company did manage to finally go public in 2005. I was working my tail off and I was promoted to managing director. But I increasingly disliked my job and felt the elevated title and the work were not worth my personal investment. It was time to make a change, but before I could leave JP Morgan, I had to figure out what to do next.

★ ★ ★

In mid-September of 1997, I met with Dan Carroll for breakfast, in Hong Kong. Carroll was tall and athletic, with a broad smile and a firm and sincere handshake. He came across as friendly and likable.

Carroll was a partner at Newbridge Capital, a private equity firm. He was only 36 but had worked in private equity for over a dozen years, most recently with a firm called Texas Pacific Group (TPG). Newbridge was a joint venture between TPG, headed by David Bonderman, and Dick Blum, a well-known American investor based in San Francisco. Established in 1994, Newbridge had been set up as a China fund with about $100 million in capital but had expanded its mandate to cover the whole of Asia. Carroll's co–managing partner had recently left, and Newbridge was looking for his replacement.

The only time I had come into contact with the private equity business I hadn't even known what it was called. Shortly after I joined JP Morgan, my boss, Tad Beczak, took me aside and told me that a vice chairman of the bank in New York had asked us to look into the possibility of investing in a China venture called ASIMCO. Since I was supposed to know China, Beczak wanted me to check it out.

U.S.-based ASIMCO had been set up to form joint ventures with various Chinese manufacturers of auto parts. It was looking to raise $400 million, and there was strong interest in Wall Street circles to invest. A colleague from JP Morgan's principal investment department and I took a tour with ASIMCO executives to investigate these potential Chinese joint venture partners. Most of them were under the umbrella of Norinco, the China North Industries Group Corporation. Norinco was primarily a defense contractor, but it also operated a vast array of other businesses, scattered across China. We visited Norinco's headquarters in Beijing and then traveled to a number of provinces to check out its auto parts makers. I was underwhelmed by what I saw. My impression was that almost all of these companies were in trouble, and Norinco was trying to find a way to save them. The proposed investment by ASIMCO seemed a perfect solution from Norinco's point of view, but how ASIMCO could make money out of these auto-parts makers was unclear to me. I wrote a report to summarize my views and, in the end, JP Morgan did not invest.

ASIMCO was able to successfully raise the funds from other sources and eventually lost practically all of the money. In 2006, Tim Clissold, who had worked at ASIMCO as a young analyst, wrote a book called *Mr. China*, which detailed the near-disastrous experiences of the company. I supposed I helped JP Morgan dodge a bullet.

I still didn't know much about private equity. But a few days after meeting with Carroll, I received a call from the headhunter who had put me in touch with Newbridge. Newbridge wanted to invite me to San Francisco for more interviews. I liked Carroll, but I still did not know what to make of the company, which I had never heard of. I did not think it would be worth it for me to travel all the way to San Francisco to learn more about the job, but I did leave the door open and indicated I would be happy to meet with Newbridge partners when they came to Hong Kong.

On Thursday, October 23, 1997, I took a day off to spend some time with my family. My wife, Bin, and I went shopping in Hong Kong's Times Square, a multistory mall in the bustling shopping area of Causeway Bay. The plaza in front of the mall was dominated by a giant overhead TV screen. On that day, Causeway Bay seemed even more crowded than usual, and I noticed that a large crowd had gathered below the giant TV screen, staring up at it. I looked up to see the stock market tickers scrolling along the bottom of the screen. Every one was showing red. In the middle of the screen was an intraday chart of the Hang Seng Index, which tracked Hong Kong's stock exchange. It was midday, and the Hang Seng was already down more than 1,000 points, nearly 10 percent. Before the day was over, it would fall an astonishing 16 percent.

It had been a difficult few months for Asian stock markets. In July, the devaluation of the Thai currency, the baht, had triggered a chain reaction of currency devaluations across the region, from Indonesia to South Korea. Investors were fleeing the market in droves. The cratering of the Hong Kong Stock Exchange meant we were now in a full-blown financial crisis. No company would be able to do an IPO, issue a bond, finance an expansion, or engage in any of the capital-raising activities for which banks like JP Morgan charged hefty fees. For investment banks, the capital markets in Asia would be as good as dead for a while.

Some 10 years later, in 2008, a similar scene would play out in the United States with the collapse of Lehman Brothers and the meltdown of the financial markets.

I turned around to see Bin, who usually could not care less about the stock market, staring at the screen. I told her, "I think I am going to join Newbridge Capital."

"What's Newbridge Capital?" she asked.

I explained to her as much as I knew at that point about private equity. The firm's business was to make investments in companies or assets, improve them, and sell them hopefully at a higher price.

"But why did you suddenly decide to switch jobs?" She was puzzled.

"There will be a long winter for capital markets, and investment banking will be in a deep freeze. There won't be much to do on the sell side," I said. "It's time to switch to the buy side."

Investment banking is considered to be on the *sell side*, selling its products and services to clients and helping clients *sell*—or market—themselves to investors to raise capital. By contrast, private equity is on the *buy side*. It is primarily involved in directly acquiring assets and businesses and turning them around. When Asian markets were hot, it was good to be on the sell side because assets and securities were easy to sell. But once the market collapsed, the buy side became more attractive. Cash was king and assets could be acquired at bargain prices. The Asian Financial Crisis brought severe economic pain but with that came rare opportunities for investors like Newbridge Capital. And the Newbridge opportunity instantly felt more interesting and appealing to me.

A couple months later I met with Dick Blum and David Bonderman, Newbridge's co-chairs, in Hong Kong. Blum I had met once before, but it was first time I had met Bonderman, although I knew him by reputation. Both were tall and rather imposing, but they came across as friendly and casual. We had a good conversation, peppered with light jokes, in a relaxed manner. While I thought there were good investment opportunities in China, I talked mainly about the difficulties of the market and all the risks involved for foreign investors. They already knew about all that because most of Newbridge's China investments were struggling by then.

Shortly afterward, Newbridge made me an offer. The cash compensation was not as good as what I could get in investment banking, but I had completely lost interest in that business and almost no offer could have persuaded me to stay. Newbridge's offer included profit sharing, known as *carried interest*. If the firm made a decent profit for its investors, it would get to keep a percentage of that profit to share among its partners. This was certainly appealing, but with it came the risk that if the firm did not make money for its investors, there would be nothing to share.

Carroll invited me to visit San Francisco, where both TPG and Blum's company, Richard C. Blum & Associates, were based. I arrived in San Francisco a week before Christmas. The next day, after I met with a number of TPG people, Carroll took me to dinner at a nice seafood restaurant. On the menu was a whole steamed crab, a dish for which San Francisco was famous. I knew one rule of business meals was to never order anything that might be messy, but I couldn't resist the temptation, and Carroll seemed too nice a guy to mind. So I had my last interview with him cracking open crab legs and concentrating on not cutting my fingers on the shells.

After the dinner I signed up with Newbridge Capital as a partner and agreed to start work in the new year.

Some time after I joined Newbridge, my new colleague Paul Chen recounted a conversation he had had with Bonderman. After my interview, Chen had asked Bonderman what he thought of me. Bonderman had replied, "This guy has no clue what private equity is about."

Bonderman was right, of course. A few years later I asked him about it. "If you thought I was clueless," I said, "why did you hire me?"

"Personalities," he said, "and I figured you could learn."

He was right about that. But there was a lot I had to learn.

Chapter 2

Project Safe

The weather in New York City was pleasant and mild in the fall. Dan Carroll, my partner at Newbridge Capital, and I walked out of the Stanhope Hotel at about 8 am as the early morning sun shone warmly on my face. Our car waited for us at the curb, and behind it, Fifth Avenue was jammed with the usual rush-hour traffic.

It was September 1998. Newbridge was raising its second fund, and we were in New York City to visit various potential investors.

Once in the car, I opened a folder of faxes I had received overnight from our office in Hong Kong. One of them was sent by our colleague Paul Chen. In it there were two brief descriptions (*teasers*, as they were called in investment banking) for the sale of two major South Korean commercial banks that had failed and been nationalized by the government. Chen explained that the government of South Korea had engaged Morgan Stanley, an investment bank, to be its financial advisor to conduct an auction to sell off control of both banks.

The Asian Financial Crisis had hit South Korea hard. By the end of 1997, the country had been on the verge of defaulting on its sovereign debt. Money was fleeing the country, and its foreign exchange reserves had plummeted to just $8.9 billion by December, barely enough to last a week or two at the rate of capital flight. The stock market had plunged by 49 percent, and Korea's currency, the won, had depreciated

15

by 65.9 percent against the U.S. dollar. The country came so close to default on its foreign debts that citizens were encouraged to sell their gold jewelry to the country's central bank to help replenish its foreign exchange reserves.

It was a humiliating experience for a proud country, one that had joined the Organisation for Economic Cooperation and Development (OECD) in 1996, the year before the crisis. It was only the second Asian nation after Japan to join the OECD, a clubby group of rich, developed nations. Until late 1997, South Korea had been one of Asia's remarkable success stories. The country epitomized the so-called Asian miracle. Once a war-ravaged, aid-dependent nation, it had transformed itself into a fast-growing, export-oriented economy. The Asian Financial Crisis threatened to wipe out nearly three and a half decades of hard work, leaving South Korea's 46 million citizens in financial ruin.

Part of the reason for Korea's success had been its banking system. Banks channeled funds to *chaebols* in industries like automobiles, iron and steel, shipbuilding, and petrochemicals, fueling their take-off. *Chaebols* are a uniquely Korean type of conglomerate controlled by wealthy families. They were favored by the government, which wanted to see them succeed, ostensibly for the benefit of the nation's economy. But there were risks that came from the government's playing favorites.

Political and personal connections, rather than business considerations, led banks to favor the government's picks when it came to lending. Export-oriented firms also had greater access to credit and lower borrowing costs than did firms that focused on the domestic market, allowing *chaebols* like Hyundai and Samsung, which had had great success selling products overseas, to use leverage, or borrowed money, to expand, while enjoying a protected domestic market. As a result, *chaebols* were highly leveraged, and there were few restrictions in place to prevent banks from concentrating their risks in a small number of corporate borrowers. Some banks lent up to 45 percent of their capital to a single borrower. Under Korean accounting rules, banks considered borrowers performing customers as long as they could make interest payments, regardless of whether they had any hope of paying off the principal.

President Chung-hee Park had nationalized all the banks when he came to power in 1961, and it was not until the mid-1980s that they were nominally put back in the hands of private management. Still, they functioned less as private companies and more as tools for national development. As such, their profitability was extremely low. A McKinsey study found that profitability among Korean banks, as measured by return on assets, was just one-tenth that of world-class banks. They were, in the words of one analyst, "managed to be weak."

Furthermore, Korea's economic success had relied on foreign borrowing. The World Bank pointed out that if Korea had relied on domestic savings alone, its economic growth rate, which was 8.2 percent between 1962 and 1982, would have been only 4.9 percent. At the end of 1997, as foreign creditors pulled back on lending, Korea faced a severe liquidity crisis. By some estimates 61 percent of the foreign borrowings of Korean banks were short term, and many of these short-term loans were invested in long-term projects by *chaebol* borrowers who had expected the loans to be rolled over every year.

Over the course of 1997, seven *chaebols*, including Hanbo Steel, either went bankrupt or sought the banks' help on loan repayment. This stoked the fears of Korea's foreign creditors, who became even more unwilling to roll over their short-term loans. The government used its dwindling foreign exchange reserves to pay back overseas money it had guaranteed.

In late November 1997, Seoul went to the International Monetary Fund (IMF) and the World Bank to ask for help. South Korea negotiated a $58 billion rescue package, the largest in history, which was agreed to in early December. But even that failed to stem the tide. An internal memorandum prepared by the Bank of Korea on December 18, 1997, suggested that the foreign exchange reserve balance on December 31 would be anywhere from negative $600 million to positive $900 million. According to economist Kihwan Kim, "No wonder foreign creditors further accelerated the withdrawal of their funds from Korea, pushing the country to the verge of a sovereign default in less than two weeks after the initial agreement was signed."

Ultimately, foreign banks agreed to extend their loan maturities, at greatly increased interest rates. The IMF rescue package came with conditions on austerity and restructuring, including a mandate to sell off to foreign investors two failed banks, Korea First Bank and Seoul Bank. Although unspoken, the apparent reason for selling these banks to foreign buyers was the need to bring a *credit culture* into Korea's banking system.

Previously, loans had been made on the basis of government policies or personal relationships, without much regard to the creditworthiness of borrowers. Selling the two banks was driven by more than the need for capital; it was part and parcel of Korea's banking reforms in the wake of the crisis.

★ ★ ★

The teasers about Korea First Bank and Seoul Bank I read in the car that sunny New York morning said: "The Government is seeking an international commercial bank to purchase a minimum of 50.1 percent interest in the bank through a new issuance of common stock." Both banks were among South Korea's largest in terms of number of customers, branch network, and market share of loans and deposits. They also had a massive amount of debt that had become uncollectible. The teasers noted that both banks held bad loans that were expected to represent 25 percent of the banks' total loans. That was an astounding number, far greater than the banks' capital, which typically was just 5 percent of their assets. With 25 percent of loans considered uncollectible, both banks were insolvent many times over.

No foreign buyer was expected to sink money into the capital hole created by the bad loans. To entice them, the government offered to put its own money into the banks, to largely fill the hole. As part of the deal:

> The Korean government has made available a government support package to potential investors . . . which provides protection against existing and future deterioration in the asset quality (on both loans and securities). This protection is in the form of reimbursement of loan loss charge-offs and government guarantees on the securities portfolio.

As the Korean government's advisor, Morgan Stanley was tasked with finding potential investors and helping the government negotiate a deal with them. The solicitation specifically stated that the Korean government was "seeking an international commercial bank." Despite this, Newbridge, a private equity investor, had been invited. Obviously, Morgan Stanley had decided to cast the net wider, fearing there would not be enough interested buyers. I did not find that surprising.

"Who would want to buy a failed bank in a failed economy in the middle of the worst economic crisis the country has ever experienced?" I wondered aloud.

Carroll was more thoughtful. "We should ask Bondo," he said. "If anyone knows how to do a bank deal, it's him,"

David Bonderman, co-chairman of Newbridge, had experience with failing banks. About 10 years earlier, as the chief investment officer at the Robert M. Bass Group, he had helped Bass acquire and recapitalize the then-insolvent American Savings Bank (ASB) during the U.S. savings and loan crisis. Bass had taken control of ASB, which had once been the second-largest savings bank in the country, in a government-assisted transaction. In such a transaction, the government is the seller, as it has already taken over the failed bank and will take the responsibility for the risks of the bank's *legacy assets* (assets that were on the bank's books before the new owners take control) by paying the bank for losses from those assets. After turning around the bank, Bass sold it, making multiples of the money invested.

Bonderman was known to be a contrarian, buying businesses most other investors would shun. Incidentally, he was scheduled to visit Korea the very next month.

Chen sent a memo to Bonderman and Newbridge's co-chairman, Dick Blum, a couple days later, outlining the information in the teasers and giving a brief summary of the pros and cons we identified in a potential deal.

Bonderman responded with his customary swiftness, by fax:

I think that your memo is precisely on point in the sense that for an opportunity to exist here the Korean government will have to give much better protections than it is proposing. On the other hand, the history of life is that well-protected failed bank deals are an excellent way to make money if you can buy them at the bottom of the cycle. Accordingly, I think it is worth your while hanging around this process to see what develops.

Asia was now in a full-blown financial crisis. As money rushed out of these economies, panic set in. At one point, the Indonesian rupiah had fallen by 86 percent against the dollar. The currencies of Thailand, South

Korea, Malaysia, and the Philippines were all down by 40 to 60 percent; stock markets suffered losses of at least 75 percent in dollar terms. In 1998, Indonesia, Malaysia, South Korea, and Thailand saw their real GDP shrink by an average of 11 percent. The whole South Korean economy declined by 7.8 percent. Many millions of people had lost their jobs. Numerous companies failed.

★ ★ ★

As the financial crisis swept through Asia, China remained relatively insulated. There was no capital flight from China, mainly because its foreign borrowing was limited and the Chinese yuan was not freely convertible. Chinese individuals and companies could not easily move their money abroad and into other currencies. Although China remained stable, asset prices in the rest of Asia collapsed. This made China the most expensive market in Asia for investors. That was not good news for Newbridge, which had been founded as a China-focused fund engaged in the business of buying and turning around undervalued Chinese companies. As investment opportunities in China got scarce, we began to look at the rest of Asia, from South Korea to Indonesia, for good businesses to invest in. The fund Carroll and I were in New York to raise money for was planned as an Asia-wide fund, not limited to China. The failed Korean banks could turn out to be promising investments.

On October 9, 1998, Bonderman and I arrived in Seoul. We were there to meet with Hun-jai Lee, chairman of South Korea's Financial Supervisory Commission (FSC), a newly established regulatory agency tasked with helping fix Korea's financial sector. The meeting took place at the FSC's offices in Yeouido, an island in the Han River, which ran through the middle of Seoul. The island was home to the National Assembly and many government offices.

Slightly built and bespectacled, Chairman Lee came across as serious, thoughtful, and confident. He held a master's degree in economics from Boston University and studied at Harvard. He spoke English with a Korean accent. He was accompanied by his staff and a team of Morgan Stanley bankers.

After introductions, Bonderman talked about his successful experience investing in ASB. He described the *good bank/bad bank* structure used in the ASB transaction, which required separating the good and bad assets of the bank into two separate entities. New investors would invest in the *good bank*, while the *bad bank*, owned by the government, would focus on resolving all of the nonperforming legacy loans. This model was not dissimilar to Morgan Stanley's proposal on behalf of the government, in that the government had offered to provide protection to investors against bad loans. Bonderman's model would create a good bank to hold the good assets, which could concentrate on conducting normal banking business. Without having to worry about managing bad legacy loans, the good bank could resume growth.

Lee listened attentively as his aides took notes. He asked a few questions for clarification, and I sensed that he had a quick mind and grasped the key points. Toward the end, Bonderman suggested that we would be interested in submitting a proposal under two conditions. The first, of course, was that the Korean government would be willing to consider a proposal from Newbridge, despite its stated preference for bids from commercial banks. Second, it would have to be willing to consider a proposal that would not fully conform to Morgan Stanley's guidelines. Even though Morgan Stanley outlined that the government would provide some protection against the inherent losses and risks of the bad loans, we thought the measures were inadequate and wanted more robust protection.

Lee was cautious. I was sure that this was in part because he had probably never heard of Newbridge. He looked at us and asked, "Do you have enough capital to buy what used to be the largest bank in Korea?"

"Capital is no constraint," I replied, without elaborating further.

Newbridge's first fund had raised less than $100 million in capital, and that money was already fully invested. Newbridge II, our second investment vehicle, had a target of $400 million, which we were still in the process of raising. Before they became insolvent, Korea First Bank and Seoul Bank each had something on the order of $40 billion in assets. Even in their slimmed-down size, it would probably require about a billion dollars to recapitalize each one of them, after the government cleaned up all the bad assets.

My thinking, however, was that if a deal was good enough, we would have no problem raising the capital we would need; but if the deal was not good enough, we would not invest a penny anyway. Therefore, I felt confident saying that capital was not a constraint. It all depended on what kind of deal we could negotiate.

Chairman Lee thanked us for the visit and encouraged us to submit a proposal.

I found the mood in Seoul gloomy. Every company we met with was trying to raise capital. This was understandable, because the entire country seemed to be deeply in debt.

The financial crisis had been particularly hard on corporate Korea. During the high-growth years, companies had become used to having their loans rolled over or renewed when due, usually annually. But now banks were so squeezed for money themselves, they would not roll over the loans. This caught many Korean firms by surprise, forcing them into bankruptcy and leaving their employees without jobs. These corporate bankruptcies added to the woes of banks and drove the tally of their troubled loans higher, further squeezing capital, and the vicious cycle continued.

Whereas the average debt-to-equity ratio of American companies stood at about 70 percent, the same ratio was more than 300 percent for Korean companies. For the largest *chaebols*, the average was an astounding 500 percent. That meant for every $100 in capital, the company had $500 in debt. By the end of 1998, 14 of Korea's top 30 *chaebols* were bankrupt or nearly so.

The $58 billion bailout package Korea negotiated with the IMF did not immediately cure the economy's woes. Furthermore, the associated austerity conditions were deeply unpopular with the Korean public. Many, ironically, blamed the IMF for their pain. What was called the Asian Financial Crisis elsewhere was popularly referred to in South Korea as the *IMF Crisis*. It was as if a doctor had saved a patient with some bitter medicine, and the patient blamed the doctor, and the medicine itself, for the illness. Despite the IMF's help, South Korea was in dire need of more foreign capital. Before the crisis, South Korea had been one of the markets most closed to foreign direct investment (FDI). The government, fearing foreign entry into the industries it had nurtured, preferred loans rather than FDI as a source of capital, which it could more easily dole out to favored industries and businesses. The crisis and the ensuing capital shortage forced the country to scrap its previous limits on foreign ownership.

But as is often the case in financial crises, just as South Korea opened its door wide to FDI, foreign capital was stampeding for the exits. To us, it signaled an opportunity.

After our visit to Seoul, we decided there was enough potential in the deal to continue to follow through. We put together a proposal, or term sheet, for the investment, which we intended to model on the deal structure for ASB. We would need an investment bank and a law firm to help us work through the complicated financial and legal aspects of the proposal, so Bonderman suggested the Financial Institutions Group at Lehman Brothers and Cleary Gottlieb Steen & Hamilton, both based in New York City. They had worked on the ASB deal and were familiar with its structure and terms.

Lehman assembled a team of experienced bankers including Phil Erlanger, Michael O'Hanlon, David Kim, and others. Cleary's team included Michael Ryan and Linda Matlack, both of whom had worked on the ASB transaction. I also engaged Dr. Jihong Kim to be our advisor. A professor at Hanyang University in Seoul, Jihong was an old friend and classmate of mine from U.C. Berkeley's PhD program. He had graduated from Seoul National University, the best university in South Korea, and earned an MBA from Harvard. He knew the country and many of its key players well, including Chairman Lee of the FSC.

As customary, for the purpose of internal use and confidentiality, we gave the proposed investment a codename, *Project Safe*, which has the double meaning of, in its adjective form, being protected from risks, as a bank ought to be, and of being a secure vault-like box.

By October 15, 1998, we had produced a first draft of the term sheet for a controlling investment in one of the two banks for sale. The major terms required the government to remove all the bad loans and assets from the balance sheet, creating a *good bank*, and then to fill the hole left by the removal of the bad assets with an interest-bearing government IOU, which we referred to as the government note. Newbridge and the government would jointly invest enough money to bring the bank's capital up to the minimum required by banking regulation, and Newbridge's ownership would be 51 percent. The government would own the other 49 percent. Newbridge would have full control of the good bank. If we discovered any remaining bad loans after the deal closed, we would also have the right to *put* them to the government, meaning we could sell them back at the original book value (i.e., 100 cents on the dollar) plus accrued interest.

In the Morgan Stanley proposal, the government offered to take all the bad loans and assets off the balance sheet of the good bank before the closing of the sale, but it offered to pay only 80 cents on the dollar for any charge-offs discovered on the legacy loan book after closing. Our proposal required 100 cents, which we thought was reasonable. We wanted to buy a ship and its cargo, but only after damaged goods were removed. The investment would work only if the seller would agree to take away and pay the buyer the original value for any damaged goods subsequently discovered in the original cargo. Otherwise, we would risk sinking money into a hole of unknown depth.

Our proposed deal structure was modeled after the ASB transaction, but, due to the many Korea-specific peculiarities, we had to modify the terms. While going over some questions about the ASB deal with Bonderman, he said, "My memory is foggy on the details. You should check with Lehman and Cleary guys for details." But it soon became clear that Bonderman remembered the terms, and the related thought process, better than anyone, so we repeatedly checked with him to make sure we did not miss anything.

Unlike the rest of us, Bonderman did not use email. We communicated with him only by fax or by phone. Wherever he might be, he would respond to any memo as soon as he read it, by dictating his reply over the phone to his secretary, who was based in Fort Worth, Texas. If it was after office hours, he spoke into a tape recorder and his secretary would transcribe the message and fax it out as soon as she received it. I now feel fortunate he was so old-fashioned, because I managed to gather a trove of physical memos that have been crucial in reconstructing the deal for this book. (It took Bonderman some time to catch up with the modern world. Ten years later he and I went together to the Beijing Summer Olympics. One day we were sitting a few rows apart in the vast and crowded stadium. Before the event finished, I got a text message from him: "Meet at gate question mark." It turned out he couldn't figure out how to type a "?" on his Nokia phone so he spelled it out.)

After more than a week of working on drafts internally, we finally dispatched our term sheet to Morgan Stanley. Our proposal did not specify which of the two banks we would acquire, as we did not yet have enough information about either to make a decision, but the deal structure we proposed would apply to either Korea First or Seoul Bank.

The term sheet outlined the good bank/bad bank model we had discussed with Chairman Lee in our meeting in Seoul. The good bank would contain substantially all of the bank's performing loans and assets, as well as its facilities, branches, and deposits. It would also hold the right to exercise a put option to sell to the government any bad loans which were discovered later on (any new loans made under our ownership would of course be excluded from the put right). All nonperforming loans (NPLs) would be transferred to a bad bank, which would be a government-owned entity.

My cover letter highlighted the merits of our proposal. The good bank, once freed from its legacy bad loans,

> would alleviate the public's anxiety about the safety of their deposits, enabling it to attract new deposits and reducing the bank's cost of funding. The restructured bank would have a drastically reduced risk of failure and would provide a strong signal to the international community that the government was serious about financial sector reforms. Its success would be critical in restoring confidence, both overseas and at home, in Korea's financial system. By retaining a 49 percent ownership stake in the good bank, the government would share the upside from our success in turning around the bank; these proceeds would offset the overall cost of banking sector reform.

I did not realize, until much later, what a difference the last point would make in the government's consideration of our offer. To save these banks, the government had already poured 1.5 trillion Korean won (about $1.125 billion) into each of them, and expected to add many times that amount, as more and more loans became impaired. The government had a strong desire to recover as much of the taxpayers' money as possible. Many officials found the opportunity to share in the upside of a recovery very appealing. We were, of course, not the only bidders. The team at the FSC was also negotiating with two strategic investors, Citibank and HSBC. Both were major international banks—exactly what the teasers specified—and were preferred over Newbridge as potential buyers. The FSC Chairman Lee recalled in his 2012 memoir (which I only read the English translation of an excerpt on KFB), "The government wanted to deal with HSBC with an expectation that we would learn advanced management methods and if we sold the bank to the world's best bank, it would better enhance our sovereign credit ratings."

The government's preference for a major bank might explain why we did not hear back from it until nearly three weeks later, just days before the bank's self-imposed deadline for a deal on November 15.

"Just an update on Project Safe," wrote my colleague Chen. "We had a conversation with Morgan Stanley earlier today to clarify aspects of our term sheet. Morgan indicated that our proposal, while different from that of the government, was nevertheless reasonable, particularly given the potentially substantial upside for the government to help reduce the cost of banking reform."

Meanwhile, I received a handwritten note from our advisor Jihong Kim, who thought that "[t]he Korean government and the FSC are more favorable to strategic investors than to financial investors [such as New-bridge]. . . . By attracting a world-renowned bank into Korea, the FSC wants to have announcement effects in the world financial community. . . . If Newbridge teams up with a major bank, I feel confident that New-bridge will be the preferred candidate."

Among our investors whom we call limited partners, Newbridge had many blue-chip financial institutions, including GE Capital, Bank of America, Merrill Lynch, MetLife, and others. We thought we might be able to entice one of them to co-invest with us if we put a good deal together, but their role would still be that of a financial investor rather than a strategic one. Few big banks had any appetite to invest strategically in a broken bank in the middle of a financial crisis. Still, to the Korean government, such a major financial institution could bring a valuable "announcement effect" to the table, even if it came in as a junior co-investor in a deal led by Newbridge.

I called Jihong and told him we would try Bank of America (BofA), whose principal investment arm was an investor with Newbridge Capital. Blum's firm had made a major investment in BofA during the savings and loan crisis in the 1980s, which we could point to, alongside Bonderman's turnaround of ASB, as evidence of our collective expertise reviving problem banks. If we could bring in BofA's principal-investing arm as a co-investor, I thought, it would make us more appealing to the Korean government.

My suggestion worked, at first. Jihong Kim sent through the FSC's initial response on November 23, 1998, which said that FSC officials were pleased about the potential to bring in BofA as a co-investor. They also made it clear that the FSC wanted Newbridge to communicate with the FSC directly instead of working through Morgan Stanley. This caught my attention. I wondered why the government wanted to go around its own advisors.

I suspected it was a signal that the FSC's negotiations with other parties were not going well, or that it was losing confidence in Morgan Stanley. It was a sign that Newbridge might be closer to making a deal than we realized.

However, the next day Jihong sent another note. The FSC had issues because BofA already held a stake in another Korean bank, KorAm Bank, which was also in trouble. We decided to instead approach GE Capital, the investment arm of the American industrial giant and also a limited partner of ours, through its office in Hong Kong. GE Capital was interested. I immediately informed the FSC, which seemed to be pleased and invited us to meet at our earliest convenience.

★ ★ ★

Almost three months after we first saw the invitation from Morgan Stanley, negotiations with the FSC seemed to be getting serious. We met on December 11, 1998, at FSC headquarters. There were seven of us on our side: Carroll, Chen, our advisor Jihong Kim, and I represented the Newbridge team; Phil Erlanger and David Kim of Lehman Brothers; and Nancy Ku from GE Capital. We met with Dong-soo Chin, director general of the Financial Restructuring Task Force of the FSC; his deputy, Sung-hun Kim; and others of the FSC staff.

Chin looked youthful, much younger than his 49 years, and scholarly with pale skin, dark hair, and spectacles. He was gentle in his manners and soft in his speech. His deputy, Sung-hun Kim, looked to be in his late 30s. Referred to as Dr. Kim, he was also a scholarly type, gentle, patient, and detail-oriented. The two of them made a good negotiating team.

We presented Chin and his team with an overview of our credentials, including our investor base, and the various bank deals we had done, including those our principals had led at TPG, RCBA, and Newbridge. We explained the merits of the good bank/bad bank model and the basic elements of our term sheet. Chin expressed appreciation for the deal structure we proposed, especially as it allowed the Korean government to participate in almost half of any upside from the deal. I could tell he really liked that.

The main sticking point, as the meeting went on, was the put option, the right to transfer back bad loans to the government after the transaction had closed. How long would the put right last? And at what price would the government be obligated to buy these bad loans? The government's original position, per the documents sent out by Morgan Stanley, was that it would allow the investor to sell back bad loans and assets for a period of three years. But now the FSC had changed its mind, saying it would agree to a one-year put. We countered by asking that it remain in force for at least two years.

The FSC also wanted the investor to share 20 percent of the losses from legacy loans when the investor exercised the put right. This was not acceptable to us; 20 percent of a black hole was still a black hole. Such loss-sharing could easily wipe out the new capital we planned to inject into the bank. Loan-level due diligence ("Due diligence" refers to a process of thorough investigation) would have been hard even in normal circumstances; in an economic crisis, when virtually all borrowers were struggling, figuring out which loans would go bad in the future and transferring all of them to the government before the transaction closed would be almost impossible. The risk was too great and too hard to quantify.

The FSC team did not seem to think our position unreasonable. However, they countered, if the good bank was given the accommodating terms we envisioned—basically, an unlimited put-back right—it would have no incentive to work out these problem loans. They were concerned about creating a moral hazard because it would be too easy for the bank to get rid of a troubled loan without incurring any losses, as opposed to making a reasonable effort to work it out. I thought the government's concern was legitimate and suggested we find other ways to address it.

Despite these differences, the meeting went well and lasted four hours. It was clear that the FSC was engaging with us seriously. After we adjourned the meeting, all of us from both sides went to a Chinese restaurant nearby for lunch. I thought it was a good sign that everyone liked fried sauce noodle, a typical Chinese dish with a Chinese name, *zha-jiang-mian*, that was pronounced similarly in Korean. At least in this dish, we found good chemistry and understanding between us.

Chapter 3

White Knight

We didn't know it at the time, but one of the reasons we seemed to be getting along so well with our new friends at the FSC was that negotiations between the government and the other banks had bogged down.

Chairman Lee of the FSC later recounted the situation in his memoir:

> *The market was chilly. Nobody wanted to buy the banks. I knocked on the doors of more than 40 foreign banks following the advice of Morgan Stanley. Citibank suggested it would want to buy 100 good branches of Korea First Bank. If so, who would buy the remaining ones? . . . HSBC, the only interested bank, showed nerve. But they were so arrogant. They required put-back options and also said, "We will own 100 percent of the shares." . . . The government argued "We have to hold at least 40 percent of the shares." But HSBC insisted "no more than 20 percent."*

As we learned, even the 20 percent of equity that HSBC was prepared to let the government own came with conditions. HSBC wanted the right, known as a *call option*, to purchase the remaining 20 percent after four years, at the bank's net asset value. In normal times, banks trade at a premium to net asset value; such a call option would have left the government without much upside. Morgan Stanley was pushing the government to accept HSBC's proposal as the only credible one, and the government was desperately in need of a way out.

The government was counting on Newbridge to make an acceptable bid. We were prepared to engage immediately once the FSC shifted its attention to Newbridge. Although we had no knowledge of the proposals made by Citibank and HSBC, our bid, which included a 49 percent ownership stake for the government, was looking more appealing. The English edition of *JoongAng Ilbo*, a major Korean newspaper, explained the Korean government's perspective in a special report a few years later:

> *Newbridge's Weijian Shan visited the Financial Supervisory Commission and offered a dossier on a plan to normalize Korea First Bank. "We know what the Korean government thinks. We will have a 51 percent stake. And the government takes the other 49 percent," Mr. Shan told commission officials. Newbridge read the Korean government's mind.*

In fact, nobody told us what the government was thinking, nor were we clairvoyant. However, we knew there would not be a deal unless the government could sell it to the Korean public. A lot of taxpayer money— 5.1 trillion won (about $4.25 billion) by then—had been poured into the two banks to save them. If an investor bought 100 percent of the bank, the government could only report to the public how much taxpayers' money it would lose—not only how much had already been put into the banks, but also the additional costs of buying back the remaining bad loans. The public wanted to know how much money the taxpayers would *get back* if the bank was turned around. The HSBC deal didn't leave much room for good news.

Our proposed deal would let the government invest on a pari passu basis, or on equal footing with us, for about half of the equity, which would allow it—and taxpayers—to capture about half of the future gain. It is understandable that a bank such as HSBC would want to control 100 percent of a subsidiary. But there were ways to structure a deal so that the investor would retain a preemptive right to acquire the shares owned by the government at fair market value *after* the bank was turned around. Such a structure would allow both parties to achieve their objectives. The politics seemed so obvious that we had never thought of a deal structure that would deny the government upside from a successful turnaround. It was surprising that none of our competitors could see this.

★ ★ ★

After our meeting at the FSC, Dr. Sung-hun Kim, Dong-soo Chin's deputy, became our interlocutor representing the FSC. I met with him again six days later, on December 17, to discuss the terms of our investment over dinner at the Japanese restaurant in Seoul's Hilton Hotel, where I was staying. Our advisor, Jihong Kim, joined us. Dr. Kim questioned me on our terms, and I explained the rationale for each of them. I listened to his responses, including his reasons for objecting to some of them. In the end, we narrowed the gap between us considerably. It was a helpful, candid conversation, and I came away from it feeling that we had built trust with the government. Dr. Kim concluded the meeting by saying "I hope we sign an MOU by the end of the year."

An MOU, or memorandum of understanding, would not be a binding contract, but it would contain the basic terms of an agreement and it would give Newbridge the exclusive right to negotiate further with the government. As much as I shared his hope, with just two weeks left in the year, we had a lot of ground to cover.

Unknowingly, Newbridge had become a "white knight" in the government's search for a buyer of its failed banks. In private equity business, the term "white knight" refers to an acquirer who comes in late but offers a better and more friendly deal to the seller. At that particular moment, we had no idea what terms that HSBC and Citibank had offered to the government. But, from the perspective of the government, our proposal was clearly more attractive than those from either of the two large global banking institutions.

The next day, the FSC was in touch to reiterate that they could agree to one year of unlimited put rights, but not the two years we had asked for. Bonderman thought a one-year put, in addition to the right to remove all the bad assets prior to closing, was acceptable. I was still concerned that we would not be able to identify all the hidden bad loans and assets within one year. If the economic crisis was prolonged, there was no telling how many legacy loans could go bad.

I decided to insist on a two-year put right, but, as a compromise, we would agree not to sell back loans exceeding a certain percentage of the loan book in the second year, based on our confidence that even if we missed some hidden bad loans in our initial due diligence, they would not represent a significant percentage of the total. For every loan we put back to the government, though, the government would be required to pay its original book value, 100 cents on the dollar, plus accrued interest. I asked Jihong to explain all this to the FSC and let them know that shortening the put period was not necessarily in their best interest. Loan quality was expected to improve as the economy recovered, which would likely take more than one year. The longer the put period, the fewer loans might eventually be put back because the bank would be given more time to work out a questionable loan, which ultimately would reduce the cost to the government.

Jihong Kim went to meet with the FSC's Chairman Lee on the afternoon of Friday, December 18, just as I was flying back to Hong Kong for the weekend. I received a call from Jihong as soon as I landed. He said that Lee was receptive to our proposal and had also spoken with his team about it.

The FSC, Jihong explained, would accept Newbridge's put condition if the post-close rights were exercised "with proper procedures." For example, the loans could be transferred back to the government only after the bank had sent several demand notices requesting payment from borrowers and had gone through other legal procedures. The bank would be expected to roll over regularly performing loans at maturity, unless it had specific reasons to refuse the roll-over of loans. That was not a problem for us. From our point of view, the bank would have every incentive to keep a performing loan because it was an earning asset. A bank's business was to make loans so we would want to get rid of a loan only if it clearly could not be recollected.

We seemed to have cleared a major hurdle. Dan Carroll and I worked over the weekend to revise the term sheet, which we completed on the morning of Tuesday, December 22. We faxed it to the FSC that afternoon, just before my colleague Daniel Poon and I flew to Seoul from Hong Kong. Our flight was practically empty; there were few business travelers so close to Christmas. I did not know where negotiations between the government and HSBC stood at that point, but I assumed Westerners would not want to work over Christmas holiday, so the FSC team could concentrate all their attention on us. It felt like Santa was on our side.

We again stayed at the Hilton in downtown Seoul, and the FSC team decided to hold our meetings there for the purpose of secrecy. This sale was inevitably going to be a high-profile affair in Korea. The press was sniffing around for any signs of progress to report. Newbridge and the FSC did not want our teams to be seen together, as neither side wanted a premature leak.

Dr. Kim and his team arrived at the Hilton the next morning at 9:30. On our side were myself, Jihong Kim, Daniel Poon, and David Kim from Lehman Brothers. We began by going through the term sheet, line by line, very slowly and carefully. At first, we avoided the major issues, trying to narrow the gap between us by resolving smaller and easier ones instead. We did not finish our meeting until about 10 pm, and there was still a lot of work ahead of us.

The next day would be Christmas Eve. Since I could not go home, my wife, Bin, our son Bo, who was 15, and our daughter LeeAnn, who was seven, flew to Seoul to join me. I was so happy to see them, but I could not spare much time for them. Bin and I always tried to emphasize to our children the importance of a strong work ethic, so Bin used me to set an example. "Putting bread on the table for the family isn't easy," Bin lectured Bo. "Look at how hard your dad works!" But if I'm honest, putting bread on the table wasn't my motivation. I was driven by the thrill of this opportunity—and beating our rivals. It was all consuming; I could barely focus on anything else.

We continued to negotiate the term sheet with the FSC, picking up where we had left off the previous night. Since we were getting reasonably close, Dr. Kim asked us to decide which of the two banks, Korea First Bank (KFB) or Seoul Bank, we proposed to buy.

Our team had only two members, Daniel Poon and myself, camped out in Seoul, along with David Kim from Lehman. We decided to divide our limited forces. Poon and David Kim went to check out the two banks and I continued to negotiate the term sheet with Dr. Kim and his team. Only 25 years old, Daniel was the youngest member of our team. But he was highly analytical and meticulous. Almost nothing escaped his sharp eye when it came to due diligence or documentation. He also had excellent judgment.

It was now a race with HSBC to see who could reach an agreement with the government first. We understood that they had a team of 20 people on the ground conducting due diligence, looking through as many loans as they could, document by document, in order to get a sense of the health of both banks. We had also heard, although we could not verify it, that HSBC was willing to absorb 20 percent of the losses on any bad loans discovered after the deal closed. Given that HSBC needed to be able to identify not only every bad loan but also every potential bad loan before closing, they had set themselves up for a massive amount of work; there were tens of thousands of loans across the two banks.

Our strategy was different. My thinking was that diving into loan-level due diligence without knowing if we could strike a reasonable deal was a waste of time, manpower, and resources. Our proposed deal would be subject to due diligence, to be completed after signing the MOU, and, under our terms, we would be able to transfer all the bad loans and assets to the government after closing, so there was no need to do all our due diligence before the MOU. That allowed our team, small as it was, to remain fully focused on negotiations with the FSC. In fact, we were all but monopolizing the FSC's time, leaving our competitor HSBC with no counterpart to negotiate with. I couldn't help but gloat a bit. It was obvious that we had the government's full attention and that it was making a serious effort to reach an agreement with us by the year-end deadline.

In reality, of course, we were never in control of the negotiation pace; the FSC team must have felt it had a better chance to reach a deal with us, and faster, than with anyone else. Our willingness to accommodate the government's wishes to meet the deadline also made a difference.

★ ★ ★

On the morning of Christmas Eve I spent an hour on the phone with David Bonderman, updating him on the negotiations and getting his guidance on the remaining issues. Then I met Dr. Kim and his team in a conference room on the 19th floor of the Hilton. Following Bonderman's suggestion, I proposed that after the bank was purged of its bad loans and assets, it would issue two types of shares, common and preferred, to both the investor and the government, as consideration for the capital we both would invest. I proposed that the split between preferred stock and common be 60:40, with Newbridge owning 51 percent of each and the government, 49 percent. Unlike common stock, preferred typically does not have voting rights, but its dividend takes priority over that of common stock.

We also offered the government warrants, the option to buy 5 percent more of each type of share issued by the bank at a future date, at a predetermined price. Via the warrants, the government would own 49 percent of the shares outright but would stand to capture another 5 percent of the upside if the shares' value rose higher than the strike price of the warrants. (The warrants were exercisable only at the time of our exit, so the government would not own more than 49 percent of the shares of the bank at any time.) Bonderman's idea was meant to give the government a better share of the upside. The warrants would dilute our own gains, but he was a big-picture man. Bonderman liked to say "In the scheme of things, this won't matter to us."

The idea had not come up before, and was probably unnecessary to bring the parties closer, but we felt it would build goodwill and trust. Sure enough, Dr. Kim was pleased by our offer, but once the door was opened, the government demanded more warrants.

Another major point of discussion involved reaching agreement on the yield on the government note, the interest-bearing IOU to the bank, issued by the government to fill the hole left by the carved-out bad assets. Owing the bank and paying interest on the money owed would be mutually beneficial to the government and to Newbridge. The government was so strapped for cash that it was in its best interest to postpone any payments. For the bank, taking the government note was much better than taking cash because the note would earn interest.

It was agreed that the note's interest rate would be set at 250 basis points (2.5 percent) over the average cost of the bank's interest-bearing liabilities (i.e., deposits, or any other borrowings on which the bank would pay interest), giving the bank an effective 250-basis point margin above its cost of funds. In the context of the economic crisis, this margin was low, but we considered it fair because the government's IOU was virtually risk free. The probability of a government defaulting on a domestic debt obligation is practically nil, because in the worst case it can always print money. I was pleased as it seemed major issues were being resolved. Indeed, I was beginning to feel merry.

Meanwhile, Poon and David Kim returned, late in the afternoon, fresh from visiting the two banks up for sale. The decision was not hard. In some ways the banks were quite similar, confirming our impression from the initial teasers sent by Morgan Stanley. They were similar in terms of total assets, number of employees, and the bad loan ratio. They were both centered in Seoul with branches scattered across the country. But after meeting both management teams, Poon and David Kim suggested that we choose Korea First Bank. They felt that not only had KFB a stronger brand, a stronger branch network, and a longer operating history, its management actually had a plan for the future and was working to right the foundering bank.

Since our deal structure required the target bank's balance sheet be cleaned up by the government, the volume of bad loans was less important to us than the quality of the franchise, and Newbridge felt KFB's quality was stronger. I also thought the name was more appealing: The name "Korea First" immediately suggested a nationwide institution of some prestige, whereas the name "Seoul Bank" could be misunderstood to mean some local city bank. We decided right there and then to pick KFB. It took us less time to decide which bank to buy than it usually would take a family to decide which car to purchase. But this was an unusual situation, and there was no time to hesitate.

I called Dr. Kim to let him know our choice. The FSC agreed that, if the negotiations were successful, we could buy KFB. Ultimately, the government did not care very much who bought which bank, and it was willing to accommodate our wishes on a first-come, first-served basis. I was glad that we moved fast and decisively. The FSC told us that, later that same day, HSBC indicated to the government that it, too, wanted to buy KFB, but they were told it was too late.

★ ★ ★

Korea has had a long history, dating back to antiquity. In much of its ancient history, the land was divided among warring states and occasionally unified as one kingdom, such as the Shilla (AD 668–935) and the Goryeo, from which the English name "Korea" was derived (918–1392).

The Korean peninsula is strategically positioned between China, Russia, and Japan (see Exhibit 1), and for centuries its sovereignty was under constant threat. Japan invaded in 1592 and again in 1597. Both times, Japanese troops were repelled by the joint forces of Korea and China. In 1894, the king appealed to the Chinese government for help to put down a rebellion. Japan, with its long-held ambitions for Korea, was not invited but sent troops anyway. After the rebellion was quelled, Japan refused to leave, fought a war with China, and won. As a result, Korea ceased to be a vassal state of China and came under Japanese occupation. In 1910, Japan formally annexed Korea. The colonial rulers were known not only for their brutality but also for their systematic effort to erase Korea's national identity and culture.

After the Japanese surrender in 1945 at the end of World War II, the Korean Peninsula was occupied by the Soviet Union in the north and the United States in the south, along the 38th Parallel. On June 25, 1950, the Korean War broke out when North Korea invaded the South in an attempt to reunify the country. The United States entered the war and pushed the North Koreans all the way to Yalu River, which borders China. China intervened and eventually fought the US forces to a stalemate back at the 38th Parallel, which stands to this day under an armistice signed on July 27, 1953.

Korea First Bank was one of the country's largest and oldest banks. It was founded in 1929, during the Japanese colonial era, as Chosun Savings Bank. It was listed on the Korean Stock Exchange in 1957 and by the end of the decade had come under the control of Samsung Group. It changed its name to Korea First Bank in 1958. In 1962, it was nationalized along with other commercial banks by Chung-hee Park, leader of the military coup that had taken power in 1961. During Park's authoritarian regime, which lasted until his assassination in 1979, he rallied the nation's energies and resources toward a series of antipoverty and industrialization campaigns. In pursuit of industrialization, the government tightly controlled access to credit, subsidizing loans to favored industries in close coordination with business leaders.

In 1971, KFB was the first Korean commercial bank to open an overseas office, allowing it to borrow from abroad. Korea's domestic savings were far below desired levels, so foreign capital was key to economic growth. In the 1980s, KFB became known for innovation. It was the first commercial bank to computerize all its internal systems and one of the first banks to introduce credit cards and automatic teller machines in Korea. In 1982, KFB was reprivatized as part of the government's economic liberalization efforts.

By the early 1990s, it was among the most profitable Korean commercial banks, with some of the country's largest and most influential companies among its clients. It was the lead bank for such big *chaebols* as LG Group, SK Group, and Daewoo Group. Loans to the top five *chaebols,* including also Hyundai and Samsung, accounted for 65 percent of KFB's portfolio.

By the middle of the decade, it emerged as Korea's largest integrated financial group. In addition to commercial banking, KFB had subsidiaries engaged in securities, derivatives, leasing, and investment consulting. By the end of 1996, KFB's total assets stood at $40.7 billion (34.6 trillion won), and the bank had 8,321 employees, 421 domestic branches, and 17 overseas branches and offices. It was considered to be one of Korea's crown jewels.

But in 1997, the go-go growth strategy that had allowed KFB to become so large began to unravel. In January a major borrower, the Hanbo Group, collapsed, brought down in part by a bribery scandal that exposed widespread corruption and weakness among some of Korea's largest companies. Amid the ensuing turmoil, six other *chaebols* either filed for financial assistance or sought protection from the commercial banks. KFB installed a new president, Shee-yul Ryoo, the former deputy governor of the Bank of Korea, the country's central bank. But by this point the Asian financial crisis was in full swing; KFB's shortage of capital overwhelmed Ryoo's best attempts at restructuring it. In the end, Ryoo simply ran out of time.

As *chaebols* continued to fail, KFB's bad loans exploded. During the first half of 1997, the bank had about $3.2 billion in nonperforming or impaired loans—approximately 17 percent of its total loans—and reported a net loss of $417 million (356.5 billion won), 10 times its year-earlier loss of $42.7 million (34.6 billion won). International rating agencies downgraded KFB's debt, reflecting the bank's deteriorating asset quality and the heightened risks Korean banks faced as corporate defaults continued to mount.

In October, as Korea's economic situation worsened, the government offered special loans to the nation's capital-starved commercial banks to forestall a meltdown in the financial sector. On December 3, 1997, just one day before the IMF bailout was announced, KFB's bad loan problem became public knowledge and the Korean government had to decide whether to let KFB fail or bail it out. Many analysts and bankers stated that the bank should be closed outright.

★ ★ ★

Daniel Poon flew back to Hong Kong on the afternoon of Christmas Eve. I decided to stay in Seoul to get the deal sealed up. David Kim from Lehman and a lawyer from Cleary, S.K. Kang, worked with me to revise the term sheet to reflect the points we'd agreed on with Dr. Kim earlier that day, and then I stepped out for a run.

It was an unusually warm winter day and the run was pleasant. About halfway through, my mobile phone rang. It was Jihong Kim, our advisor.

There's been a change, Jihong said.

Lehman's chief representative in Seoul was Kunho Cho. He was not much involved in our deal discussions but somehow, unbeknownst to me, he had met with Chairman Lee earlier that day and indicated that New-bridge would be willing both to accept loan-loss sharing and to increase the number of warrants granted to the government. I was disturbed to hear this, and suddenly felt a lot less merry. I had not expected to be undercut at the 11th hour, by our own financial advisor, no matter how well intentioned Cho had been.

It was awkward, but I had to call Dr. Kim to explain that Cho was not involved in our internal deliberations and what he had said did not accurately represent our position. In the end, Dr. Kim accepted my explanation, but I was working until very late on Christmas Eve, while my family went out to celebrate.

Christmas is the second biggest holiday in South Korea, after the Lunar New Year. Despite being a Confucian society by tradition and culture, South Korea is about 30 percent Christian. Although the country was facing its worst economic crisis since after the Korean War, all the buildings were brightly lit, and all the shop windows were adorned with colorful ornaments. The streets were packed with traffic as merrymakers drove from party to party. From the windows of my hotel room, I could see Seoul's buildings covered in festive, bright lights. Below, cars filled the streets in every direction. Bin and our children tried to go to a skating rink that was, peculiarly, inside a shopping mall, but the traffic was so bad they gave up and came back to the hotel.

★ ★ ★

Bright and early on Christmas morning, I received a fax from Bonderman, asking me to halt negotiations and call him immediately.

He was perturbed that the deal might not work for us anymore after the compromises I had made. I thought I had been careful, and I would never make a material concession without internal consensus, and especially without his consent. But small concessions could add up, and, from a distance, Bonderman was worried that the deal might have materially changed from our initial proposal. I updated him on what had transpired in our negotiations the previous day. He suggested that we regroup via a conference call to make sure that we were all on the same page before proceeding further.

The call was scheduled for late in the evening Christmas Day, so I spent some time with my family. Bin and I took the children to Lotte World, a huge indoor amusement park in Seoul. The place was so packed with children that it was hard to imagine that South Korea was in the throes of an economic crisis, but despite the crowds we had a great time. We ended an enjoyable Christmas Day with dinner at the teppanyaki counter of the Hilton's Japanese restaurant.

After the children had gone to sleep, I headed upstairs to the conference room to join the conference call. On the line were the members of our team, including Carroll, Chen, and Poon; the Lehman team, led by Erlanger; and the Cleary team, led by Michael Ryan. We were all in different places and in different time zones, and it was Christmas Day for all of us, which we were supposed to be celebrating with our families. Still, united by the project at hand, we methodically worked through each item on the term sheet and laid out the outstanding issues. It took us until 1 am, Seoul time, to finish.

The next morning, I returned to the 19th-floor conference room and phoned Bonderman. Although he hadn't been on the previous evening's call, he had been briefed by Erlanger. Overall, Bonderman was satisfied with where we stood. His only suggestion was regarding the government note, which we expected in return for the troubled loans we would be moving over to the bad bank. Bonderman suggested we extend the maturity of the government note beyond three years if its size was greater than $6 billion. He was concerned that if the government paid back the note before the economy improved, we might not be able to turn the cash into new loans quickly enough. It would be costly for the bank to hold cash, which would not earn interest (to cover the costs of its liabilities), whereas the government note would pay us 2.5 percent over the bank's average cost of funds. By proposing to extend the term, Bonderman meant to give us more time to grow our loan book based on our judgment about the timing and strength of Korea's economic recovery.

After lunch, Bin and our children went with Jihong's wife and children to Yongpyong, a popular ski resort about a two and a half hour drive east of Seoul. I so wished I could go with them, but duty wouldn't allow me. My disappointment was tempered by the fact that I knew, before they arrived, that work would consume most of my time. Even though I couldn't join them, I was happy that they could find something fun to do. Jihong Kim, David Kim, and I headed for the FSC's office to meet with our negotiator, Dr. Kim. As this was a holiday, the FSC's office was empty except for us.

The meeting began at about 2 pm and ground forward as we painstakingly reexamined each of the terms. I did most of the talking, while David Kim took notes. We negotiated late into the night. The FSC officials certainly earned my respect. They were professional, dedicated, and hardworking, no less so than our side. They fought hard for everything and did not give up until they had pushed us to the limit. We once again went through the terms one by one, eventually reaching agreement on all of them.

At the last minute, Dr. Kim requested an increase in the warrants we'd agreed to grant the government. In my opinion, we had already been unduly generous in offering them at all. After a drawn-out discussion, I reluctantly agreed to increase the warrants on the preferred shares from 5 percent to 5.5 percent. Dr. Kim gave me a look of incredulity and reproach—*how stingy can you be?*—but he did not push further.

As the night wore on, David Kim, who had not slept much for days, began to noticeably nod off. We finally finished at about half past midnight and I retreated to my hotel, while an exhausted David Kim still had to back to his office to revise the term sheet based on the results of our negotiations and to send the latest revisions to Bonderman and other members of our team.

The next morning, relieved to have some family time, Jihong and I took off for Yongpyong ski resort, arriving in time for lunch with our families. Yongpyong, which means *Dragon Valley*, is the best-known and largest ski resort in South Korea; it even hosted the 2018 Winter Olympics. Yongpyong spanned four peaks and more than a dozen lifts. There were trails for skiers of all levels, which was good for me. No one in our family was an experienced skier, so we planned to stick to the less difficult runs and just have fun. Dragon Peak, the tallest of the resort, was nearly a mile above sea level. It was for advanced skiers, but we all admired the stunning backdrop it provided. Breathing in the icy air, I could feel the stress of the negotiations began to subside, and I was eager to hit the slopes.

After lunch, I rented some ski gear, but just as I headed for the lift to make my first run of the day, Bonderman called, quite upset. The term sheet was far worse than the previous day, he said. He would not agree to follow through with the deal.

This was perplexing to me because I did not think the terms were any worse, so I wondered how he had gotten that impression. But before I could ask him to clarify, the battery on my phone died, drained by the cold weather, leaving me scrambling to find a landline and call him back.

By the time I got in touch, I had also taken another look at the term sheet David Kim had typed up after the previous night's meeting. I discovered a number of mistakes in his notes, no doubt made as he was sleepily typing on his laptop. In a couple of places, the sleep-deprived Lehman banker had nodded off, literally typing a string of *zzzz*'s. In some places, the language was unclear and ambiguous. For example, during the negotiations we had agreed that, after the government had replaced KFB's bad assets with cash or government securities and turned it into a clean bank, both Newbridge and the government would recapitalize the bank by putting in money in agreed-upon proportions. But our revised terms sheet read as if the government would simply receive shares without paying for them. No wonder Bonderman was nonplussed.

I abandoned all hope of skiing that day. Working from our hotel room at the resort, I carefully reworked the term sheet to reflect what I had agreed upon with Dr. Kim the night before. Then I wrote a long note to explain the changes. In keeping with my bad luck that day, our hotel did not have a fax machine, so Jihong Kim had to drive me to another hotel to fax the lengthy documents to Bonderman. Then I emailed the same documents to the rest of the team, including our advisors. It was past midnight by the time I finished.

The next morning, December 28, dawned clear and beautiful. I took the family out skiing under blue skies and bright sunshine. The air was crisp and being with Bin and our children in the snow-covered mountains filled me with joy. We arranged for our daughter LeeAnn to have lessons with a Swiss ski instructor who spoke good English. I was so pleased that LeeAnn soon learned to go up the lift and ski down on her own. By the end of the day, she was arguably the best skier in our family, despite being only seven years old.

But the deal went on. After a morning on the mountain and lunch at the hotel, I spent the rest of the afternoon on a conference call with Bonderman and others. When we finished, it was about 2 am in Colorado, where Bonderman was, and 4 am on the U.S. East Coast, where other members of the team were working. Before we finished the call, I said to Bonderman, "David, don't freak out when you see something wrong. It stresses me out. Just call me and we will fix it."

All of us were working nonstop that holiday season to move the project forward. I thought to myself there was no way HSBC could possibly compete with us to meet the government's year-end deadline, which was only three days away. Our team had an intensely strong work dynamic and we were far nimbler than most of our corporate competitors, so we were able to have productive discussions and make decisions in real time, even during Christmas. I had worked in two major banks in my previous life, the World Bank and JP Morgan. I knew the bureaucracy of a large bank would not allow efficient decision making on a major project like this. I was confident we would be able to beat HSBC to the finish line.

I called Dr. Kim that afternoon and promised that I would send him our revised term sheet the next morning. He told me the government was prepared to sign the MOU on December 30.

Despite his words and intention, it would not be a smooth ride to the finish line.

The next morning, December 29, David Kim faxed Dr. Kim the revised term sheet. I was skiing with my family, when, shortly before 11 am, someone at the FSC called Jihong, requesting that I immediately return to Seoul. Jihong and I left together at about 6 pm to drive back. On the way, I called Philip Gilligan of White & Case (W&C), the law firm advising the government. I learned that, at the advice of W&C, the FSC had raised a number of issues with the term sheet and suggested several changes. Negotiations would be tough once I got back to Seoul.

Once again we met Dr. Kim and his team in the 19th-floor board-room of the Hilton, at about 9 pm. David Kim and Jihong joined me on our side. We discussed each of the terms revised by W&C, about seven or eight of which I considered to be outright deal breakers. For example, in our original term sheet, we had included a drag-along right, which would allow Newbridge to sell the shares of the bank owned by the government, on behalf of the government, when we sold our own. Literally, it would "drag along" the government into the sale we would be able to negotiate. This clause would be critical for when we ultimately sold the bank. Many buyers, especially other banks, would be interested in acquiring 100 percent of the company. If we could deliver only the portion that Newbridge owned, we might not be able to attract the best buyers, nor get the best price. The lawyers from W&C had removed this clause.

I explained to Dr. Kim that the drag-along was critical for both sides to be able to maximize value of the investment. But the FSC had its own concerns. "What if you sell too cheaply and take the capital to invest in something more profitable?" Dr. Kim asked.

I tried to assuage his fears. "That could not happen," I said. In the private equity business, we only got to invest the capital from our fund once. When an investment was sold or realized, we had to give the pro-ceeds back to our limited partners. Once a fund was fully invested, we had to raise another in order to make further investments. Usually, we would not be able to recycle the capital. Because Newbridge, as the manager of the capital provided by our investors, received a cut of the profit made from investing each fund, we would not exit from an investment until we thought the growth potential had peaked and we had maximized our return. There was every incentive for us to maximize the return on each investment.

Finally, Dr. Kim accepted my reasoning, and we kept our drag-along right, but we spent three hours on that term alone.

There were compromises on both sides, and the negotiations took hours. Finally, sometime after 8 am on December 30, we reached agreement once again on all major issues. We adjourned the meeting so

Dr. Kim could go back to check with his own people at the FSC to see if they could reach internal agreement on the changed terms.

Meanwhile, I called Erlanger of Lehman to consult with him on the changes. Then I called Ryan to get the Cleary lawyers' take. Finally, I called Bonderman to update him. He was agreeable, with two major exceptions: One, we must insist that the government exercise all its warrants at the time of our exit. Two, we had to be able to put the bank's nonperforming loans to the government in a timely manner.

After a quick shower I headed to the FSC with Jihong to meet with Chairman Lee. In our negotiations so far, the chairman had been stiff and formal—in fact, I had never seen him smile. But I could tell he was pleased with our progress, and I sensed that he wanted the deal to be reached before the year was out as much as I did.

President Dae-jung Kim's cabinet, the Council of Ministers, met that afternoon to discuss the merits of our negotiated deal. I knew that there were only three ministers whose opinions counted: Chairman Lee of the FSC; President Kim's chief of staff; and the head of the Ministry of Finance and Economy (MOFE). Lee and the chief of staff were both in favor; the finance minister voted against. However, I was relieved to discover that the motion to pursue a deal with Newbridge carried with a simple majority.

The opposition from MOFE wasn't entirely a surprise. I knew the ministry had made some last-minute requests to change the terms. Whereas the FSC was in charge of restructuring the banking system, MOFE was the one to provide the government funding for all the bank-bailout packages. However, I was told by the FSC officials that I did not have to accept MOFE's last-minute request unless I wished to.

Meanwhile, I had been busy exchanging draft documents among our team members and with our advisors for internal sign-off. It was not until dinnertime that I realized I had completely forgotten to have lunch that day, which was unusual for me, as I always have a good appetite.

At 9 pm, Dr. Kim and his team came to the hotel for further negotiations. For the most part they were minor details, except for the changes requested by MOFE. I had to reject all these changes, however, as we did not have any further room to concede. It was about 11 pm before we reached agreement on all the terms. I had been working on this deal without a break since Jihong and I had returned from our ski holiday more than 24 hours earlier, and I was hoping that this would be the final round of revisions before signing.

At five minutes past midnight on December 31, New Year's Eve, I circulated what I hoped was the final term sheet to our team. It felt good to have a document that seemed final and represented our weeks of work. My cover note summarized the major terms as follows:

- *The transacting parties would be Newbridge and "the Government of the Republic of Korea, acting through its Ministry of Finance and Economy, the Financial Supervisory Commission, the Korea Deposit Insurance Corporation and other agencies, as appropriate."*

- *At closing, KFB would retain substantially all of its performing loans, cash, investments and deposits, as well as any of its facilities and hard assets—office buildings, branches, furniture, and so on—that Newbridge wished to keep. All the nonperforming loans and assets would be transferred to the government or the "bad bank" owned by the government.*

- *All assets and liabilities of the bank would be subject to thorough due diligence by Newbridge. Each asset and liability initially selected to remain in KFB would be "marked to market" on an individual basis by Newbridge—in other words, they would be valued based on what they were worth in the current market.*

- *The hole in the balance sheet as a result of the transfer of the bad assets and of the mark-to-market exercise would be filled by cash or the Government Note issued by the government, in an amount sufficient to restore the balance between assets and liabilities.*

- *The Government Note would bear an interest rate that would be not higher than 2.5 percent over the bank's own average borrowing costs and, would mature, initially, in three years.*

- *Following an equalization of the assets and liabilities of the bank through the use of cash or the Government Note, the government and Newbridge would both make a capital contribution to recapitalize the bank, by subscribing for shares of the common stock and the preferred stock, resulting in 51 percent ownership by Newbridge and 49 percent ownership by the government.*

- *The government would receive a warrant or an option to buy more shares of KFB, representing 5 percent of the total shares of the common stock and 5.5 percent of the preferred stock outstanding as of closing. The exercise prices for the warrants would be determined by multiplying the purchase prices of the stocks by a growth rate of 10 percent per annum compounded for the period from closing to the time of exercise.*
- *Newbridge would be given the right to exercise sole voting rights with respect to the government's shares of the common stock, except with regard to specific issues having a material adverse economic effect on the government's interests as a shareholder.*
- *In the first year after closing, KFB would have the right to transfer to the government an unlimited amount of loans and other assets, which were collectively defined as "Put Assets." All such transfers would be at the original book value of the assets plus accrued interest. In the second year, KFB would have the right to transfer to the government Put Assets in an amount not to exceed 20 percent of the total loans of KFB as of closing, also at original book value plus accrued interest.*
- *There would be special treatment for the loans to top five chaebols (Hyundai, Daewoo, Samsung, LG, and SK), whose transfer to the government would be unlimited, but each of the top five chaebols would be treated equally if KFB was to retain any of their loans.*
- *The government would provide a guarantee on the principal of all the fixed income securities portfolio and on the book value of the equities portfolio retained by KFB.*
- *KFB would retain 100 percent of all benefits resulting from all existing tax losses held by the bank at closing as well as all benefits arising from future losses recognized by KFB—in other words, future income could be offset by the amount of the accumulated losses for the purpose of computing corporate income taxes.*
- *Newbridge would have the sole and complete right to appoint and terminate members of management and employees.*
- *The government and Newbridge would develop a plan to ensure the stability of the bank and preserve its value during the*

transition period between the signing of the MOU and closing. This would potentially include some kind of joint supervisory transition team overseeing the bank as Newbridge prepared to take control.

The exclusivity of our MOU would be valid for four months, expiring May 2, which was expected to give the parties more than enough time to negotiate the final documents and to close the transaction. May 2 seemed to be in the distant future. After all, the most contentious points of negotiation had already been hashed out for the MOU. Anything that was decided there should be unlikely to change much, we thought.

By the time I'd sent off the final, final document to our team members and advisors, I had been up for 43 continuous hours, beating my previous record of 31 hours straight, which happened in my youth, when I was digging a canal in China's Gobi Desert. For some reason, however, I did not feel tired. I was exhilarated. When I bite on something, I don't let go, and this deal excited me. It seemed our persistence had paid off, and we might just have wrestled this deal to the ground.

Although I had not gotten to bed until 1 am, I got up at 6 the next day and went for my regular morning run. At breakfast, I noticed the major English-language Korean papers were reporting that the KFB sale was "making progress." Although much of it was speculation, it was clear the press was now aware that Newbridge was the only party making headway with the government.

All morning I waited to hear from the FSC, but there was complete silence. I had no idea what was happening on the government side and didn't know whether I should worry. It was the last day of the year, the final deadline the government set for itself to sign the MOU. There was nothing more for me to do, and the energy that had sustained me through the deal making and negotiating finally faded. I dozed off. At about 10:30 am, I was awakened by a call from Jihong Kim, who said that the FSC was prepared to sign our agreement. The ceremony would be held at 1:30 that afternoon.

Elated, I began to get ready. However, Jihong called again an hour later to say there had been a snag. MOFE had another request, this time to raise the amount of the warrants we had offered the government— something we had already increased beyond what we wanted. The ministry had not been involved in the negotiations up until this point, so it was unaware of how many concessions we had already made. It seemed like a last-minute effort to squeeze as much out of us as it could. I knew that at this stage the government wasn't going to walk away over such a minor point, so I ignored it.

I arrived at the FSC building in Yeouido at 1:30 pm to find the FSC team already waiting for me. Unlike our previous meetings, the atmosphere was quite relaxed. With the tough negotiations behind us, we all felt relieved and accomplished—slightly more like colleagues than adversaries. We stood around chatting with each other, waiting for the signing ceremony to begin.

After a few minutes of chitchat, however, an FSC official drew me aside. The request to increase the warrants came directly from the finance minister, he explained. This changed things somewhat: I had to take a personal request from the minister seriously. While I knew we did not have to make any further concessions, in order to show respect to the minister I offered, as a gesture of goodwill, to increase the government's warrants for preferred shares by another half a percentage point. Fearing that another concession on my part would only invite more requests, I added that the offer was valid only for one hour, after which it would be withdrawn. The agreement was on the table, waiting to be signed, and we were literally running out of time. It was time to bring all this to an end.

The FSC team delivered my offer to Chairman Lee, who in turn talked with the minister to get his consent. It was accepted. We were all set.

At about 2 pm, Director General Dong-soo Chin and I sat down in front of the table, where a stack of documents was placed before us. We primed our pens and got started, Chin signing on behalf of the Korean government and I on behalf of Newbridge Capital. We signed the stacks in front of us, swapped piles, and signed again. The whole process took 10 minutes. After weeks of grinding work, many sleepless nights, and the stress and suspense, it was official. (See Exhibit 2.)

Chapter 4

New Faces at the Table

As reporters say, we made great copy. The announcement of the deal touched off a media frenzy. Not only was the timing of our agreement dramatic, coming as it did on the last day of the year, but it also catapulted Newbridge to prominence from relative obscurity. Some just did not believe that a relatively unknown private equity firm could have outmaneuvered HSBC, one of the largest banks in the world, to accomplish such a feat.

Among those who apparently did not believe it was a reporter for the *New York Times*, who filed a dispatch, dated January 1, 1999, giving credit to GE Capital as KFB's lead investor: "The South Korean Government signed an agreement today to sell a controlling stake in Korea First Bank to a consortium led by GE Capital, the world's largest nonbank financial services company, and Newbridge Capital."

The reporter clearly hadn't done any fact checking. While we had originally proposed bringing in GE Capital as a way to build credibility with the FSC, we ultimately did not include it in the deal. The *New York Times* reporter probably presumed that only some big, well-known company could pull off a deal like this one.

News of Newbridge's deal was splashed across the front pages of all the major Korean and English newspapers. Many foreign investors considered it risky and adventurous to invest in a failed bank in the middle of a financial crisis with no end in sight. Others called to congratulate us. The deal had certainly put us on the map.

The *Wall Street Journal* editorial board hailed the deal as a "bold stroke" on the part of the Korean government. "Triumphant Pragmatism in Seoul" read the headline. It congratulated the Korean government for its courage:

> [I]f the new owners turn Korea First Bank around the government's 49% stake could end up being worth far more . . . than the 94% it now holds. That prospect ought to please taxpayers who coughed up for the recapitalization. It was difficult to put a price tag on the value of good publicity and the amount of money a smooth Korea First deal might attract into Korea in the form of other investments.
>
> The Korea First Bank deal is a bellwether. . . . No doubt the government is bracing for some kind of tempest, though the press and public outcry may not be so loud as it would have been a year ago. And to those wailing about Seoul giving away the "crown jewels" here: Listen, Korea First Bank ain't no jewel. But now it has a chance to become one.

The government must have felt like a bowl of fried ice cream. The warm reactions toward the deal in the international financial community outside Korea contrasted sharply with the ice-cold sentiments held by domestic critics.

Only with hindsight could I fully appreciate the extent to which nationalistic sentiment influenced the government's attitude and approach to the deal. The effects of the financial crisis, and the subsequent imposition of IMF austerity measures, were humiliating. The sale of one of its largest financial institutions to foreigners was a high-profile target for public anger. The attacks against the government came swiftly. It had made "too many concessions," according to an article in the *Korea Times* on January 5, including "[agreeing] to shoulder the burden of additional bad loans to take place over the next two years."

But while the deal itself might have met with some skepticism, the reaction of the international community was impossible for Koreans to ignore. The MOU was a strong vote of confidence in the Korean economy, and the knock-on effect on investor sentiment was immediate. On the first working day of 1999, the credit rating agency Standard & Poor's revised its outlook on Korea to "positive" and signaled a possible upgrade of Korea's sovereign credit rating. Among the reasons it cited was the KFB deal: "The completion of the Korea First Bank sale, coupled with the expected government divestiture of Seoul Bank, should mark a turning point in resuscitating Korea's weakened banking sector," S&P said, citing the MOU as an indicator of the government's willingness to embark on "sweeping structural reforms."

The upgrades were a big help to a country still in the grip of the financial crisis and would lower the government's borrowing costs in international markets.

The positive reporting by foreign press started to turn the tide of public opinion. Both the *Wall Street Journal* editorial and the S&P announcement were translated and carried in all major Korean newspapers, bolstering the government's position and to some extent silencing its critics.

The announcement of the deal also brought competitors out of the woodwork. About a week later, our advisor Jihong Kim told me there were as many as five new bidders who had stepped forward, including the representative of one major bank who had approached a KFB director and told him it would have bought the bank outright if it had been offered the same terms we had negotiated.

What a difference a week made. While we had helped improve investors' sentiment toward the Korean economy, the renewed interest, perversely, did not bode well for our own deal. Although we were pleased to have beaten the competition to sign the MOU, we all were keenly aware that, while it laid out the major terms of our investment in KFB, it was not legally binding. Much needed to be done to nail down the transaction. And, all of a sudden, there were other suitors in line. David Bonderman warned it was critically important to finalize the project by May 2, when the exclusivity period would end. Otherwise, the government might be tempted to renegotiate.

Paul Chen, Daniel Poon, and I had dinner with Dong-soo Chin, head of the FSC's Financial Restructuring Task Force, and his deputy Dr. Sung-hun Kim, the FSC's chief negotiator. They had news: Chin was going to be promoted to work in the Blue House, the office of Korea's president. Someone else would replace him as the head of the task force. I was sorry to see him leave but I was happy for him. He had earned my respect as a reasonable, fair-minded, practical, and dedicated government official.

★ ★ ★

I first set foot in KFB headquarters on January 6, 1999, a sunny winter day with the temperature hovering just above freezing. Though I had been negotiating for this bank for months, I had not visited it until now. KFB headquarters was a 22-story building in the Jongno-gu district in the center of Seoul. Built in 1987, it reminded me a bit of the United Nations building in New York City. Although it was not quite as big, it was broad and imposing, with a white stone façade framing tinted windows. The KFB logo, a big red thumbs-up sign, was perched atop the building, visible from miles away.

We were yet to finalize the formal contract, but as I walked through the enormous, high-ceilinged lobby, I already felt like an owner, on behalf of Newbridge Capital, of course. We were warmly welcomed by Shee-yuel Ryoo, the bank's government-appointed chairman and CEO, and his senior staff. Ryoo was a white-haired gentleman in his late 60s. He greeted me with the air of an embattled general who was glad to see reinforcements arrive. Educated in the United States with a degree from Columbia University, he spoke fluent English.

At that point KFB was severely hampered by a lack of capital. A number of its major customers had simply stopped making payments, including Kia Motors and companies affiliated with Daewoo Group. The bank had only stayed afloat thanks to occasional injections of funds from the government.

After being put in charge of the bank in 1997, Ryoo had hired Andersen Consulting to produce a restructuring plan. He downsized the bank, cutting the workforce from about 9,000 to about 4,000 and shutting down a number of money-losing branches. He also slashed management salaries by 30 percent and staff salaries by 10 percent. To improve the bank's lending and risk management practices, Ryoo had formed a 10-person credit review committee, of which he was not a member, to independently review loans. This kind of independent decision making on credit was standard in more advanced markets, but it was almost unheard of in Korea, where management almost always had the final word. As a result,

Ryoo told us, the bank had begun to generate income from operations in the last two months of 1998, even though the economy was far from being stabilized.

I took an immediate liking to Ryoo. I was impressed with the actions he had taken to improve the bank, given the circumstances in which he found it. I could imagine the pain and suffering its employees were going through and the sacrifices they were making. When Newbridge's MOU was announced, Ryoo had told his staff, "The sale to a foreign investor is the only course left for the bank to be reborn." He and other employees were looking forward to a new life under a new foreign owner. They were eager for a change for the better.

Chairman Ryoo graciously offered us a whole floor in KFB's headquarters building to use as our temporary offices while we worked on the transaction. We needed the space. For a deal of this nature, Newbridge would need to engage a small army of advisors, working on everything from documentation to financial modeling to evaluating good and bad loans to legal and regulatory issues.

Lehman was tasked with helping us build financial models and advise on valuing the bank's assets. E&Y, one of the world's leading accounting firms, would lead our efforts to *mark to market* the bank's assets, which meant determining how much they were worth in the current market. It sent an initial team of between 60 and 80 Korean-speaking professionals, bolstered by a team of analysts from Samjong Houlihan Lokey, an asset valuation specialist. Bain, the consulting company, was to examine KFB's operations and management to diagnose any problems we needed to address after taking control. On the legal side, we continued to use Cleary and also retained Kim & Chang, the most prominent law firm in Korea, to help us navigate the local laws. In total, there were probably more than 100 professionals working with Newbridge on the transaction.

On the afternoon of January 19, 1999, we assembled representatives from all parties for an organizational meeting at KFB. Paul Chen, who was more experienced in private equity than I was, presided. He and Daniel Poon led the execution of the deal, while my main responsibility was to lead the negotiations with the government. For more than two hours, we went over the scope of the project, our timetable, and the responsibilities of each of the parties. To keep tabs on everyone's progress, all the parties were required to be present or call in every Tuesday and Thursday for coordinating meetings. Our floor at KFB was like a factory, with piles of paper and teams of people working day and night.

The officials from the FSC did not seem to share our sense of urgency. It wasn't until two weeks after I'd first set foot in KFB's offices that we were able to organize an official negotiating session.

On January 20, 1999, Dick Blum flew to Seoul with Dan Carroll. We brought him to visit with Chairman Ryoo at KFB's offices, where we sat through a management presentation and then had lunch together. The next day, Blum, Carroll, Jihong Kim, and I went to the FSC building in Yeouido to visit with Chairman Lee. It was a courtesy call. Each side thanked the other for the conclusion of the MOU and pledged to work as hard as possible to make progress.

During that meeting we were met with an entirely new team on the Korean side, led by So-woo Noh (not his real name), a director general in the FSC, and his deputy Director Bo-sung Kang, also known as BS Kang (not his real name).

Noh and Kang were linked by school ties, which are very important in Korea for being part of the "old boys' network." Both were graduates of the elite Kyunggi High School, Korea's most prestigious school for boys. Both went on to study economics at Seoul National University, one of the most competitive programs at the best university in South Korea. Many senior government officials, including Chairman Lee, were graduates of these two elite schools.

The change in personnel concerned me. After months of negotiating I understood and had grown accustomed to the chain of command across the table: Dr. Kim had reported to Director General Chin, who in turn reported to Chairman Lee. As far as I could tell, Kim had Chin's confidence and trust, and Chin in turn enjoyed the confidence and trust of the chairman.

Now, however, Chin had moved to the Blue House, and Dr. Kim had apparently been sidelined. I never knew whether Dr. Kim had been forced out or stepped aside voluntarily, but he was no longer the FSC's lead negotiator and, some weeks later, would leave the organization entirely. It was the first indication that opposition to the Newbridge agreement might not be confined solely to newspaper headlines. There was a little more than three months left in our four-month exclusivity period, and the May 2 deadline began to feel tight. We would need to start from scratch to establish rapport with the FSC's new negotiating team, and that would take time.

We tried to negotiate with the new FSC team on the specifics of the contract, based on the MOU. But the new team seemed ill-prepared and not particularly interested in the terms of the MOU. They seemed reluctant to even engage with us. Unlike Chin and Dr. Kim, whom I could talk with at any time, Messrs. Noh and Kang remained somewhat aloof. Noh spoke limited English, and almost all our discussions required a translator. It took weeks to set up a meeting with them. It was not until February 3, 1999—more than a month into our exclusivity period— that we were able to sit down for a substantive conversation. The meeting lasted from the morning until 4:30 in the afternoon, but we made no progress.

On February 11, in an attempt to get everyone better acquainted, I hosted a dinner, inviting BS Kang and two of his colleagues. Kang, the most senior of the three, arrived 45 minutes late and without much in the way of an apology. This was unheard of in Korea, where people bowed to each other when meeting on the streets and young people would hold the right elbow with the left hand when extending the right hand to shake hands with an older or more senior person. In my experience, Koreans were exceedingly courteous with outsiders and tended to be punctual, if not early. I could only interpret his behavior as a deliberate snub.

On Friday, February 12, David Bonderman arrived in Seoul with Dan Carroll. We met briefly that morning to discuss the situation and then met Chairman Lee for lunch.

Bonderman was not known for being subtle. As soon as lunch got under way, he turned to the FSC chairman and told him that our team did not think the negotiations were going well and that we felt the FSC team was not being cooperative. Chairman Lee, who was probably expecting a pleasant and courteous lunch, seemed taken aback. He turned around and spoke in Korean with his own team for a couple minutes. Turning back to us, he said he would look into it, assuring Bonderman that the deal was a high priority for the government.

Bonderman's complaint had an impact. After the lunch , the Newbridge and FSC teams sat down for another meeting. At the table on the FSC side were Director General Noh, Director Kang, and Myung-chun

Lee, whom we called "Junior Lee" internally so as not to confuse him with the FSC chairman. The mood was tense. But I was relieved to see a familiar face: Dr. Kim, our former chief negotiator, was also in the room.

"Noh was mad as hell over the message you had delivered to Chairman Lee," I wrote Bonderman in a subsequent memo. "I suppose he felt he had personally lost face."

I told Noh that I was the one who had informed Bonderman of the current negotiation dynamics, and it was my view that we had reached a crisis point, which, without resolution, could derail the deal.

This caused a flurry of Korean on the other side of the table. Our advisor, Jihong Kim later explained that Junior Lee was getting scolded over his "attitude and personality" problems and was told to be more flexible. I then spent some time talking about the necessity of trust between the two sides and asked them to be honest with us if they felt we were not being fair on any issue. The FSC negotiators agreed, and said that they also appreciated the level of trust we had established before the MOU.

For the rest of the meeting, we discussed one specific deal-related issue: the assumed maturity we would use when marking to market KFB's rolled-over loans. When one-year loans were rolled over, their maturities were effectively extended, and therefore their interest rate should be changed to that for longer-term loans, we proposed.

"In the past two days of 'working level' discussion, Mr. Lee has become much more patient and engaging," I told Bonderman in a memo. "He still does not agree with us on the maturity issue, but he is now willing to move on to other issues, leaving the difficult issues to a higher-level discussion. This has allowed us to make modest progress."

★ ★ ★

The following week marked the Lunar New Year holiday, which was a big deal in Korea, as it is in China. While some Koreans worked on Christmas, as had Dr. Kim during our negotiations over the MOU, the Lunar New Year holiday was a time to be spent with family.

With little expected to happen on the deal for a full week and with schools in Hong Kong closed as well, Bin and I decided to take the family to Korea's Jeju Island, off the southern tip of the Korean Peninsula, for a holiday. I was studying Korean history and saw this as an opportunity to learn more about the country. I also wanted to be close to Seoul, where I would be headed immediately after the break.

On Jeju, we checked into a spacious and bright room at the Shilla Hotel, right by the ocean. The view of the endless blue sea was splendid. The weather in Seoul had been frigid when our flight left, but, just an hour south by plane, Jeju was mild, about 50 degrees Fahrenheit (10 degrees Celsius). It was as if we had landed in another world. The island had been formed by volcanic eruptions, and evidence was apparent everywhere. Lava rocks covered much of the island. Over the centuries, locals have used chunks of them to build the dry-stone walls that snake across the windswept landscape. Where the lava flowed into the sea, it froze into strange and beautiful shapes. In the center of the island was Mt. Halla, a dormant volcano and Korea's tallest peak, which was lush with green vegetation.

Jeju was famous for its female divers. Even in wintertime, these intrepid women dove into the sea with no equipment but a wetsuit, a mask, and a heavy weight tied to a rope around their waists. There they would stay for several minutes, emerging from the depths with bushels of shellfish, sea urchins, and sea cucumbers. It was hard work. They sold what they collected from the bottom of the sea to the passing tourists, who would sit on the rocks and eat it raw with some wasabi and soy sauce.

The divers were exclusively female, and I learned that they had taken up their trade out of necessity. In the old days fishermen often perished in storms, leaving their widows to make a living on their own. The women learned to dive to collect edible sea life from the ocean floor. All of the female divers I saw appeared quite old and I felt sure this tradition would soon die out, as I could not imagine younger women taking on such a hard and perilous job. But even if the widowed divers disappear into history, their spirit would live on. Watching them plunge into the cold surf, I felt they represented the audacity, resilience, and pride I had seen in the Korean people in the face of adversity and hardship. This is a nation that will emerge stronger from the economic crisis, I told myself. That was what we were betting on by acquiring Korea First Bank.

Every day on our vacation in Jeju, I worked the phones and joined conference calls with our teams to discuss the KFB deal. One day my daughter ran into the room. I put the phone on mute and called out to her,

"LeeAnn, I love you!" All of a sudden the chattering on the conference call stopped. After a brief silence came the voice of Paul Chen: "Shan, we love you too!" Everyone on the call laughed. It turned out the mute function on the hotel phone did not work.

★ ★ ★

The month of February, interrupted by the long Lunar New Year holiday, came and went quickly, and there was no progress in our negotiations with the FSC. By the terms of the MOU, we had about two months left to reach a deal.

The mark-to-market pricing issue was a major sticking point, complicated by the fact that, in the middle of an economic crisis, there was hardly a market for these loans to be marked against. I spent the week negotiating with the FSC team, led by BS Kang, but we could not resolve how the mark should be determined. Under the current market conditions, if the bank sold a loan, even a performing one, it would have to sell it at a discount to book value. As for nonperforming loans, the situation was even worse; nobody wanted to buy them. Without a market, how were we to determine the market value of a loan?

Our advisors at E&Y proposed the parties use the current international standard, which employed a forward-looking methodology to classify loans. This meant that a loan would be classified according to how likely it was to be paid back to the bank. There were several major loan categories: normal, precautionary, substandard, doubtful, and loss. The last three classifications—substandard, doubtful, and loss—are generally considered to be nonperforming or bad loans and are often referred to as *classified loans*.

Under the forward-looking methodology, if a borrower's ability to repay seemed impaired, the bank would set aside *provisions* (reserves) to prepare for potential losses. For example, if the bank's credit officer determined that the bank could recover only 80 percent of the loan from a borrower, the bank would make a provision of 20 percent, marking down the value of the loan on its books to 80 percent of its original value.

At the time, Korean accounting practices were not forward looking. Rather, they focused on a borrower's record of meeting its interest-payment obligations. As long as borrowers were able to keep making interest payments on time, their loans would be classified as normal, and no provisions would be made for them. Continuing with this practice was, in our view, foolhardy. Thousands of Korean companies were struggling with massive debt loads, slashing staff and expenses to make their loan payments even as their cash flow dried up. But as far as their lenders were concerned, everything was just fine. The FSC still insisted on using this Korean standard, despite the number of failing borrowers that were crippling the banking industry.

Take, for example, Hanbo Steel, a former client of KFB's, whose collapse had helped precipitate Korea's financial crisis. To anyone aware of what was going on, it was clear that the company was overleveraged and that it would be only a matter of time before it collapsed under the weight of its debt. Still, Hanbo had made interest payments up to the moment it declared bankruptcy. A prudent bank would have classified its loans to Hanbo as either substandard or doubtful long before, and set aside reserves for it. The failure to do so by KFB and Hanbo's other creditor banks brought those banks down once Hanbo ran out of cash, because its loans had to be written off.

The Korean regulators were fully aware of the issues with the Korean standard of accounting. The Financial Supervisory Services, a sister organization of the FSC, was already planning to adopt a new, forward-looking methodology. Even so, the FSC was unwilling to implement this international standard in our contract for KFB. To us, this was like saying that an apple, rotten at the core but not yet on the surface, was still a good apple.

This was also a major deviation from the terms we'd agreed upon in the MOU, which called for both sides to use international standards to define good and bad loans. I soon discovered that this was not the only deviation.

During our previous negotiations, wanting to make absolutely sure of our right to put any bad loans to the government, I had secured a side letter from Dr. Kim, the chief negotiator, dated December 30, 1998, which read: "The Government allows the Investors to separate any loans to the bad bank whether they are normal, precautionary, or not before the transaction's close."

Crucially, the FSC team would not acknowledge our right to choose the loans for the pre-close put, nor would they agree that Newbridge had an unlimited right to put a loan after the closing. Not only did this about-face ignore the terms in the MOU, but it also made the economics of the deal unworkable.

The FSC was working with its financial advisor, Morgan Stanley, and accounting consultant Samil PriceWaterhouse (PwC). Both the Morgan Stanley and PwC teams told us privately that they were in basic agreement with us on our put right but they could not persuade their client to honor the MOU. Thinking that reason would prevail, I proposed that E&Y, representing Newbridge, and PwC, representing the FSC, work out the methodology between themselves without the interference of their respective clients. I hoped their professional standards would lead them to an agreement without Newbridge having to negotiate directly with the FSC team.

★ ★ ★

All of a sudden, we had even more reason to hurry. In late February, the FSC and HSBC made an announcement that they had agreed upon their own MOU for HSBC to acquire Seoul Bank. HSBC would pay the government $200 million up front and also put about $700 million in new capital into the bank.

HSBC had lost to Newbridge in the race to acquire KFB primarily because it limited the government's ownership stake to 20 percent. Now, in part because of our MOU to acquire KFB and the ensuing upgrade of Korea's sovereign debt, the government's bargaining position had improved significantly. The terms outlined in the announcement were much more favorable to the government, allowing it to retain 30 percent of the shares in Seoul Bank, with the right to buy another 19 percent, bringing its potential ownership to 49 percent. The announcement also said that HSBC would conduct a strict audit on Seoul Bank's assets and liabilities and would expect to close the transaction by late May.

It was clear that the government's deal with HSBC was more favorable for the government than our deal for KFB, especially given the up-front $200 million payment HSBC was to make.

With pride in his voice, Director General Noh told me that he had personally negotiated the HSBC deal. I felt that this only stiffened Noh's resolve to get more concessions from Newbridge, regardless of what we'd agreed upon in the MOU. This also raised serious doubts about whether the government wanted our deal anymore.

My fears were not unfounded. A few days after the announcement of the HSBC deal, I met privately with Dr. Kim, the former FSC chief negotiator for the MOU. Though he was no longer part of the negotiation team, he had some insight into their thinking.

He told me that there was now strong opposition to our deal within the FSC. "You had better conclude the deal within the exclusivity period," he told me, "or you might lose it altogether."

It seemed, however, that the more urgently we needed to push forward, the slower negotiations became. We had a big team now. In addition to Dan Carroll, Paul Chen, Daniel Poon, the Lehman team, and me, we had added a few new faces. Jim Warner, an associate at Bonderman's firm, TPG, was seconded to the Newbridge team to help finalize the deal. Bob Barnum, the former president and chief operating officer of American Savings Bank, came over to advise on operational issues. Bob, a veteran bank executive with deep operating experience, recommended a few hires of his own, including SH Lee, a Korean American credit analyst who specialized in the local loan market and was familiar with the credit and financial capabilities of many Korean corporate borrowers.

The government's team was also growing. Whereas we had originally negotiated with the FSC alone, their side of the table now included representatives from the Ministry of Finance and Economy and the Korea Deposit Insurance Corporation. This made meetings even more unwieldy. We often argued for hours without making progress on any of the major issues, especially on how to value the loans. Every term we had spent so much time on with the predecessor team now seemed to be viewed as subject to renegotiation, as if the MOU had not existed. And if we proposed any new terms or methodologies, the government rejected them without consideration or discussion.

★ ★ ★

March arrived. With two months left in the exclusivity period, we still had not established much trust with Noh's team. It seemed the government team was afraid to accept any of our proposals, lest they should give away too much. Perhaps they considered us to be more financially sophisticated and were afraid we would take advantage of them.

Newbridge's financial model showed that the deal would be economically and financially untenable if we couldn't achieve the bare minimum of terms as agreed to under the MOU. This model was, essentially, our projection for how KFB would perform under our control. It was based on our team's accumulated knowledge and analysis of KFB, its business, and current market conditions. We applied this information and made various assumptions or projections about the bank's future performance, including assumed loan losses. It had been the basis for all of our negotiations so far. Meanwhile, the new FSC team seemed concerned that Newbridge would be making too much money out of the deal.

I realized that we needed to find a way to balance this information asymmetry if we were going to build trust. Before we adjourned our March 2 meeting, I proposed to share our financial model with the government side, so they could see how we looked at the economics of the whole deal and judge for themselves whether it was fair and reasonable. This would be a major reveal, and was almost unheard of in a negotiation of this nature. It was like revealing your battle plan to your opponent in the middle of a war. But I thought transparency would build trust. We needed them to understand that what we had proposed was fair and reasonable.

The FSC team was happy with our willingness to share our model. The next day, we spent the bulk of the day explaining it to them and walking them through the numbers. They listened attentively, without much comment, although the atmosphere became more relaxed. Nonetheless, we consistently received only one response to everything we had proposed: *No.*

Meanwhile, the question of how to mark to market KFB's loans was also stalled. My brilliant idea of punting the question to E&Y and PwC to sort out had failed. It turned out that the two accounting firms could not agree with each other on a methodology either. E&Y was focused on what our team needed, while PwC was worried about compromising the FSC's position. Although I was counting on their objectivity, each firm felt it was so important to prioritize the best interests of its clients that no agreement could be reached.

Recall from the terms of our MOU that this mark would be very important for both sides. The government would not only be responsible for filling the hole in the balance sheet created by the bad loans that KFB had made prior to Newbridge's purchase, it would also have to reimburse KFB for the mark on the loan book that we chose to retain. In other words, the government would have to pay KFB the difference between par and whatever we mutually agreed to mark our retained loan at.

Upon reflection, this disagreement on the mark-to-market methodology was probably inevitable. Even if we had come to an agreement regarding the methodology, we would have produced different results in our respective models. The Newbridge team would probably have considered it necessary to project more downside than upside for the immediate future of the Korean economy, which was still in the grip of a crisis. This would have resulted in a lower proposed mark on each individual loan, and thus a greater reimbursement from the government to bring each loan back to par. By contrast, the government's team would likely be more optimistic about the timing and the extent of an economic recovery. This would have led to a higher proposed mark on each loan, and hence less required reimbursement. Either side, I realized, could be right as nobody had a crystal ball to the future.

After some internal discussion with our advisors, Newbridge proposed an entirely new approach. Instead of pricing every single individual loan or asset to its fair market value, we would move to a portfolio approach. We would effectively buy a bundle of goods of mixed quality at a discount. We would take all the performing loans and negotiate an average value for the entire portfolio, using a top-down mark.

The markdown not only necessary for reimbursement, or hole filling, purposes, reflecting the fact that even some retained loans might be impaired. It was also important for the purpose of *yield maintenance*, meaning the principal of the loans had to be marked down so that the original contracted interest rates would provide a higher and sufficient yield, reflective of changed market conditions and the increased riskiness of some borrowers. The FSC agreed to consider this new approach, but the percentage of the markdown for the total portfolio was still subject to negotiation.

★ ★ ★

Two days later, my team and I met again with Director General Noh. I made two proposals. The first was to mark the loan portfolio KFB would retain 87.5 percent of book value, or a 12.5 percent discount. This took into consideration all the potential losses, as of closing, in KFB's retained loan book. Under the second proposal, we would mark the loan portfolio at 97.5 percent, but we would keep 50 percent of the reserves that KFB already had on its balance sheet. Reserves are taken by banks for potential loan losses and are normally paid for by existing shareholders. In the instance of KFB, a failed bank with negative shareholders' equity, such reserves had effectively been funded by the Korean government. In both proposals we also would keep the right to transfer to the government, at original book value plus accrued interest, any existing loans that should go bad after closing, as described in the MOU. By our model and calculations, the two proposals were economically equivalent, so we would be indifferent between them.

I thought that the choice we now gave the government was reasonable and, in fact, generous. Under the MOU, we could have kept all the reserves that KFB had already taken and for the difference between par and our proposed 87.5 percent mark. Now we were giving them the choice between either 87.5 percent mark but no reserves or 97.5 percent mark with half of the reserves, which was a major concession on our part. Noh seemed to like the new approach and said he would come back to us after further study.

Anticipating that we would give up the mark-to-market approach on a loan-by-loan basis, I told our accounting advisors that we would not need as many of their staff as previously thought. As some of them cleared their desks, KFB management became somewhat alarmed. They thought the Newbridge team was preparing to move out. We didn't bother to correct them. It might help us to send a signal to the FSC that we were preparing for the worst. If negotiations continued to stall, we were ready to pull out.

We met with Noh and his team the next day. Our proposal was intended to be constructive and I hoped he would respond likewise, so I was dismayed to hear his response. Instead of taking one of my two proposals, he took the best part of each. His counterproposal was that the mark for the retained loan portfolio would be 97.5 percent of par and that KFB would turn over 100 percent of the reserves to the government.

It was as if I had offered to buy a broken watch at a good discount or a new watch at the full price, but the shopkeeper would only agree to sell me the broken watch for the price of the new.

Our team was stupefied by Noh's audacity. His proposal was obviously unreasonable. He was violating the principles of good-faith negotiation, and, given the quality of the loans, his counterproposal was more than absurd. While we were making an effort to bridge the gap between us, he just refused to budge at all.

In my frustration, I suggested that we invite an international organization, such as the IMF or the World Bank, to adjudicate the value of the loan portfolio. Noh would have none of it, and the meeting was adjourned.

Afterwards, I called Dr. Kim to ask him what was going on within the FSC. He wouldn't tell me, but he admitted he was "not optimistic" about our deal. We seemed to have come to a dead end.

★ ★ ★

By now my team and I were camping out in Seoul all week and very often could not go home to Hong Kong even for the weekends.

On Saturday, March 6, we met with Director Kang and his team. I made a third proposal. We would accept pricing the loans at their original book value, but KFB would keep 100 percent of the loan loss reserves that KFB already taken.

This time Kang made a counterproposal: Put the mark at 97.5 percent of book value and let KFB keep 3.4 percent of its reserves. This essentially meant their proposed mark was 94.1 percent (97.5 minus 3.4), compared with our original proposal of 87.5 percent. The gap was still too wide, but it was at least some progress.

There were other signs that we were beginning to get through to the FSC team. That week's negotiations were the first time that Director General Noh became personally involved in the process, which we saw as an indication that the FSC team realized Newbridge was reaching a breaking point. We also learned that they worked until 1 am the night before to go through the analysis with their advisors.

As the talks went on, I began to understand that the FSC team would continue to test our limit because they did not know where it was.

I requested a one-on-one meeting with Noh and told him in no uncertain terms that my last one was our final proposal and we would make no further concessions. I followed up by writing him a letter that reiterated that our position was in accordance with the MOU and suggested his side was abandoning the MOU for political reasons. He disagreed, calling my assessment of the situation an "inaccurate accusation."

I reported all this in an internal memo to Blum and Bonderman. "Interestingly," I wrote, "Noh is particularly sensitive to my suggestion of us jointly inviting an international agency, such as IMF/World Bank, to supervise the MOU execution process and indicates that he absolutely does not want that to happen." Which was precisely why I suggested it.

On Monday, I received a fax response from Bonderman:

Shan, Thank you for the fax and the attached materials. I continue to believe that we have to hang very tough here and stick to the MOU. I also think that we have to tell the Koreans exactly what we are prepared to do and then behave in such a way. We also probably need to explain to them once again what it is that they are trying to do here—convince the rest of the world that they know how to run a banking system, and why this is the right method to prove that to everyone. If need be, Dick [Blum] or I can come back to Korea for a day to have a conversation with the Blue House and Chairman Lee.

Blum arrived in Seoul the next day. He went to meet with Chairman Lee. It was a friendly meeting. They both pledged to make an effort to get the deal done. Chairman Lee suggested that if we weren't close to a breakthrough by mid-April, two weeks before the expiration of exclusivity, the chairmen from both sides would meet again. Despite the understanding between the two chairmen, however, I detected no improvement in the way the FSC team conducted the negotiations on the ground.

Meanwhile, the representative of the World Bank in Seoul, Per Jedefors, reached out to us. He wanted to find out where the negotiations stood before the bank released the next tranche of its loan to South Korea. The World Bank and the IMF had a keen interest in our negotiations succeeding. One of the conditions of their $58 billion rescue package was that South Korea had to sell at least one of its two failed banks. We met so I could brief him on the status of the negotiations.

The World Bank knew the major terms of the MOU, and I explained our difficulty in finding common ground with the government. At the end of the meeting, he agreed we were following the MOU and had, in fact, made concessions in the government's favor. Jedefors said he would help push the deal process along in his conversations with the relevant Korean officials.

★ ★ ★

With six weeks until the end of the exclusivity period, I was following a grueling schedule. I would spend 10 to 12 hours a day negotiating with the FSC or working on the deal, then spend another several hours writing detailed memos to update my colleagues. On March 12 I circulated a memo to the Newbridge team to summarize the difficulty of our situation:

> *At the working level, we have made no meaningful progress since last Wednesday. There is some notable change in their attitude and tactics, however, after Dick's meeting with the chairman. Whereas in the past, they cited political reasons, the HSBC/Seoul Bank deal and public sentiment as their excuses to reject our proposals, now they describe our differences as a "genuine disagreement" on the interpretation of the MOU. In other words, they claim that they, too, are following the MOU and the difference is simply a matter of interpretation. They have used negative press to put pressure on us for weeks.*

Bonderman, in typical fashion, responded via fax the same day: "I think we are being dunced around by people who have figured out that they cannot walk away from the MOU but who do not really want to proceed," he wrote. "I think a very strong letter in which we make it clear that we understand what they are up to is in order more or less now."

It was becoming apparent to me that our team in the United States was beginning to lose faith that the deal would ever get done. There was a lot of frustration all around. The following Monday, March 15, I spoke with our lawyer, Michael Ryan, who had worked with Bonderman on the ASB transaction, which we were using as a model for our KFB deal. He thought the deal was not going to happen, and he had shared his pessimism with Bonderman. We discussed possible ways of forcing the government's hand, including taking legal action.

"We have to force these guys to make a decision, one way or another, and sooner rather than later," I wrote to him following our call. I suggested that our lawyers deliver an ultimatum to the FSC: Either accept Newbridge's minimum position, or we would hold the government in breach of the MOU and reserve the right to take legal action:

> Of course, I defer to your professional judgment on whether or not we have a case against them either in the U.S. court or in Korea. I somehow feel that if the deal collapses, we have indeed relied on their promise to do a deal with us to our great detriment. The damages are real. At the end of the day, even if we do not win a lawsuit, the threat to sue may help focus the top leaders' attention.

My wording here was deliberate. I was referring to a legal concept in contract law in the United States, namely, *detrimental reliance*, which means that if one party has relied on a promise made by another party to do something and has, in doing so, incurred costs or detriments, the court may find the promising party obligated to make good on its promise, even though no formal contract exists between them.

My thinking was that, although our MOU was not legally binding, we might nonetheless have a case against the FSC because we had relied on the promises made in the MOU to incur considerable expenses. This reliance had undoubtedly been to our detriment, considering the legions of lawyers, analysts, and accountants already working on this deal, in addition to our own time and effort. Newbridge had already spent millions of dollars pursuing KFB, and the meter was still running. A legal challenge could help prove to the government how serious we were. And if worst came to worst, we had to protect our interests.

Chapter 5

Deadline Looming

I considered legal action against the Korean government an absolute last resort, and for the moment it seemed as if I might not need it. The following day, March 16, we had a six-hour meeting with the FSC in its office, during which the FSC team finally agreed to using forward-looking international best practices instead of Korean standards for assessing and classifying loans. We agreed that the guidelines would be worked out by advisors of both parties and implemented by the management of KFB.

This meeting also brought an interesting change in the negotiation dynamics: Gokul Laroia, a vice president at Morgan Stanley, took the lead during our discussions. The FSC team members did not say much. According to Laroia, the Morgan Stanley and PwC teams had spent a lot of time working with the FSC to agree to use forward-looking standards. Unfortunately, there remained a sizable gap between our positions on the mark-to-market and other issues, so I had no choice but to reject their offer. But at least, I thought, this was a start.

My optimism did not last long. The next day we returned to the conference room of the FSC's office to pick up where we had left off. At the beginning of the meeting I began to propose that advisors from both sides work out the guidelines for forward-looking loan classification, as we had agreed a day earlier. This time, however, BS Kang, who was leading the FSC negotiations, said that he needed to consult with his superiors before he could agree to using the forward-looking classification methodology.

I had barely recovered from my surprise when Dr. Sang-mook Lee chimed in. Dr. Lee was a deputy director in the Banking System Division of Korea's Ministry of Finance and Economy (MOFE). He had recently joined the negotiations as an observer.

"The FSC did not share its latest proposal with MOFE prior to discussing it with Newbridge," Dr. Lee said, noting that the ministry was "disturbed" by the offer and considered its terms to be too generous to Newbridge. He hinted darkly that we were unlikely to get approval from the various ministers for the deal without significant changes.

"That's fine," I responded, "because the current proposal was equally unacceptable to Newbridge." Then I turned to Kang and asked, "Does the FSC have the authority to negotiate with us or not?" Kang assured me it did. However, he went on to state that his latest proposal was indeed final, even if it meant the deal would collapse.

At this point I saw no reason to continue talking. As we were leaving the building, I passed Chairman Lee in the hall. "How are the negotiations coming along?" he wanted to know.

"Not well," I said.

* * *

For the first time we had gotten a taste of the internal politics inside the Korean government with regard to the KFB deal. To begin with, it was clear that some rivalry existed between the FSC and the MOFE. The ministry had not been directly involved in negotiating the MOU, and I knew that the finance minister had voted against the deal. Just minutes before we signed the MOU, he had also insisted we sweeten it by increasing the amount of warrants KFB would grant the government. Now, it seemed, the MOFE wanted direct representation in the negotiation process. And its representative, Dr. Lee, wanted to turn back the clock.

Then there was the problem of Director General Noh. I found all the Korean officials we had come in contact with to be professional, hardworking, and courteous. Noh was the exception. In meetings he sat looking aloof and stern. Square-jawed, with jet-black hair combed over to one side, he would stare at visitors with narrowed and expressionless eyes behind a pair of light-rimmed glasses. He never smiled. He presented himself as being important and distant, yet he seemed incapable of making decisions. His negotiation style was to reject everything we proposed—on the rare occasions he came to a session. It was almost impossible to engage in a real discussion with him to resolve any issues. It was obvious he did not like the MOU and I felt he was hostile to the deal from day one.

According to our advisor Jihong Kim, it was going to be very difficult to ask the higher authorities to replace Noh as the lead negotiator. Jihong knew most of the players in this drama well, and he explained to me that Chairman Lee remained supportive of the deal, but his hands were tied. Noh was from a rival political faction, one that often did not share President DJ Kim's agenda.

To get around the issue, Jihong proposed that Chairman Lee create a steering committee to help oversee the negotiating process. There were people in the Korean government who were loyal to the cause of President Kim's banking reforms. A committee with some of those supporters would undermine Noh's authority and help alleviate the current stalemate. While I was a bit concerned that having the wrong people on the steering committee would more deeply entrench the FSC in its position, Jihong assured me that the chairman was eager for a chance to neutralize Noh in order to push this deal through.

But until that could happen, we needed to prove to Chairman Lee and to everyone involved in the KFB negotiations that Newbridge meant business. Recently, our team had discussed sending a strongly worded letter to Chairman Lee, outlining in blunt terms our concerns with the current state of the negotiations and emphasizing that we were running out of time. It was time, I felt, to send that letter.

The letter, which I had drafted for Blum's signature and which was sent on March 18, 1999, began by stating that, from our perspective, "the negotiation has all but collapsed." It went on to highlight that the terms of the MOU were a key part of communicating Korea's determination to restructure its banking sector to adhere to international best practices. Blum noted:

> But during the past ten weeks since the MOU was signed, the FSC has repeatedly challenged key concepts in the proposed transaction. . . . This pattern of negotiation, which does not appear to have changed materially since our meeting, is of great concern to Newbridge as it calls into question the viability of the entire transaction.

Blum concluded, "I believe we have come to a critical point in the negotiations and that further delay would be fatal."

★ ★ ★

Just as I was trying to light a fire under the Korean negotiators, I was trying to put one out in Newbridge's backyard. Jim Warner, the TPG associate who had been seconded to the Newbridge team, wrote a memo to Bonderman and others at TPG, expressing his concern that my last proposal to the FSC was too generous to the government side.

"My primary concern is making sure we mark correctly the loan portfolio we decide to keep," he wrote. We proposed to the FSC a weighted average mark of 87.5 percent on the loan portfolio. This price, Warner thought, "does not seem to mitigate the fact that 55% of the loans within the *won*-denominated loan bucket (the largest bucket) have 1997 EBITDA/Total Interest coverage of less than 1."

EBITDA stands for *earnings before interest payment, taxes, depreciation, and amortization*, which is a broad measure of the operating cash flow of a company. In plain English, Warner was saying that the borrowers of 55 percent of KFB's loans were not generating enough cash from operations to pay even the interest on their loans, let alone the principal. He wondered how we could justify marking down KFB's loan book to 87.5 percent of book value, when it was clear more than half of its loans were at risk of default. Warner concluded that I was making "irresponsible/unauthorized economic trade-offs in order to get the deal done."

For some reason, Warner had not spoken with me about his reservations. I only found out about them when Bonderman showed me his memo and questioned me about the points Warner raised. I thought it was ironic that a member of our own team thought we were compromising too much, while the government side thought we were compromising too little. We had to sort out our differences internally before we could further negotiate with the FSC team. The gap between us and the government, it seemed, was not narrowing but widening.

Warner's data was correct, but he did not see the whole picture. It was true that most of KFB's loans were in bad shape, but under the terms of the MOU, these loans would no longer be our problem. They would be put to the government either before or a year or two after the deal was closed.

While it went without saying that a deeper discount would be more beneficial for Newbridge, the real question was what the correct mark should be. According to our analysis, an 87.5 percent mark would produce an adequate yield to reflect the borrowers' credit risk and provide sufficient downside protection if a borrower's ability to repay was impaired. Our proposal also meant that we would get a discount of 12.5 percent even on the good loans, and, given our existing put right, we would get a year or more to look at all of the loans to see whether we could work them out, or restructure them in such a way to enable the borrowers to repay. Meanwhile, we would be getting an attractive yield, on a risk-free basis, through the interest payments on the loans.

As I wrote to Bonderman, "whether we can live with a particular mark, whatever the agreed methodology produces, depends, as you point out, on the quality of the loans we get to keep or on how much freedom we have to select the loan portfolio by using pre- *and* post-close put rights." The last point was critically important. If we could not exercise our right to put bad loans back to the government, almost no mark would work for us. Turning around a failed bank was like starting from a deep valley to climb a tall mountain. To make it to the top, KFB would need to unload its heaviest baggage—the bad loans.

Warner and I met with a few others in the team to talk, and we quickly reached consensus that our proposed mark would work for us.

Meanwhile Bonderman, had invited a few close advisors to provide analysis. He wrote: "In a nutshell... this deal could work nicely... but it will be a longer and tougher slog than we might think. Our success would rely on diversifying KFB's customer base, which hinged in part on the growth of Korea's overall economy. That could mean our projected three-year turnaround time was overly optimistic. There was also the issue of finding a new CEO for KFB. Not everyone would be up to the challenge."

★ ★ ★

On March 23, 1999, with five weeks left to make a deal, my colleague Paul Chen; two bankers from Lehman Brothers, O'Hanlon of Lehman and Jack Rodman of E&Y; and I met with Noh and his team at the FSC. In my notes from that day I characterized the conversation with Noh as "shadowboxing." Noh told us he liked the "top-down mark" approach, which we had proposed as the alternative to valuating every individual loan. Even though he did not agree with our proposed mark, he concurred that we should value the portfolio as a whole. It was a good chance for me to test a theory I had about how Noh negotiated.

The reason we proposed the methodology of a top-down mark was because we had expected the parties to agree to our mark quickly. But if we couldn't agree to the mark, then the top-down approach had failed and we might as well go back to the bottom-up methodology.

"Mr. Shan, I think the top-down mark is the right way to do it," Noh replied. "We insist on using this methodology."

The more I argued to withdraw Newbridge's own proposal, the more insistent Noh became on using the methodology. And this was, in fact, just what I wanted. I had learned how his mind worked. He did not really know what he wanted, so he would push to test our limits. If I said yes, he would think there was still room to push us and wouldn't accept a deal. But if I said no, he would think he had squeezed the last drop out of us, so he would insist.

Whether it was our new approach to dealing with Director General Noh or some impetus from within the FSC, we finally seemed to be making some headway in our negotiations. I suspected that this was due in part to the fact that it was difficult for the FSC to publicly defend its opposition to international best practices at a time when the international market was watching closely for signs of structural reforms in the Korean economy. Therefore, despite the objections from the MOFE's Dr. Lee, assessing loans based on the concept of international best practices was at last back on the table, although the parties still could not agree on what exactly those practices should be.

We met with Director BS Kang and his team on the afternoon of March 25. I told them that our proposal of a mark of 87.5 percent remained valid, but then we moved on to discuss other issues. We agreed to let the advisors on both sides draft the loan classification guidelines and other relevant documents.

"I would characterize today's meeting as 'constructive,'" I wrote in an internal memo later that day. We had been so stymied by the uncompromising positions taken by the FSC team in meeting after meeting, we were happy to see any sign of loosening on their side. A second memo, drafted by Paul Chen, listed the issues discussed at the meeting. We reported, with some glee in our tone, that we had "actually made progress" and that Noh had agreed to gather his advisors to discuss the issues we wanted to have resolved. It seemed as if we were finally getting back on track.

★ ★ ★

By March, the Korean press was keenly interested in the progress and status of the negotiations between the FSC and Newbridge, and coverage was picking up. The government negotiators were influenced by public opinion both at home and abroad. They were concerned with the views expressed by the Korean press, fearful of getting savaged in public for giving away Korea's crown jewel. However, the sentiment of foreign investors was important to Korea's economic recovery, so the government didn't want to be perceived as reneging on the MOU either.

For decades, the press in South Korea had been heavily censored. Its authoritarian president, Chung-hee Park, shut down most of the country's major newspapers in the 1960s; his successor, Doo-hwan Chun, nationalized the news agencies and television broadcasters. But in the late 1980s, as the country began to liberalize, Korea's media expanded. By the time of the KFB deal, the nation had a freewheeling and influential free press, although I learned with some difficulty that journalists still deferred to the government in certain matters.

As the period of exclusivity dwindled, I met with a reporter from the *Korea Times*. Our interview would appear in an article titled "Newbridge to Fully Respect MOU." The reporter called me to say that the FSC had asked to review the article before publication—something unthinkable in most Western countries—but didn't request any changes and let the article go to press as the reporter had written it.

We knew the FSC used the Korean press to sway public opinion and send us not-so-subtle messages. Noh, in particular, was quite fond of planting stories, though he did it rather clumsily, leaving no doubt as to who had planted them. He also did not seem to want to share the media spotlight. In an effort to present a united front to the media and to better sell our deal to the public, I'd set up a lunch meeting with the FSC spokes-woman, Sandy Park, only to learn that the meeting was canceled at the order of Mr. Noh. I did not know what Noh was afraid of, but he obvi-ously did not want the FSC spokesperson getting to know us.

We knew that if the government wanted to walk away, it would not want to be blamed for the deal's falling apart. Therefore, it was often difficult to tell whether a slight softening in Noh's position was an earnest effort to reach agreement on difficult issues or merely a way to shift blame from his side. What we were reading in the press was cer-tainly at odds with some of the positive signs we observed across the negotiation table.

On March 26 a leading Korean newspaper, *Chosun Ilbo*, published an article under the headline: "Is Newbridge the Only Option?" The question was obviously rhetorical. The article first quoted an unnamed "branch manager of a foreign investment banking firm," who pointed out that the MOU was not a legal contract and opined that it gave Newbridge too good a deal. The article relied on other unidentified sources and cited a reported rumor that unnamed people at the IMF "joked that Newbridge has found an easy target in Korea First Bank." It then blamed the IMF for requiring that the Korean government sell two distressed banks in order to receive bailout assistance. It suggested that it would be better for the country to get rid of Korea First Bank and set up a new one rather than injecting so much capital into it. The article went on to say:

> Financial authorities who had been part of the Korea First Bank sell-off talks said, "It is true that the MOU signing was done hurriedly, but Newbridge was the only candidate at the time and we had no other choice," but added, "The government's pledge with the IMF to sell off two troubled banks—Korea First Bank and Seoul Bank—was a com-plete blunder in terms of M&A strategy."

It was a hatchet job, and it had Noh's fingerprints all over it. The thinly sourced, anonymous quotes were a staple of Korean business reporting, which at its worst was little better than gossip. The remark about getting rid of the bank and setting up a new one revealed the writer's ignorance. Apparently, the writer did not understand that the government was responsible for repaying all the deposits and liabilities of the bank and could not simply get rid of them. But I thought the attempt to disguise the true source of the article by citing anonymous sources at foreign firms was laughable. No one in the international community, especially at the IMF and World Bank, thought South Korea should walk away from the deal.

The article's conclusion was telling, and probably as indicative of Noh's true intentions as anything we'd been able to get from him across the bargaining table: "A negotiation expert"—it wasn't difficult to guess who that was—"says that if the deal is not working out, you do not have to comply with the MOU, but you have to come up with proof that it is not Korea's fault. Otherwise, departing from the MOU will undermine Korea's credibility."

That was the bind Noh found himself in. Newbridge had consistently pushed to abide by the MOU, and had said so publicly. It was *his* side that wanted to walk away from it. But Noh also knew that to do so would make Korea look bad to the international community, which would potentially jeopardize the loans and investments that the country was depending on to help get back on its feet. Therefore, we suspected Noh was only pretending to accept such concepts as international best practices; in fact, he might not have had any intention of following them.

In spite of the progress we'd seemed to be making in recent days, the *Chosun Ilbo* article raised new doubts in my mind as to whether the FSC team was negotiating in good faith. Bonderman drafted a letter for Blum to send to Director General Noh on March 26, highlighting our continued belief that the core principles of the MOU were vital to the agreement and that we would not accept anything less. The letter read at least partly as a rebuttal to the *Chosun Ilbo* article. We thought it much better to let Noh know we were not falling for his tricks and that we had every intention of holding the FSC to the principles of the MOU. As we were losing confidence that any progress could be made in our negotiations with Mr. Noh and as we wanted to put some pressure on him, the letter concluded by referring to the suggestion made by Chairman Lee in his last meeting with Blum:

> *Accordingly, while I accept Chairman Lee's decision that the senior people would wait until mid-April to get together to resolve the transaction in the absence of agreement by the negotiating teams, I think you should advise Chairman Lee to reserve several days on his calendar in mid-April since it now appears likely that this transaction will only be negotiated at the most senior levels absent of major progress in the coming weeks.*

As we entered the month of April, I felt like we were punching air every day in our meetings with the FSC. As the deadline drew closer, there was much speculation in the press about what was holding up negotiations. Many articles in the Korean press, citing government sources, suggested that the lack of progress was due to Newbridge. We were concerned that the position of the FSC team and the negative press were reinforcing each other.

On April 2, in the middle of another fruitless meeting with the FSC negotiators, I was summoned to Noh's office. Seated behind his desk, he rattled off a list of points he wanted to impress upon me, while an interpreter sitting next to me translated. First of all, he said, the government would never forget that Newbridge stepped up to sign a deal during Korea's most difficult time. This was something I had been waiting for him to remember, but his behavior still contradicted this claim. He also stated that the government was committed to a successful transaction *with Newbridge*. The emphasis, surprisingly, was his. However, he was concerned by the timing and content of our recent letters that took issue with how the deal was being portrayed in the press and questioning the FSC's intentions. The government remained staunchly in support of the MOU, and intended to stick with it, regardless of what the press said. If the government was misquoted in the media on this subject, he told me, they would take the necessary steps to clarify.

Just before I was called into my meeting with Noh, the FSC negotiators had insisted to me that no one from their team had spoken with the media. This would have been more believable if I hadn't had to wait outside Noh's office while he was finishing a meeting with a group of reporters.

★ ★ ★

Winning the battle for public opinion was critically important, and the press was an important weapon. But so far we had been operating at a disadvantage. The FSC team wanted a much better deal than the MOU but couldn't be seen to be walking away from the table; it had to make it look like it was Newbridge that was at fault. The public did not know the true story, and the local press naturally reflected nationalistic sentiment. I decided it was important to build a good relationship with the press and to correct any misperceptions. It was tricky to manage: We had to keep the specifics of the negotiation confidential. Nonetheless, communicating with the press and, through it, with the public, became an important part of my job.

There was a good deal of interest among the reporters, both Korean and foreign, in speaking with us and learning about the progress in negotiations. From time to time I met with reporters from most of the major English publications and got to know many of them well. Hyung-min Kim, a journalist at the *Korea Times*, was in the habit of calling me "Dr. Shan" or occasionally just "Doctor," which I found quite amusing. It reminded me of a cartoon in the *New Yorker* magazine, in which the maître d' at a fancy restaurant was talking into the telephone: "A party of four at seven-thirty in the name of Dr. Jennings. May I ask whether that is an actual medical degree or merely a Ph.D.?" As a mere PhD, I found Hyung-min's deference a little over the top, but I appreciated his earnestness.

Back in January, the *Korea Times*, the nation's leading English-language daily, had been critical of our deal. But after Hyung-min Kim spent some time with me learning the ins and outs of the MOU, the paper's coverage was much more balanced.

One day in April, he faxed me an advance copy of an article, scheduled to appear in his newspaper the following day, with a note that he would be happy to talk with me again, whenever I wanted. The article was essentially a report on an interview he'd conducted with a director of the World Bank. It clarified that the position of the World Bank was that the deal outlined in the MOU was the deal the international community was expecting—and one that had strong global support. Sri Ram Aiyer, director of the World Bank in Seoul, was quoted: "A deal is a deal. Whether it is an MOU or a final contract, it is something agreed to be respected by the two sides." Aiyer went on to explain that foreign investment in Korea was still seen as incredibly risky, making it unappealing to many investors. This was an important reminder, considering the optimism many Koreans were feeling since the HSBC deal had been made. Finally Aiyer pointed out that just a year ago, Newbridge had confidence in Korea's economy—while all other foreign investors were fleeing.

I had never met or even spoke with Aiyer, but I was impressed not only by his views but also by how candid he was. I sent the article around to my colleagues and remarked in the cover note: "Uncharacteristic of these multilateral agencies, he is refreshingly vocal on our behalf."

★ ★ ★

With less than a month left in the exclusivity period, there was still no sign the FSC team was making an effort to reach a final agreement with us. To all appearances, they were running out the clock until our exclusivity expired. We decided to set up a meeting among Chairman Lee, Blum, and Bonderman, our two co-chairs, in the hope of resolving the key issues. This chairmen's meeting was scheduled April 16, just two weeks before the end of our exclusivity period.

As the date approached, we made careful preparations for the meeting. Carroll and I wanted to establish a friendly atmosphere as early as possible. We suggested that Blum and Bonderman each bring a small gift that reflected a bit about them personally. Both Chairman Lee and Bonderman had connections to Harvard—the former attended the university's Advanced Management Program and the latter was its law school's trustee—so we decided that Bonderman would bring some memento from Harvard—a pair of cuff links with the Harvard crest on them. Blum, an avid mountaineer, would bring a book about the first successful conquest of Mount Everest, the summit by Edmund Hillary, a New Zealander, and Tenzing Norgay, a Nepalese, in 1953. He would attach a photo of himself on the mountain to reveal a little bit about his personality in hope of making a deeper connection with Chairman Lee and breaking the ice.

While we were preparing our peace offerings, it seemed as if the FSC was getting ready for war. The pressure only increased as we drew closer to the date of the meeting. In the days leading up to the chairmen's meeting, I received numerous phone calls from reporters inquiring about the status of the negotiations. These included not only Korean reporters but also foreign journalists from the *Wall Street Journal* and the *Financial Times*. Local newspapers were awash with articles predicting the collapse of negotiations and blaming Newbridge for the failure. Indeed, the *Korea Times* seemed to be the only domestic English newspaper expressing support for the deal. Sensing a small advantage, I briefed the *Korea Times* reporters and told them that, contrary to the press speculation, the gap between the two parties was narrowing.

A few days before the meeting I also received a call from Harrison Young, a managing director at Morgan Stanley, the FSC's advisor.

"You are about to lose this deal," he told me flatly. He didn't say anything else, but the implication was clear: We would have to make more concessions to salvage the deal.

Until that point the FSC had delivered most of its threats through the press, so I took the word of a senior executive at Morgan Stanley very seriously. We didn't think he would pass the message along without truly believing it, a fact that filled us with anxiety, but there wasn't much else we could do. If the threat was intended to wring more concessions from us, we did not have anything to give. The chairmen's meeting seemed our only hope to save it.

★ ★ ★

Blum and Bonderman arrived from San Francisco on April 15, and the next day we met with Chairman Lee and his team in the biggest conference room at the FSC. I entered the meeting in a hopeful frame of mind. We were seated at a long table on our side of the room, and the FSC team sat at their own long table on the other side of the room, with a wide space between us. Bonderman and Blum presented their gifts to the chairman and he thanked them, then we turned our attention to business. I had sent the FSC team our revised term sheet and issue list in advance, to allow Chairman Lee some time to prepare.

To our great surprise, instead of reviewing the key issues, Chairman Lee read a prepared statement. He began by accusing Newbridge of speaking with third parties, such as the World Bank. Apparently he had been infuriated by the *Korea Times* interview with Aiyer of the World Bank. There was no opportunity for me to explain that I had never spoken with Aiyer and that I was as surprised as Chairman Lee to see the article.

Lee continued, "Money isn't a problem for us. We want Newbridge to bring two things, experience and management." He explained that the Korean government and citizenry didn't have faith that we could deliver either one.

Bonderman responded, after a brief pause, that Newbridge and the government shared the same objectives. In an attempt to get the meeting back on track, he said, "Going back to the chairman's comments and the MOU, our question is: what is a clean bank? If the mark-to-market is resolved, all the other issues are easy. Let's focus on that one issue and get it resolved."

But Lee would not engage. Instead he said, "Don't burn down a house to kill a tick."

I'd never heard such an expression before, and under different circumstances I might have found it charming, but it revealed the chasm between Newbridge and the government. We had considered the mark-to-market factor to be the most important issue in the deal, but the chairman considered it a "tick," a tiny irritation.

Blum spoke up. "The bank should be made good by international standards. But, of course, the market is in Korea. The difference between the two parties is like arguing about if the glass is half empty or half full."

Lee said nothing further. He stood up and left the meeting, leaving our two co-chairmen staring across the room at Director General Noh, who responded with his usual aloof gaze.

We were all quite shocked by Lee's angry tone and abrupt departure. We had nothing to do with the views expressed by the World Bank director, who was unlikely to do our bidding in any case. Korean government officials were clearly angry that the World Bank's view resonated with ours, which made walking away from the MOU much harder for them, because selling at least one of the two nationalized banks was one of the conditions for the $58 billion rescue package the IMF and the World Bank had provided to South Korea.

Once Chairman Lee was out of the room, Noh presided over the rest of the meeting. Junior Lee began to go through a list of the government's positions on a number of issues, including how to value the liabilities of the bank, which included its deposits or any other borrowings on which the bank might owe interest. I was surprised to learn that the FSC team now wanted to mark down the value of the demand deposit on the liability side, which would have the effect of marking up the value of the assets. (For example, if you owe a creditor $1,000 less, then your net worth becomes $1,000 more.) I thought the argument was bizarre because if the bank owed a depositor 100,000 won, there were no grounds to argue it owed less than 100,000 won. As in the United States, deposits were fully insured by the Korea Deposit Insurance Corporation, so their full value would be paid to depositors. By the time Junior Lee was through with his list, the FSC had rejected all of our proposals. As in the past, they did not give us reasons for their rejections.

After Junior Lee finished, Bonderman noted, "If there is no mark to market on the assets of the bank, there shouldn't be any mark to market on the side of liabilities." We thought there was no reason why any of the bank's liabilities should not be marked at par and nothing could justify a different approach.

Instead of addressing Bonderman's point, Noh said, "I take issue with Mr. Bonderman's statement." Then he began his own diatribe, blaming Newbridge for the stalled negotiations.

Just before entering the room, Blum had taken me aside and said, "Shan, when you negotiate with their team, it is important to keep your cool and be patient." Apparently he had heard that I had lost my cool on a couple of occasions. I knew he was right, so I nodded in agreement.

At this point in the meeting, as Noh went on and on making accusations against us for stalling the negotiations, I could tell that Blum was getting more and more agitated; his expression was tense and his eyes became sharp. When he finally had the chance to speak, he began to pound the table. Sitting next to him, I gently pulled his sleeve to calm him down. Red in the face, he abruptly turned to me and bellowed, "How have you put up with this shit for so long?"

The meeting was adjourned, and, again, nothing was achieved. We all felt quite dejected. After months of negotiations, it looked as if the FSC team was preparing to walk away from the transaction. It felt like all of our efforts—the late-night meetings, the time away from our families—had been in vain. It was Friday, the beginning of the weekend. We all left Seoul without knowing what would come next.

★　★　★

On Sunday, back in Hong Kong, I bumped into Philip Gilligan on the street. Philip was a lawyer at White & Case, the firm acting as legal counsel for the FSC. His partner, Eric Yoon, had been at Friday's meeting and thought it had gone well. Needless to say, I was baffled. Philip explained that Lee's stern statement was merely positioning because the FSC was concerned we were going to pull out of the negotiations.

To me, the FSC's interpretation of our position defied common sense. Our two chairmen had flown all the way from the United States to try to save the deal. How could the FSC have thought we were about to walk away?

I conferred with Harrison Young of Morgan Stanley and thought his interpretation was more logical. Views within the Korean government were still divided, he told me, and even Morgan Stanley, the government's advisor, did not know where things stood. He said we should wait until we knew exactly what the government side intended to do.

★　★　★

Nearly a week went by before we heard anything from the FSC. Then, on April 22, we were surprised to receive a proposal from its negotiating team. Even though many of the terms were unacceptable, it showed that the FSC still wanted to talk. Perhaps the situation was not as bad as we had thought.

We met with the FSC team the next day. The purpose of the meeting, from our point of view, was to get clarification on the terms included in their proposal. Noh started the meeting by saying that he hoped our discussion would end in a good result. I think he was expecting to hear whether we would accept the FSC's proposal. As it became clear that we were only seeking clarification and would reserve feedback until we had a chance to review the discussion points, Noh, apparently bored with the technical details, left the meeting not long after it began.

The rest of the discussion was cordial and engaging. The FSC's negotiators were willing to explain their rationale and answer our questions. They seemed also willing to listen to what we had to say. We agreed to meet again the following Tuesday, April 27, to give them our response.

After the meeting I reached out to one of the FSC team members whom I had gotten to know well. In spite of the progress we'd just made, he was worried. He told me confidentially that the FSC was not going to be flexible on the terms of its proposal. He told me that the FSC's position was hardened by what it perceived as a real improvement in the financial markets and credit conditions in Korea. The latest proposal, he said, was pretty much the best his team could do.

The market sentiment was, in fact, improving. Earlier that month the *Wall Street Journal* reported that Goldman Sachs would invest about $500 million in Kookmin Bank, one of Korea's largest retail banks, to become its largest shareholder. The deal would give Goldman Sachs a 16.8 percent stake in the company and a seat on the board, although it would not get management control. This was seen as a signal to the market that the worst was over—or at least that foreign investors were willing to buy into a Korean bank at a premium, instead of at a discount, to its net asset value. I was afraid the new deal would also raise questions in the minds of the government and the public as to why the KFB deal, which included Newbridge's taking management control, was still necessary.

I proposed stepping up our public relations effort by holding a briefing session with reporters. This would serve the dual purpose of informing the public of our position, which we considered reasonable and in line with the MOU, and showing the FSC that we would not put up with being blamed for slowing down or disrupting the deal. The new proposal from the FSC gave us reason to question whether my plan was prudent. There was some concern among the Newbridge team that a press briefing would be seen by the FSC as a deliberate provocation, causing it to respond in the same way Chairman Lee had after he read the interview with Aiyer of the World Bank about the deal. If that happened, it would prompt an unfavorable backlash, causing the FSC to dig in further or decide to walk away from the deal. We'd already seen how badly they'd responded to positive news coverage about our position, and some of my colleagues feared the press conference would undo the progress we had just made.

Still, I decided to proceed because I was convinced the deal was not going to happen without public support. And I believed the deal was in the best interests of all parties. Not only did we need it, but the government needed it too. The press conference was scheduled for the morning of Tuesday, April 27, just a few hours before our afternoon meeting with the FSC.

In the days leading up to the press conference, I frequently spoke with reporters, especially Michael Schuman of the *Wall Street Journal*, John Burton of the *Financial Times*, and Hyung-min Kim of the *Korea Times*. I kept them informed of the status of the negotiation while making sure not to disclose any specifics. In return, they often let me know what they were hearing from the government side. I found the quid pro quo to be beneficial. It was clear that the FSC was not only managing the Korean press but the foreign press as well.

The longer the negotiations stretched on, the worse Korea First Bank's situation became. In early April, the FSC had notified KFB to prepare to receive a capital injection of another 2 to 3 trillion Korean won (about $1.7–2.5 billion), in addition to 2 to 3 trillion won it had already received from the government. All the infused capital was to fill the hole created by loan losses as the equity capital had long been wiped out before the bank's nationalization. The bank was in dire need of capital, and, as negotiations stalled, the government had to pump in more money to keep the bank afloat and operating. Meanwhile, Won-kyu Choi, a member of KFB's management team, told me that the employees' union of the KFB was strongly supportive of a takeover by Newbridge. Knowing that the bank's employees were in favor of our deal could sway local public opinion in our favor and would be another thing the government had to acknowledge.

That same week as our press conference, South Korea's president, Dae-jung Kim, met with the heads of the top five *chaebols* and other important Korean business leaders. Shee-yul Ryoo, the head of KFB, was there, as was Chairman Lee. The president asked Lee about the KFB deal with Newbridge and requested that Lee provide a report on our progress. The Newbridge team was encouraged by the news because it showed that support for our deal still existed at the very top level of government. That was a sign that the FSC would have a hard time walking away.

The day before the press conference and FSC meeting, both the *Wall Street Journal* and the *Financial Times* published articles saying that the Korean government might pull out of the sale of KFB to Newbridge. Dow Jones, Bloomberg, and the *Korea Economic Daily* all called me for comment. Clearly, the government side was beginning a press offensive against us.

At 11 am the following day, in a room at Korea First Bank's head-quarters that was packed with reporters, I began my press briefing. Choi of KFB, who spoke English fluently, translated for me. Choi was a good man, candid and strongly supportive of the deal. Noh had called the bank prior to the press conference in an attempt to dissuade him from acting as my translator, but Choi ignored Noh's pressure and accompanied me. I thought it took a lot of courage for a bank employee to defy a senior official from the bank's own regulator, and it signaled that Choi was strongly supportive of the transaction.

I began by apologizing for not being able to speak more than a few words in Korean and for having not met with the press sooner. Then I said:

> But I am studying the language, the history and the culture of Korea. We didn't hold a press briefing earlier because we thought it was better to do more and talk less. However, we see much misperception of Newbridge in the press and we feel a responsibility to explain to you what we are and what we are not.
>
> We are not a hedge fund. We are not short-term investors. Short-term investors don't invest in a down market. But we do.
>
> We are a private equity investment firm. We are turnaround specialists. We typically make a long-term investment to create value for stakeholders. We are good corporate citizens. We have the capital and experience to recapitalize and turn around Korea First Bank. We have a successful track record, which is why Morgan Stanley invited us to bid for the bank. The government signed the MOU with us because our proposal was the best the government had received.

I went on to explain why Newbridge wanted to invest in Korea:

First, we have strong confidence in the Korean people, who are industrious and who have the potential to compete successfully in the world market. Second, we believe in Korea's commitment to reform. Third, we know how to turn around failed banks better than anyone. We have a world-class team.

During the back-and-forth with reporters, I emphasized that we shared two common goals with the Korean government: running a clean bank and adopting international best practices. I highlighted the significant upside for the government in the deal and the fact that it would be a benchmark for banking reform in Korea. I described the credit culture that we were poised to build at KFB and how that would launch the bank to be a worthy international competitor.

"Would there be layoffs?" a reporter asked. I explained that we didn't have plans to fire anyone and that we looked forward to working with KFB's existing employees and management. By that point KFB's chairman, Shee-yul Ryoo, had made significant cuts to payroll so we didn't think further reductions would be necessary.

Everyone knew that our exclusivity under the MOU would expire in about a week, so reporters were eager to know how the negotiations were going.

I held my tongue and focused only on the positives. I described the deal as a perfect and respectful marriage with the Korean government. Of course, there were some disagreements, I said, but we respected the FSC negotiators. Besides, it would be a lose-lose outcome if the deal fell apart.

"What is the cost of not doing this deal?" I asked rhetorically. I didn't need to answer the question because the implication was clear: If the deal fell through, the government would be in violation of its agreement with the IMF and World Bank for the $58 billion rescue package. Taxpayers would be on the hook for all the money they had sunk into KFB. Plus, it would take more money to keep the bank afloat.

What would happen to the deal after the exclusivity period expired? That I refused to discuss. In truth, I had no clue.

The next day, all the major newspapers, domestic and foreign, covered my statements. In general, the reaction was positive. It seemed the press briefing was a success. At least, it managed to crush all the lies about Newbridge being greedy and unreasonable. Even Korea's finance ministry responded to my press briefing favorably, issuing a statement to say it supported the Newbridge-KFB deal. Only the FSC was unhappy with my press conference, as I heard, although it kept quiet.

★ ★ ★

Despite the economic pressures faced by KFB and the sustained top-level attention to the deal, the FSC team's negotiating strategy was very much the same when we sat across the table from them once again on the day of my press conference. Once again things stalled, and it became clear that we wouldn't make any headway.

As the negotiations broke down, we felt intense pressure to figure out what was going on within the government. To do so we had engaged a New York–based advisory firm to help us. Its two principals, whom I will not name, were said to be well versed and well connected with Seoul's political scene. They imbued an air of secrecy, intrigue, and paranoia in our minds, regaling us with tales of scheming as they described the political factions that were fighting for or against the reform agenda of President Dae-jung Kim.

They also told us that our phones and fax lines were bugged and that the government negotiators would know of any strategies or gambits we had discussed on internal conference calls. The hotel phones and our mobile phones were equally unsafe. After this, we were careful not to discuss confidential information over unsecured lines. Unfortunately, that left us without any secure means of communication, other than running out to find a public phone to make calls. I remember a few times Paul Chen had to run out in the rain to a phone booth across the street from the hotel to make a confidential call. All we could do was to minimize the risk of leaks by not saying much in our calls and memos until we were out of Korea.

Our advisors told us that South Korea's intelligence apparatus not only listened to our conversations but also had a codename for each of us. David Bonderman, apparently, was known by the codename "Kim Chee," after Kimchi, the spicy pickled cabbage found in every Korean kitchen. In order to keep our secrets, our advisors gave each of us a codename to use. They even assigned codenames for us to use for each of them. One advisor's codename was "Tall Guy" and the other was "Short Guy." I was "Thin Guy." Dan Carroll was "Handsome Guy."

Even with all these measures of secrecy, I did not exactly feel like James Bond. If these conspiracy theories were true, I thought, Korean intelligence agents were likely much more creative and professional than we were. Our codenames weren't going to fool anyone. If you were to put us all in a lineup, my seven-year-old daughter would easily tell who was Tall Guy, Short Guy, Thin Guy, and Handsome Guy. If anything, it was probably easier to identify us by our codenames than by our real names.

Tall Guy and Short Guy brought a couple of people to see us. They claimed to know what was going on within the government and that they could connect us with those who could influence decision making in the National Assembly and the Blue House. But I never knew whether what the visitors told us was true. I did visit some Assembly representatives and Blue House officials, as arranged by Tall Guy and Short Guy, to brief them on the deal status and on our plans for KFB. I had no idea if those visits did any good. But I thought they were useful nonetheless because if we wanted to educate the public by briefing the press from time to time, we might as well do the same with politicians. At this point, the KFB deal was drawing so much public attention that it felt like Korea's national pastime. We did not know who was for or against the deal, but it was prudent to win as many friends and as much support and sympathy for it as possible.

In the days running up to the expiration of exclusivity, Tall Guy and Short Guy repeatedly told us that ours was a done deal. They even had specific predictions for when the government would sign, but I had my doubts. There was no hint of willingness across the negotiation table, and there were no documents to sign. Each time, the closing date that Tall Guy and Short Guy identified came and went without a deal, and each time our advisors found some plausible explanation for the failure.

I spoke with Short Guy on May 2, 1999, hours before the midnight expiration of our exclusivity. He continued to insist it was a "done deal," but he warned me: "The deal cannot be won at the table, but it can be lost at the table." I did not really think about what he said at the time, but in retrospect I realized the import of what he meant. If we completed the deal, I would not be able to take any credit, because "the deal cannot be won at the table." But if the deal did not happen, it would be all my fault, because the deal "can be lost at the table." As I wrote in my notebook later, "so the strategy is to hold the line and wait for things to work out behind the scenes."

The two days leading up to the May 2 deadline were unnerving and somewhat confusing. The FSC had flatly rejected our most recent proposal and, in fact, widened the gap by proposing to mark down the value of the bank's deposits by 1.5 trillion won (about $1.2 billion).

We did not know what to make of these theatrics. The FSC had pushed their position so far from our proposals that it seemed impossible that we would find a compromise. It seemed, in fact, like the FSC team had no intention of trying to bridge our two positions.

Meanwhile, other bidders began circling: Regent Pacific, a Hong Kong–based hedge fund, publicly announced on May 1 that it would send in an offer with much better terms than Newbridge's after our exclusivity expired.

After strategizing among ourselves, we decided to let Mike O'Hanlon of Lehman lead the discussions on May 1. The hope was that the FSC team would be a bit more relaxed and wouldn't feel as if each comment during the negotiation was a statement for the record.

The strategy achieved some measure of success; the FSC side did seem a bit less tense when they felt that they were dealing with a slightly neutral third party. But they remained as unyielding as ever and continued to demand that we accept their April 22 proposal, which we had already rejected. O'Hanlon informed them we could only negotiate on the basis of our most recent proposal, made on April 27. The gap between those terms and the ones that the FSC had proposed in earlier negotiations was relatively narrow and seemed easy to bridge. Left unsaid was how far the FSC had moved away from its own bargaining position in the intervening month. Before we wrapped up for the day, O'Hanlon left on the table a compromise offer, which we followed up on in writing later that day.

That afternoon, with some eight hours remaining before the deadline, the entire Newbridge and Lehman team went to the FSC's office for a final meeting. We had learned from a source there that Chairman Lee had attended every internal meeting held that day on this transaction. This was the first time we heard that the negotiation team on the other side might have received some signal from the top.

Before we finished exchanging pleasantries, I was summoned to Noh's office. O'Hanlon and I went together. O'Hanlon briefly explained our new proposal to Noh, and Noh replied that the government would need some time to review it and give us feedback. O'Hanlon then brought up the subject of an extension of exclusivity. Noh immediately asked if that was an official request.

"I could make it an official request," I replied. Noh asked his staff to note down the request and asked me to send it to him in writing.

Noh's body language telegraphed that he had been trying to use the pending expiration of exclusivity as leverage against us, to force us to accept his proposal. He probably had expected us to capitulate right before the expiration. For that reason, I thought there was no way he would want to extend the exclusivity for us.

That was as far as we got with Noh on that day. I sent him a request for an extension of exclusivity for 10 days, to agree on major terms to be incorporated into a new MOU, followed by three weeks for the documentation and to close "as soon as practicable."

Then we waited.

Our exclusive right to negotiate with the Korean government for KFB expired at midnight on May 2, 1999, with no word from the government. By the following morning we still had not heard from them one way or another. I filed an update to Blum, Bonderman, and the team noting our lack of progress. But just before I sent out the update, I received a letter from the FSC. After reading it, I added a paragraph at the beginning of my note: "I received the official letter from the FSC rejecting our request for extension of exclusivity. They say they will continue to discuss with us on a non-exclusive basis until May 12."

Chapter 6

The Ambassador

Seoul, the capital of South Korea, is situated slightly south of the dividing line between North and South Korea in the middle of the Korean Peninsula and at about the same latitude as Tokyo, Athens, and Richmond, Virginia, in the United States. May is probably the most pleasant month of the year in the South Korean capital. April is still somewhat chilly, and by June the city starts to bake in the still heat of summer. It rarely rains. All the trees are fully dressed in new green leaves that seem to be polished with wax and glitter in the sunlight.

The Newbridge team had made Seoul's Shilla Hotel home. It was there that we stayed each time we visited Seoul. The Shilla was perched at the top of a long driveway right up against one of the many hills surrounding central Seoul, this one called Namsan, or South Mountain. Its main building was a slab of reddish-brown brick, about 20 stories tall. The hotel itself was rather old, and its age was starting to show. In the back of the hotel were the remains of Seoul's old city wall. It was connected to a historic guesthouse, an old government building in the Chinese style, where generations of Korean leaders had entertained foreign dignitaries. Over the main door hung a plaque with three big Chinese characters: "Welcome Guest House." In between this building and the hotel was a large lawn that I could see from my room. There was a wedding on the lawn almost every weekend in May.

Being able to read Chinese gave me a greater appreciation of Korea's history. Many historical sites, including palaces, temples, pavilions, and museums, used Chinese characters, as did some of the streets. Chinese characters were called *hanja* in Korean (just as they are called *kanji* in Japan) and had probably been introduced to Korea more than 2,000 years ago, at the time when the Qin dynasty unified China and the defeated rulers of the north who had lost their kingdoms fled to Korea. Chinese characters were the only written language in Korea until the 15th century, when King Sejong the Great and his scholars developed an alphabetic writing system known as *hangul*. In the 1970s President Chung-hee Park largely banned the use of *hanja*, promoting *hangul* instead. When I first visited Korea in the late 1980s, many street signs were still in *hanja*. Today the characters have largely disappeared, except for most Korean names, which are still written in *hanja*. Many among the older generation of Koreans are still well versed in Chinese characters and can write in Chinese calligraphy.

As a runner, I liked running in the pleasant May weather along the mountain path zigzagging all the way to the peak of Namsan, where Seoul Tower stands. From there I could enjoy a panoramic view of the sprawling city. Cutting through the city like a shining belt is Han'gang, the Han River.

★ ★ ★

The FSC announced to the world on Monday, May 3, that it would continue to negotiate the sale of KFB with Newbridge until May 12, but on a nonexclusive basis. I dispatched a memo by fax from Hong Kong on Sunday, May 7, 1999, with the subject "Safe—Towards Another Deadline." The project codename was still "Safe," although at that point the deal looked anything but.

Despite assurances from Tall Guy and Short Guy, I wrote, I still didn't see any sign of flexibility across the table. Although the other side now seemed more willing to meet with us than it had over the past two months, there was no change in their position on major terms.

"Given the large gap between us," I concluded, "I cannot see *how* the two sides can suddenly agree to a deal on so many major open issues at the eleventh hour. I am afraid that even though the other side wants to do a deal with us, it may continue to expect us to accept its deal, which is not acceptable to us."

At 10:30 in the morning on May 11, one day before the government's new self-imposed deadline, we had a last-ditch meeting with the FSC team at their office to hear their feedback on our proposal. Noh came into the meeting only ceremonially, for about five minutes, and then left. Without making any comments on our proposal, the FSC team insisted we should give them a new proposal.

Mike O'Hanlon of Lehman, whom I asked at that point to lead some negotiation sessions, was an infinitely patient man. "Shan, please don't ever take it personally," he counseled me, after one particularly frustrating negotiating session. "It's just a deal." His patience, I thought, was our best weapon against the other side's maddening and seemingly endless quibbles on every issue.

But now even O'Hanlon seemed to have had enough. "Please don't view yourselves as regulators. This is a commercial negotiation," he told the FSC negotiators. Bob Barnum, another member of the Newbridge team, asked whether it was the economics or the structure of the deal that was not acceptable. The reply was: "Newbridge's proposal is not acceptable. Come back with a better proposal."

The Newbridge team regrouped in a conference room at the Shilla Hotel's business center to discuss how to respond to the government's request. Short Guy came in to tell us, once again, that the deal was done, no problem, and all we had to do was submit our best proposal to the other side. Incidentally, a few people, including a *Korea Times* reporter, called to congratulate me, saying that a local newswire had just reported that the KFB deal was Newbridge's to clinch, and the government was only making a last-ditch effort to improve the terms.

I found all this hard to believe. It was as if I had gone out for a date with a girl who refused to talk to me and slapped my face, only to be told by friends, when I returned home, that she was ready to marry me. How was that possible?

We all felt that we had spent the past four months negotiating against ourselves, submitting proposal after proposal at the government's urging, undercutting our own terms at their every request.

That afternoon we made a bold decision, hoping to drastically change the course of negotiations. We decided to take a new tack, proposing to use a *covered assets model,* which we had considered earlier but never proposed. We hoped using such a model would eliminate the two key issues: the valuation mark on the loan portfolio and the methodology used to classify troubled loans when deciding which would be put to the bad bank.

Under the covered assets model, Newbridge would eliminate any puts of loans to the government. Instead, we proposed a five-year, yield-maintenance agreement for all of KFB's loans. In other words, we would accept a guarantee from the government of the principal and interest of the loans. After the five years were up, KFB would give the government a price at which it would buy any classified loan at that time. The government could either accept the price and pay KFB the difference between the price and book value, or buy the loan outright at book value.

We liked this model for a couple reasons. To start with, we would avoid sending a negative signal regarding any company whose loans were being put to the bad bank. For another, except for the initial transfer of nonperforming loans, all other loans would be kept. This avoided the need for loans to be marked to market.

At the end of the five-year period, impaired loans would be classified according to the then-prevailing standard adopted by the Financial Supervisory Services of Korea rather than international best practices. (We expected that by that time the Korean standard would converge with international best practices anyhow.) The government would then have two options. If it agreed to the impairment value as determined by KFB, it would pay KFB the impaired amount. If the government did not agree (i.e., if it determined the impairment was smaller than what was assessed by KFB), it could buy the loan at the original book value and sell it in the market, hopefully at a price better than what KFB valued it at. The government would thus be protected against any possibility that KFB would undervalue the loans, since it had the option of taking or leaving our price. Under this arrangement KFB would have no incentive to undervalue a loan, because it would risk losing a customer if the government decided to purchase the loan; neither would it overvalue a loan, because it would then make a loss.

The arrangement could also work in reverse. In this scenario the government could name the loan value, and KFB would have the option to either accept it or to sell the loan to the government at the original book value. Again, each party would be protected against any opportunistic behavior of the other.

We called this a *buy/sell arrangement*, which is typically used to dissolve a joint venture. Suppose two parties jointly own a property but they wish to terminate the joint ownership. Which one of them should be the buyer and at what price? In a typical buy/sell arrangement, one party names the price, while the other party has the right to either buy or sell at that price. It does not matter which party names the price because the other party has the option to either buy or sell, depending on if the party thinks the price is lower or higher than fair market value. This is probably the best way to find the fair market value. For our purposes, the buy/sell arrangement would eliminate any need to value the loans at the present time, thus removing what had been a major point of contention between the FSC and Newbridge.

Our new proposal attempted to address the concerns of the government without making things riskier for KFB. The government feared that we would not roll over loans at maturity and that we would use the put right to transfer those loans to the government. As we knew, many of KFB's borrowers used short-term loans for long-term projects, because the old practice of Korean banks was simply to roll over these loans upon maturity. If these loans were not rolled over, the borrowers might default, which would trigger our right to put the loan. Under the new proposal, KFB would generally roll over such loans, because they were guaranteed by the government. By rolling over the loans almost automatically upon maturity within five years, we also would take care of another concern of the government: that KFB would send a negative signal to the market about the borrower if its loan was put.

The ingenuity of the proposal was that both the government and Newbridge would be better off with it, because it would be less risky for both sides. As the buyer of the bank, we were concerned about the potential deepening of the economic crisis, which might render even good borrowers bad in the future. Therefore, we would need to value current loans conservatively. The government, meanwhile, was hoping that the economy would recover and the loan would be worth more tomorrow than it was today, so it would be opposed to valuing loans conservatively at the present time. With completely divergent expectations, the two sides could not hope to reach an agreement. Our new proposal eliminated the need to put a value on the loans at the present time. It gave KFB borrowers five years to recover from the economic crisis and improve their financial health. If they did so, loans would be worth more, which would be beneficial both to the government, which provided the guarantee, and to KFB, which would have retained good customers. It is rare for a new proposal to be better than the old for both sides. We thought ours was. I just hoped that the FSC team saw it that way as well.

We went back to the FSC at about 6:30 that evening, May 11. O'Hanlon took the lead, carefully explaining the new proposal. The FSC team looked stunned. They raised a few questions, then said they would study it. Gokul Laroia of Morgan Stanley called later to ask a few follow-up questions. My hopes rose that the government team was receptive to the concept, if not the proposal, as yet.

That evening Dick Blum arrived in Seoul on his private plane. The purpose of his visit, arranged by our political advisors, was to meet with a Woon-ji Choi the next day. Choi was said to be affiliated with United Liberal Democrats, to be the treasurer of the three political parties that formed the coalition government, and, critically, to be FSC chairman Hun-jai Lee's mentor. Short Guy and Tall Guy told us that Choi would meet with Blum and bring Chairman Lee to the meeting. During the meeting Lee would apologize to Blum for being rude during their last meeting back in April. Then the deal would be struck.

The next day, May 12, all of us waited for confirmation of a meeting time between Blum and Choi, but the morning passed without word from our advisors. By then we knew that Tall Guy and Short Guy worked in secrecy, so we waited patiently. Finally Blum and Carroll went to KFB to pay a courtesy visit to Chairman Ryoo. At about 2 pm Short Guy and his Korean friends told us that Blum was requested to call Mr. Noh, who was waiting for the call.

Blum dialed the number, but the man who answered had no clue who Blum was or where to find Noh. In his exasperation, Blum said over the speakerphone, "All the big shots are here waiting." The man on the other end of the line did not know what Blum was talking about, but he politely replied, in poor English, "I know you are a big shot." All of us who were sitting around the speakerphone had to cover our mouths with our hands to muffle our laughs.

When I finally tracked down Noh, he was not expecting a call from Blum. The men spoke for no more than three minutes, and Noh said only that the FSC was still studying the new proposal. Despite all that, our political advisors insisted that the deal would be done by midnight.

Earlier in the day Yonhap, a Korean news service that was practically a government mouthpiece, reported that Newbridge had made a new proposal that the FSC was studying. "The new terms are expected to hold many traps," it helpfully explained, citing unnamed government sources. We did not have to guess who had planted the story.

Another newspaper, *Munhwa*, had run with the headline "Newbridge/ KFB Deal Completed—Government Decides to Bear 4.5 Trillion Won." According to that article, the contract would be signed at 12 noon and announced in the evening, but the parties were still negotiating, because, it reported, the government was concerned about its sovereign credit rating. How a deal that *helped* the country's sovereign rating should be a source of concern was not explained in the article. This report was eerily similar to the story told to us by our advisors, and I suspected that someone involved in their circle was behind it.

It seemed that many people knew better about the prospects for our deal than we did ourselves. I had stopped trying to handicap the various outcomes. In the end, the May 12 deadline passed without further contact between the FSC team and ourselves, other than that three-minute call between Blum and Noh.

At 4 pm on May 12 Blum left Seoul to return to San Francisco, having spent less than 24 hours on the ground. He hadn't had the promised meeting with Mr. Choi and Chairman Lee and had had only a three-minute call with Noh. What a waste of time.

Already skeptical about the repeated assurances given to us by Short Guy and Tall Guy that the deal was done, I was curious to hear their explanation as to what had happened. They had one. They said that the political opposition had mounted a counterattack on the night of May 11 and turned the tables on the deal. The opposition, they said, was led by none other than Woo-choong Kim, the chairman of Daewoo.

He opposed to the deal, they claimed, because KFB was Daewoo's lead bank, and he was concerned that foreign owners would be less inclined to do Daewoo's bidding.

I was certain that if Chairman Kim had understood our deal, he would not have opposed it. Our new proposal to the government was intended to preserve customer relationships by giving customers time to recover from the current financial malaise. I decided to pay him a visit to explain the situation. Regardless of whether the rumors were true, it was prudent to win such a powerful and influential *chaebol* head to our side.

Luckily, I knew Chairman Kim personally. Our relationship dated back to 1987, when he sought my advice while I was still a professor at Wharton, and was such that I could just pick up the phone and call him. We arranged to have lunch the following week, on May 18.

To prepare for the meeting, I wrote up a confidential memo that explained, in summary form, the key terms and major benefits of our new proposal. I had it translated into Korean, even though Chairman Kim spoke good English.

There was one element of our proposal I knew would be of interest to him. Under our new covered assets model, there would be no further transfer of loans after the close of our acquisition for at least five years. Borrowers like Daewoo would not have to worry about a disruption in their banking relationship with KFB.

I told Chairman Kim the deal would be a win–win and that we wanted our customers to succeed. If the deal fell apart, it would create a lose–lose outcome for all concerned.

Kim listened attentively. In front of me, he read our briefing memo carefully, twice. Then he said he would try to find out where things stood.

Coincidentally, Dick Fuld, chairman and CEO of Lehman Brothers, was in town a few days later. He and Mike O'Hanlon were meeting with regulators and Lehman's major clients, including Chairman Lee of the FSC and Chairman Kim of Daewoo. O'Hanlon and I spent some time preparing a script for Fuld to use in his meetings concerning the KFB situation.

O'Hanlon returned to the hotel at about 6 pm, after having spent the day making the rounds with his CEO. He looked dejected. Chairman Lee had told Fuld that he was committed to the deal and that he remained positive about its prospects. But the main issue now, Lee said, was not price but the bank's management and customers. Fuld explained that the new management team identified by Newbridge was ready but, without a deal, it could not be moved into place. Further, he noted, the covered assets model in our latest proposal meant there would be no disruption of corporate client relationships for five years. It was clear to both O'Hanlon and Fuld that Chairman Lee knew nothing about this new proposal.

The meeting with Chairman Kim was even worse. Although I was under the impression that my meeting with him a few days earlier had been productive, the Daewoo chief bluntly told Fuld that he thought it was too late and that there was no hope to save our deal. O'Hanlon reported that Chairman Kim was so negative that he spoke of the deal in past tense.

The next morning Chairman Kim called to invite me to meet with him at the Hilton Hotel. The meeting was brief; he had only one message for me. He asked me to keep in contact with him directly, without the knowledge of any third party. He wanted to keep our communication strictly confidential. He said he was going to meet with Chairman Lee at 4 that afternoon.

I had heard from some Korean friends that Lee had once been Kim's chief of staff and therefore they knew each other well and had a good personal relationship. I took this as a positive sign.

At about 9 pm Chairman Kim called again, and I went to meet him at the Hilton. Chairman Lee was not negative about the deal, he said, but he was worried we'd get rid of half of KFB's customers. This feedback, consistent with what I'd heard from O'Hanlon, was further proof that Lee had zero knowledge of our new proposal. It became clear that Noh had never shared our proposal with his chairman, nor had he provided any feedback since we submitted it, more than a week earlier.

★ ★ ★

I suspected that one reason we had not heard from the FSC was because it was distracted, negotiating with HSBC for Seoul Bank. I had heard from Michael Schuman of the *Wall Street Journal* that the talks between the FSC and HSBC were moving ahead. If the FSC and HSBC struck a deal for the only other major bank up for sale, the government probably would not need Newbridge anymore. It could walk away and blame us for the deal's failure. Still, I found it hard to believe that things with HSBC could be progressing any better than they were with Newbridge. My suspicions were soon proven to be well founded.

"HSBC's deal has run into trouble," Won-kyu Choi told me as soon as we sat down for lunch on May 20, the day after my private meeting with Chairman Kim. I had held Choi in high regard ever since he'd defied Noh by translating for me at our April press conference, and I found the KFB executive to be quite well informed on all that was going on surrounding the two bank deals.

HSBC had submitted a new proposal, Choi said, with a number of new demands. Many of these sounded familiar and had been in Newbridge's original discussions over KFB: using international best practices instead of Korean bank standards to classify troubled loans, for example, and marking down the value of the workout loans, as opposed to accepting them at book value. But supposedly HSBC had not included these terms in its MOU. Furthermore, HSBC wanted to value the office building of Seoul Bank at a steep two-thirds discount from its book value.

"The FSC team was shocked by HSBC's new proposal," Choi told me. "In fact, they were flabbergasted. HSBC's terms are worse for the government than Newbridge's. Now the FSC doesn't know what to do with HSBC anymore."

"Guess what?" Choi went on. "Now the FSC thinks Newbridge people aren't bad guys after all, because compared to HSBC, you guys have been up front and reasonable."

I was glad to hear that the FSC team seemed to appreciate our honesty—finally—but I wasn't entirely surprised by these developments. It seemed inevitable that HSBC would have to change its terms from what it had negotiated under its MOU, unless it had calculated that the inevitable losses from keeping bad loans was the price it had to pay to acquire Seoul Bank. Even so, I doubted HSBC or anyone else would be willing to pay that sort of price. The economy was still so fragile that it was almost impossible to quantify how large the hidden losses might be.

It seemed that HSBC had taken the opposite approach to ours in negotiating with the Korean government. We'd put all our cards on the table negotiating the MOU. In subsequent negotiations, we never deviated from any of the agreed terms to ask for more. We only loosened our terms, making concessions. HSBC, by contrast, now seemed to be the ones demanding the Korean government make concessions.

Bankers are known to sometimes use the tactic of bait and switch or of trying to take a second bite of the apple. They justify it not as intentionally misleading but as a way to squeeze themselves in the door when the counterparty is more demanding than discerning. The approach is risky because it can backfire, and it requires a desperate counterparty that is willing to accept worsening terms. Those who fall for it once rarely will do so again.

We did not play that kind of game. Bait and switch made it impossible to build a long-term relationship. The only way to build trust, I still believe, is to be up front and honest, even if it means losing some opportunities. We earn our credibility in the long run.

I thought back to Noh's glee, celebrating the HSBC MOU he took credit for negotiating. In truth, he had been more than a little naïve. Anyone with experience would know that no investor in his right mind would offer to lose money before it could make money, as the terms of HSBC's MOU seemed to imply.

"Now the FSC doesn't know what to do," Choi repeated. If what he was telling me was true, our chances had improved markedly. He also said that "DJ's men," referring to those working with President Dae-jung Kim, were building pressure to push forward with banking reforms. He hoped that these powerful allies of the president could override the opposition and provide political cover for the FSC to do the deal.

"Unless the FSC has a good reason not to do the deal," Choi told me, "DJ's men will prevail because the deal is in the national interest."

"But what deal?" I asked. "I am not sure if the president's men even know what our new proposal is."

Choi disagreed. "I think they know."

He cited two articles in that day's newspapers which reflected frustration over the lack of progress with the KFB deal. Both articles were critical of the FSC. One questioned its competence. The other reported that KFB's employees were losing morale. It even quoted Choi himself as saying "Whenever there is talk of capital injection by the government, employees become concerned because they are regarded as takers of taxpayers' money. And the morale goes down."

Choi concluded that he was confident in our eventual success, advising us to sit tight and wait for the FSC to show another card. His unwavering confidence in us and in our deal lifted my spirits.

Later that afternoon I received an invitation from Kevin Honan, the economic counselor at the U.S. Embassy, to visit him and Ben Fairfax, his boss. My colleague Daniel Poon joined me, and we briefed them on our new proposal. To my surprise, they seemed quite well informed of what was going on. They also told us that the U.S. ambassador, Steve Bosworth, took a keen interest in the deal, viewing it as a litmus test of South Korea's resolve to restructure its banking system. I did not know the source of their intelligence, but it hadn't come from Newbridge, as none of us had met with the U.S. diplomatic team before. It seemed that Choi was right again; the president's men were following the negotiations closely.

Before I left, Honan also shared with me a cartoon clipped from a local newspaper. It depicted an ugly girl sitting on the ground, crying, in the middle of a village. She was holding a traditional Korean fan labeled "KFB." There were two ladies in traditional Korean costumes standing in the background chatting with each other. One says to the other, "They tried plastic surgery to marry her off quickly. . . ." The other woman replies, "I heard she needs another three trillion to finish the job!" At the right side of the frame, a woman, also in traditional Korean dress, chases after and tries to pull back a Western man with a briefcase labeled "Newbridge," who is walking away with sweat dripping off his face. The thought bubble above his head reads "She doesn't look anything like her photos." (See Exhibit 3.)

I had to admit the cartoon was pretty clever, and it suggested that the public sentiment was turning. Faced with the prospect of another 3-trillion-won bill to taxpayers, on top of the 2 to 3 trillion won previously, to keep the bank afloat, a deal with Newbridge was looking far preferable to no deal at all.

Even so, negotiations with the FSC had gone quiet. We had received no further word from the FSC negotiators after the May 12 deadline had expired. So, with nothing further to do in Seoul, Daniel Poon and I left the U.S. Embassy and headed for the airport to take the next flight back to Hong Kong.

As soon as I arrived home, I checked my voicemail and found a message from Jin Park, a lawyer from Kim & Chang, the Korean firm we had engaged soon after signing the MOU. He informed me that his senior partner, Ambassador Hong-choo Hyun, would like to get in contact with either Blum or Bonderman.

★ ★ ★

I had first heard of Ambassador Hyun over breakfast with a group of Kim & Chang lawyers more than a month earlier, when the deal seemed to be in peril. They told me about a senior partner at their firm who had been South Korea's ambassador to the United Nations, and to the United States, in the early 1990s; he had been a National Assembly representative before that. Everyone referred to him as *the ambassador*. He was a highly respected figure in Korea, they told me, and suggested he would be a good addition to the K&C team to help communicate Newbridge's position to the top levels of the FSC.

I had met with Ambassador Hyun at Kim & Chang's offices in mid-April. In his late 50s, Hyun wore rimless glasses and a well-tailored suit. He had just enough gray in his hair to look distinguished. Smiling warmly, he greeted me with a firm handshake. He spoke fluent, indeed masterful, English, probably better than any Korean I had met. He had a slow, gentle style of speech, which gave one the impression that his every word was considered. He came across as an impeccably polished diplomat and gentleman, which he was.

The next day, on May 21, I followed up by phone with a Kim & Chang partner. He told me that the FSC was somehow still unclear as to Newbridge's current intent with regard to the KFB deal and Ambassador Hyun's mission was to help us better communicate with the FSC.

Perhaps not so coincidentally, Gokul Laroia of Morgan Stanley called me that same afternoon.

"Shan, this is unofficial," he said. He didn't know for certain, but he believed the FSC was preparing a counterproposal to our covered asset model to show us next week. However, he cautioned, the FSC team was still being unrealistic, so we should temper our expectations. "I hope they don't come up with something totally bizarre," he said with a sigh.

Whether it was public sentiment, the HSBC deal going south, or pressure from "DJ's men," something had changed on the FSC side. After a long silence, they were coming back to the table. But we had to remain cautious, I believed. The negotiations were not going to be any easier. As I related in a memo on the same day to prepare Blum and Bonderman for a visit by Ambassador Hyun:

It seems that the FSC now feels the pressure internally to do a deal with us. But they probably do not know what to propose. They want to get the best deal but they do not know where our limit is. We know they do not do the kind of analysis we do, and neither do they use their advisors. The only benchmark they go by is how far they can push, i.e., testing our limit. That is why they have consistently said no to whatever we have proposed so far. . . . Therefore, the only way for them to take our proposal seriously is for them to understand that <u>we are already at or beyond our limit in terms of economics with our latest proposal</u>. As long as they believe we can make further concessions in terms of economics, it is unlikely for them to accept anything we propose. This, unfortunately, is typical Korean brinkmanship negotiating style, as we have learned. Therefore, we need to be careful, holding firm our position while show- ing flexibility to accommodate the political and other sensitivities of the other side.

Bonderman responded via fax the same day:

Thanks for your memo of May 21 on negotiating strategy. I am in total agreement. Specifically, I think our position with Ambassador Hyun should be that, while we are always willing to move pieces around to help the FSC, our economic bottom line is exactly as set forth in our most recent proposal.

With that thought in mind, we were prepared to start talking with the Koreans again. It was time for Blum and Bonderman to meet the ambassador.

Chapter 7

Presidential Visit

The meeting between Ambassador Hong-choo Hyun and Dick Blum took place in San Francisco on May 24, 1999. My partner Dan Carroll and our advisor Bob Barnum also participated. Blum enjoyed meeting Ambassador Hyun and took an instant liking to him. To our surprise, the ambassador proposed, on behalf of Chairman Lee, a "summit meeting" between Lee and both Blum and Bonderman in June. He insisted the meeting should take place outside of Korea, and Hong Kong seemed to be the most logical and convenient location. I felt encouraged by this request. Ambassador Hyun would not have made the offer unless Chairman Lee was serious about wanting to do a deal with us.

Meanwhile, back in Seoul, Noh requested a meeting with Kunho Cho, the Lehman Brothers chief representative. It seemed that the FSC, having allowed its deadline to lapse, needed some graceful way to come back to us. Instead of communicating directly, however, it sent messages through advisors.

The messages, as per usual, were confusing and conflicted. On one hand, Noh expressed a firm desire to do a deal with Newbridge. "There hadn't been any talks with any other potential bidders" he said. The FSC wanted "to give it a last push before changing the course of action," Cho told me afterward. "It wants to cross the bridge."

On the other hand, Noh was dismissive of our latest proposal and said that it still showed a lack of understanding of how business is conducted in Korea. The FSC's biggest concern, he told Cho, was that we would restrict the business activities of KFB's borrowers. This seemed to echo what Woo-choong Kim of Daewoo had told me during our late-night meeting at the Seoul Hilton—that the head of the FSC, Chairman Lee, was concerned that we wanted to get rid of half of KFB's existing borrowers. At the time I'd thought this was because Lee was misinformed or because Noh had simply not told him about our proposal. Now I had no idea what Noh was talking about.

Noh also asked Cho to find out what Newbridge's "bottom line" was. The FSC seemed intent on finding out how much farther it could push us. Cho replied that Newbridge was unwilling and incapable of giving more in terms of economics but that we were flexible to structure certain aspects of the deal to accommodate the needs of the FSC.

When Cho asked what these needs might be, however, Noh turned cagey. He did not have either a counterproposal or formal feedback, he said, because "whatever gets put on paper cannot be taken back."

Though we had made a great effort to accommodate the FSC with our new covered assets model proposal, Noh saw no change from our previous position, because "Newbridge will continue to have discretion and management power over the loans." Newbridge wanted the government to protect its downside, but it wasn't willing to take the risks, he complained. Covering the assets for five years was too long. Saying that we were unwilling to budge on economics but flexible on structure was neither consistent nor helpful, he remarked.

In the end, Noh told Cho that we should simply trust the government. "We will not allow this investment to go sour," he promised.

The messages from the FSC through Laroia of Morgan Stanley, Cho, and others all seemed to tell the same story. The government wanted to engage, but it was not prepared to accept our proposal. It wanted us to come up with a better one.

A few pieces of the puzzle were beginning to fall into place, however. A few days earlier, we had seen a report that Chairman Lee of the FSC would be called to the Blue House to brief President Kim on the status of the Newbridge-KFB deal. Subsequently, I learned that Lee had given his presentation and was also scheduled to meet with an advisory group, the vice ministers council, to make a similar report.

Chairman Lee would not be appearing before the vice ministers without the approval of the president, I was told. While we didn't know what exactly President Kim had approved, we reasoned that Chairman Lee would not have gone to him with a deal he couldn't get done.

Meanwhile, HSBC's talks with the government over Seoul Bank seemed to be on the rocks. The *Maeil Business Newspaper* (the Korean equivalent of the *Wall Street Journal*) reported that HSBC and the government were at loggerheads, predictably, over the mark-to-market issue, and that the final close of their deal was expected to be delayed. While the FSC had issued a statement denying the report, I received a call from a *Wall Street Journal* reporter telling me that the news was in fact true.

There were other movements in the shadows. We'd heard from a reliable source that BS Kang, the FSC director, was growing increasingly frustrated with his boss, Director General Noh. Kang had privately complained that Noh was totally incapable of making decisions, a frustration we'd also heard from the FSC negotiating team. Unfortunately, the same source said, it was impossible for Chairman Lee to make a decision to go ahead with the deal without a recommendation from Noh, since the chairman wasn't involved in the details.

Against this background, I thought it was significant that Chairman Lee wanted to meet with either or both of Newbridge's chairmen. "Given our experiences with him in the past, I know we run the risk of wasting your precious time," I wrote to Blum and Bonderman. "However, if there is going to be a breakthrough, this seems to be the right time and opportunity. If Lee really wants to sit down to talk, it might be the only chance to make him understand that our proposal does not cause and actually takes care of many of his or the FSC's concerns."

★ ★ ★

Following his curious, if cryptic, meeting with Noh, Cho of Lehman Brothers became a conduit between our team and the FSC—at Noh's request. The director general had told Cho that he found it easier to convey subtleties in Korean. Not wanting to waste what seemed like a good opportunity, we were happy to oblige.

A few days later, Cho met for dinner with Noh's subordinate, Director Kang. Once again, Kang affirmed the FSC's desire to do a deal and that they weren't talking with anyone else. But as government officials, there were certain things they could not do or were afraid of taking responsibility for. Specifically, he said that they could not give us the mark that we proposed on the loan portfolio. Nor could they give us the put right. If we insisted on the mark on the asset side, they had to insist on the mark on the liabilities side. The bottom line would be at par.

Kang did, however, have favorable things to say about Newbridge. After spending so much time together, the FSC team was beginning to like us. Earlier, they thought we were taking advantage of them or scheming against them. Now, they knew we were being fairly honest and straightforward. In contrast, Kang told Cho, the FSC team was now angry with the HSBC for having backtracked from its earlier positions.

Later that week, we also got a bit more information on what had transpired between Chairman Lee and President Kim. According to our sources, Lee reported to the president that the FSC thought Newbridge's proposal of May 11 (covered asset model) looked promising and that it was an improvement from the MOU. Lee further suggested that the Newbridge deal would have an impact on the HSBC deal and that therefore the FSC needed to drive the hardest possible bargain with Newbridge. Finally, he informed the president that it was unavoidable that the government would have to inject another 3 trillion won (nearly $2.5 billion) into KFB to keep it afloat, but such a move would have no effect on the negotiation with Newbridge.

"I think it is very clear from all the hard evidence that they very much intend to do a deal," I wrote to Blum and Bonderman on May 26. "It is equally clear that they do not know how good a deal they can get. Therefore, they keep trying to test our bottom line." I felt that the ball would start to roll even faster when Noh, Kang, and Chairman Lee finally realized that we indeed had no further concessions to give, other than moving pieces around.

★ ★ ★

Cho met with Noh again a couple days later, on May 27. The two sides were still far apart on specifics. The FSC's complaints were the same as before: that the put right would adversely affect KFB's biggest customers and that Newbridge stood to make unfair and excessive returns from the deal. Cho's response was also the same. Our proposal of May 11 (the covered assets model) was final, and the FSC should make a decision. Noh said that he was disappointed but that the FSC would come back to Newbridge with a counterproposal. Noh's last comment was "Take that as a sign of sincere interest to do a deal."

The same day I received a bit of useful intelligence from Kevin Honan, the economic counselor at the U.S. Embassy. The U.S. Ambassador, Steve Bosworth, had arranged a meeting with Chairman Lee of the FSC to discuss the latest news regarding the two bank deals.

Ambassador Bosworth told the chairman that he was concerned about the effect on reforms if both deals fell through. Lee reassured him that both deals were still alive. Lee thought Newbridge now understood the FSC's concerns.

Lee was still worried about the optics, however. He knew the press was going to come after him when the deal was done, and he needed to prove that whatever agreement he'd reached was for the good of Korea and its people. He also wanted the deal to close as soon as possible, because he worried that it was going to be difficult to go back to the market and find another buyer.

He was also concerned that if KFB classified a loan differently from other banks, then other banks would follow suit regarding the same borrower. That would create trouble for both the customer and other banks. Further, the five-year arrangement under our covered assets model proposal would create moral hazard, Lee suggested, presumably in the sense that we would have no incentive to collect loans if they were guaranteed by the government.

"We will resume discussion soon," he told the ambassador.

Newbridge had a fine reputation, Ambassador Bosworth assured Lee, and had turned around many companies. Newbridge should be fully capable of turning around Korea First Bank.

★ ★ ★

On May 30, we received a request from the FSC team through its advisor Morgan Stanley to meet at 10:30 am on Tuesday, June 1, to discuss our most recent proposal. This would not be a negotiating session, they cautioned, and asked us not to mention this meeting to the press. It was the first direct meeting between our two sides since May 11, nearly three weeks earlier. Short Guy reported exuberantly that, according to his contacts, a deal along the lines of our last proposal would be done within the week. At this point, I didn't give that much credence.

The week began with some ominous signs. An FSC spokesperson was quoted in the English-language press, although not in the Korean press, saying that the FSC would give Newbridge a counterproposal—one that specifically disregarded the terms of the MOU—and, if Newbridge rejected it, the government would walk away. "FSC Will Give Newbridge an Ultimatum" read the headline in the *Korea Herald*. The Yonhap news service quoted another FSC official as saying that the government would guarantee the loans for no more than two years, but they have to be marked at book value.

When we arrived in the meeting room at FSC headquarters Tuesday morning, however, the atmosphere was quite different. On our side were Paul Chen and me from Newbridge and Mike O'Hanlon and David Kim from Lehman. On the other were BS Kang and Junior Lee.

The FSC team had quite a few questions about our most recent proposals, which seemed to indicate that they were taking them seriously. They also had what I judged to be legitimate concerns, which fell into four main categories.

Their first concern was the five-year window. Under our covered assets model proposal, the government would guarantee the yield and interest for five years on all the loans KFB decided to keep. The FSC side was concerned (a) that the government might not be able to set up a facility at the end of those five years to manage the loans KFB didn't want and (b) whether that time frame was going to be too long for the government to risk. While some loans may indeed improve in value as the economy recovered, they pointed out, loans otherwise classified as normal at the end of two years might actually deteriorate over the next three, increasing the risk to the government.

Their second concern was the 96 percent mark. We needed the markdown to give the loan portfolio sufficient yield even if it was guaranteed by the government under the covered assets model. But the government negotiators still considered the 96 percent mark too big.

The third source of contention was Newbridge's return on investment. The government, probably sensitive to public perception, worried that we stood to make too much money on this deal. They proposed to cap Newbridge's return on equity at 25 percent.

Finally, the buy/sell arrangement was another complication for the FSC. We explained how it would work again and the rationale behind it. One party would name the price of the asset to be put, and the other party would decide whether to buy or sell the asset at that price. The FSC decided to table the issue for further discussion.

Afterward, I saw Ambassador Hyun to get his take on the meeting and to finalize plans for the summit meeting in Hong Kong between Chairman Lee, Dick Blum, and David Bonderman, which was scheduled for the following week. The ambassador thought the negative press reflected the weakness of the FSC's position, if anything, and Chairman Lee seemed by all accounts to want to do the deal.

I told him that we continued to talk with the country's politicians and opinion leaders in our effort to win their support. "Don't say too much, but provide them with punch lines and pithy quotes," Hyun advised. I very much appreciated his wisdom.

The chairman's visit was going full steam ahead.

It was certainly encouraging that President DJ Kim seemed strongly motivated to restructure Korea's banking system and retool the economy, and was exerting pressure on officials to carry out his policies. On June 4, he stated emphatically, in a meeting with foreign bankers, "we will sell Korea First Bank and Seoul Bank to foreign investors." Such a public statement was quite unusual and only put more pressure on the FSC. Two opposing forces were at work, and Newbridge's KFB deal was at the crux of this tug-of-war.

The week, which had started out so ominously, ended with some positive news coverage. *Chosun Ilbo* quoted a senior FSC official as saying that Newbridge's new proposal was more workable. The remaining issue was the duration of the yield protection. It further said that the interest rate yield protection in our proposal required neither marking to market of the loans nor additional reserves, which would reduce the taxpayers' burden.

★ ★ ★

The summit meeting took place on Tuesday, June 8, 1999, at the Island Shangri-La Hotel in Hong Kong. At about 5:30 that morning I went out for a run on Bowen Road, a quiet running trail near our home. Bowen Road hugs the side of Victoria Peak about halfway up, meandering across the steep, green sides of the mountain and offering panoramic views over the city's skyscrapers and high-rises. When I was about halfway through, it began to rain heavily. By the time I finished my run, I was soaked with sweat and rain.

I arrived at the Shangri-La at 8 am and met with the team to brief Blum and Bonderman on the key points of our proposal and the major points of contention with the FSC team, which we hoped the chairmen would resolve. It was a full house. Bob Barnum was there, as were Mike O'Hanlon from Lehman and Dan Carroll, Paul Chen, and Daniel Poon from Newbridge.

Shortly afterward, Chairman Lee came down to the hotel's business center, where we were waiting. Blum, Bonderman, and Ambassador Hyun went into the meeting room to meet with Chairman Lee. The rest of us waited in an adjacent room. From time to time Bonderman came out to consult with us on some issues and deal points.

At about noon the meeting was adjourned and Lee left for the airport. Bonderman wrote up his notes from the meeting and confirmed them with Ambassador Hyun. In typical Bonderman style, they were brief and to the point:

Meeting Minutes: June 8, 1999, Hong Kong

Discussion:

1. *KFB portfolio to be divided into three pools:*
   a. *non-performing [loans], as determined by Korean Government ("NPL")*
   b. *performing loans as determined by Newbridge ("PL")*
   c. *all others, termed "gray area" loans*
2. *NPLs taken by Government; PLs marked to 96 [percent of book value] and kept by KFB; gray area loans marked to 94 [percent of book value] and subject to paragraph 3*

3. *"Gray area" loans treated as follows:*
   a. *with respect to all workout loans and any other loans with maturity longer than 2 years*
      i. *for a period of 3 years if there is a payment default, loan can be put to the Government; and*
      ii. *if during this period additional provisioning is required by [Financial Supervisory Services] guidelines as applied by agreed-upon third party, Government will pay for provisioning by a receivable [i.e., an IOU] to be monetized [i.e., paid down by cash] at the end of the period*
   b. *with respect to all other "gray area" loans, they are treated as in (a) but with a two-year period*
4. *Concentration of chaebol loans will either be excluded from new regulations or KFB otherwise protected from regulatory default on pre-existing loan concentration. [This was to accommodate new regulations that would limit the concentration of loans or exposure by a bank to a specific chaebol; KFB's legacy chaebol loans would be grandfathered in.]*
5. *Returns, if any, to the parties will be determined by the market. Korean Government will not guarantee Investors any minimum or maximum return.*

Note: Mark on NPLs and PLs subject to further discussion.

Afterward, the Newbridge team had lunch with Ambassador Hyun in the hotel, and we all felt encouraged by the progress we'd made. The framework outlined by Chairman Lee and agreed to by both sides seemed like a positive, workable agreement and was consistent with the covered assets model proposal we'd suggested.

Our optimism proved premature.

★ ★ ★

That afternoon, my family and I, along with Blum and a few others, flew to Bali in Blum's private jet, to attend Newbridge's annual investors' conference. Bali, an idyllic island in the Indonesian archipelago, was known for its beaches, surfing, and laid-back culture. Unfortunately, I wasn't going to enjoy much of any of those on this trip.

At the conference, held in the ball room of a grand hotel, which over-looked the sparkling blue ocean, our investors were keen to hear every-thing we could tell them about the much-publicized KFB deal. I made a presentation on the deal's status, using a few cartoons to illustrate the dif-ficulties of our negotiations and break the ice. KFB was often depicted as an unwed or undesirable Korean bride with Newbridge as a disappointed suitor (Exhibit 4).

The cartoons lightened everyone's mood, but there were still plenty of questions as to how good a deal we would be able to cut and what the chances were that the deal would happen. Finally, Bonderman spoke up. We did not have total confidence the deal would come together, he said, but if it did, we were sure we could turn the bank around.

In the middle of our conference, I received a fax from BS Kang at the FSC, containing a new proposal from the government side. I read it with growing astonishment.

The FSC's new proposal bore no resemblance to what Chairman Lee proposed in Hong Kong. Specifically, it would cap our return on invested capital at 12 percent, would eliminate any mark on the loans by treating them all at full face value, and would eliminate our right to put bad loans back to the government. If the terms Lee proposed in Hong Kong were a step forward, the FSC's new proposal was 10 steps back. It was both puzzling and infuriating.

On June 10, I wrote a letter to Ambassador Hyun, who was now our main conduit of communication with the top at the FSC, outlining our position and our reaction to the newest proposal from the FSC:

> I hope that you understand that both Dick and David were quite upset and disturbed by the proposal we received. Not only does it not reflect any of the discussion and understanding with Chairman Lee, it rep-resents a major step back from FSC's own proposal of April 27 on MTM [mark-to-market] and put right. April 27 proposal was a step back from the FSC's March 16's one and the new one retreats even further from April 27's! They ought to know their proposal is simply economically not viable. It does raise the question of whether or not the FSC is genuinely interested in doing a deal, or if it simply wishes to

provoke us. Many of our advisors now tell us that the bureaucracy does not really wish to do a deal although President DJ Kim remains firmly committed to reforms of the banking sector. Squeezed between a rock and a hard place, they say, the bureaucracy is simply buying time. We have doubted this theory for a long time, but it seems that the evidence is not on our side.

You, of course, can best advise us, especially Dick and David, if that is the case. What I am most afraid of is that their patience, and that of our shareholders, is running out, as we continue to spend our resources and time on this deal without seeming to get closer to agreement. They find it difficult to understand how the directives of Chairman Lee, a cabinet member, can be disregarded by his own staff, and that the FSC does not seem to be able to recognize a very good deal when they have one, especially compared with the other deal [i.e., HSBC's]. All this stretches our credulity. We have always believed that this transaction is good for all the stakeholders, the government, taxpayers, the bank, customers and investors. We do not want to get into a lose-lose situation as our investors will not allow us to quietly walk away after having expended so many resources on this transaction, having relied on an explicit understanding with the government. We desire a win-win situation. We have worked hard hoping to win the trust of the staff of the FSC and we wish to work closely with them, now and in the future. However, we do not see how this deal can get done if the FSC does not even honor the words of its own chairman. So, the question is, does it have the political will to do a deal?

Ambassador Hyun, all of us highly respect and trust you. Your words carry heavy weight with Dick and David. I very much appreciate your advice, which I know will significantly influence our thinking and the decision-making process.

I received a call from Ambassador Hyun on June 11. He said: "I spoke with Chairman Lee after I received your message, and asked him what was the meaning of all this. I said to him, 'This is backtracking from your own proposal. It is against the understanding you had with Chairmen Blum and Bonderman in Hong Kong. The Newbridge people are puzzled. I am puzzled too.'"

Lee's response was that some points needed to be clarified, and that he wanted to talk further with Newbridge, Hyun told me. However, Lee asked that we not send a formal response to the "working-level people," meaning Noh and the FSC negotiators. He wanted Newbridge to communicate directly to him, through the ambassador.

"I think, although he might have a different understanding on some points from the Hong Kong meeting, he still wants to handle this in good faith," Hyun advised me. "I don't see a major reason for concern, and I don't detect anything that indicates he doesn't want to deal in good faith. Please give him all your thoughts in a detailed manner in a letter, and we will proceed from there."

I also received a call from David Kim, who told me that the collective advice of the Lehman team—Kunho Cho, Mike O'Hanlon, and himself—was to avoid sending a point-by-point response, as it would only dignify FSC's latest proposal, and give them another month to get back to us.

Following this advice, I refrained from responding directly to the FSC counterproposal. Instead, I drafted a letter from Blum and Bonderman to Chairman Lee. After reviewing and making some revisions, Bonderman sent it on June 15:

Dear Chairman Lee,

We were encouraged by the progress we achieved in our meeting with you and Ambassador Hyun on Tuesday, June 8, 1999. We continue to believe that the suggestions you made as embodied in the discussion memorandum circulated after the meeting (copy attached) can be the basis of a successful conclusion of our negotiations with respect to Korea First. We were, therefore, profoundly surprised by the nature of the letter received by our colleagues from Director [BS Kang] dated June 9, 1999. [Director Kang]'s letter did not appear to us to reflect any of your suggestions embodied in the discussion memorandum or in our conversations with you and Ambassador Hyun the preceding day. Indeed, the letter from [Director Kang] of June 9 not only contradicts the very items you proposed in our meeting in material respects, but also retreats in significant ways from major items offered by the FSC in its past proposals. A brief summary of these differences is attached for your perusal.

Accordingly, we don't believe it would be productive to re-engage in an item-for-item re-argument of the issues raised by [Director Kang]'s June 9 letter. However, since we continue to believe . . . in the importance of completing the transaction we are negotiating, we remain open to using your proposal as set forth in the June 8 meeting memorandum as the basis of finalizing our negotiations. To that end, we suggest that those proposals, together with certain of the items and conditions that we submitted to the FSC on May 13, form the basis of our continued discussion. We are, of course, willing to meet again with you and Ambassador Hyun in order to finalize our agreement.

★ ★ ★

At this point, I really did not know what to make of it. Did Chairman Lee instruct his people at the FSC how to take the deal forward or did he not? Why was his message so completely different from his own team's?

I decided to step up our own public relations campaign. On the morning of June 14, I sent a brief note to Michael Schuman of the *Wall Street Journal* to update him of the deal. The next day, the *Journal* published an article under his byline: "US Firm Hits New Snag in Bid for Korean Bank." It read in part:

SEOUL – The troubled acquisition of a nationalized bank by U.S. investment firm Newbridge Capital Ltd. hit a major setback as a new proposal from the South Korean government widened the gap between the two sides.

The new proposal, said a Newbridge executive, backtracks from the government's earlier positions on the method of valuing Korea First Bank's assets and the right of Newbridge to sell nonperforming loans to the government in the future. These issues have been among the main sticking points in the negotiations.

"It raises the question of whether they want to do the deal at all," said the Newbridge executive, who still expressed optimism that the acquisition will be completed.

The FSC could tell immediately that we were the source of this story, but I did not mind. I wanted to set the record straight. The FSC team had been using the local press to put pressure on us, and I had been working hard to undo these misunderstandings. It was difficult to get the Korean press to write anything sympathetic toward us, nor was it possible to ensure accuracy of local newspaper reports. But the government also cared about international opinion, and I knew we could rely on the professionalism of the journalists at the *Wall Street Journal* and other foreign media outlets to accurately report our message and the facts.

I spoke with several other reporters that week. They told me that the HSBC team had been encouraging them to write negative stories about the Newbridge/KFB deal. I laughed it off but thought it was quite sneaky of them to advance their own cause at our expense, even as they tried hard to hide their own troubles in their negotiations with the government. I could not imagine that Newbridge would do the same to any of our competitors. We, ironically and maybe somewhat naïvely, believed in the *English* spirit of fair play.

After the Newbridge meeting in Bali, I returned to Seoul with our team members. We met with the FSC team on June 17. By then they had learned about the content of the minutes of the June 8 meeting, although I suspected they did not know where the meeting had taken place or who had led the discussion, in view of Chairman Lee's desire to keep the summit a secret.

After the meeting, O'Hanlon and Cho of Lehman went to talk with Noh, because he had asked to talk to the Newbridge advisors only. At the meeting, the director general told the Lehman team three times that they should persuade Newbridge to accept the government's proposal. It was as if he sensed a willingness on our part to start negotiating with ourselves again and couldn't resist the urge to push us. Ambassador Hyun, who also spoke with Noh that day, said to me that he had emphasized to the director general that Newbridge was already at its limit and was about to abandon the deal. He told me that Noh seemed surprised to hear it.

★ ★ ★

The following day, Ambassador Hyun faxed me a copy of a letter from the FSC chairman, Hun-jai Lee. It was addressed to Hyun but clearly intended as a response to Blum and Bonderman. In the letter, Lee denied that he had agreed to the terms contained in the minutes of June 8 chairmen's meeting, suggesting that these were only points raised by Blum and Bonderman. He said that he had not endorsed the plan to put certain loans into a gray bucket. Then he urged us to consider and respond to the June 9 proposal from Director Kang.

I found it bizarre that Chairman Lee disavowed his own proposals at the June 8 summit in Hong Kong as if it had never taken place. Instead, he endorsed Kang's proposal, which Bonderman, in his letter to Lee, had already rejected because it represented a retreat from the FSC's previous proposals. In fact, each of the FSC's three proposals to date was progressively worse. It seemed as if negotiating with the FSC team was like nailing water to the wall—as soon as we tried to accommodate them, the government side moved farther and farther away.

After sharing the letter with us, Hyun called Lee again and asked him point blank if he thought the deal was doable.

"I really want to close this deal," the chairman replied. He seemed as committed to the deal as he had ever been, Hyun told me afterward, and it seemed that Lee thought there were no major differences between Newbridge's position and the government's. However, Lee told Hyun to ask us to try to come closer to the FSC's position, if we could.

In light of Lee's letter, I felt we had no choice but to let the FSC team know our own position on the various issues Lee raised. However, Hyun had another idea.

Hyun's advice was that, while we should make sure we got our point across, we should consider making our term sheet look as much like the FSC's documents as possible. By using their format, we would give them the impression that we had taken their proposal seriously, and it could help narrow the perceived gap between us. We should also refrain from using any new terminology or introducing any new concepts in our communications. As a case in point, he noted the FSC's strong response to the term "gray area." "Try to use their vocabulary," Hyun advised.

I thought the ambassador's advice was excellent. He was, after all, a veteran diplomat, and he knew how to make the other side feel good without bending his principles. Also, despite Chairman Lee's apparent amnesia regarding our summit in Hong Kong, I had to admit that the tone of our recent negotiations with the FSC had been more positive.

The ambassador believed Chairman Lee wanted to negotiate in good faith and pointed to the big difference between Lee and his own people in their desire to do this deal. The ambassador also believed Chairman Lee might be open to another chairman-to-chairman meeting. Over the next few days, we put together a revised term sheet in line with the ambassador's recommendations, and refined it further on the back of a long discussion with him and his colleagues from Kim & Chang. They suggested several changes that would not affect our economics but would make the term sheet appear more accommodating to the FSC's sensitivities. Regarding their concern that putting loans into a gray-area bucket might send a signal to the market that the borrower was in trouble, we proposed a compromise: Eliminate the "gray" pool entirely, and mark all the loans to be retained by KFB after the close of the deal at 95 percent of the face value, which was the middle point between 94 percent for nonperforming loans and 96 percent for performing loans as discussed in the June 8 meeting.

We sent the document to the FSC on June 23. "This term sheet reflects the discussions we have had with the FSC and represents the best Newbridge can do in terms of economics in an effort to close this deal," I wrote in the conclusion. "We would be happy to have detailed discussions with the FSC on the basis of this term sheet."

Meanwhile, Kunho Cho, who was still acting as intermediary between our team and the FSC, got an update from BS Kang on the internal differences within the FSC over dinner.

Kang told Cho, confidentially, that he felt Noh was a major obstacle to the deal, and that he was also fed up with Noh. As long as Noh continued to filter the information Chairman Lee received, the deal was going nowhere. The only way to get it done, Kang believed, was to go around Noh directly to Lee. He advised Cho to request another summit meeting with the chairman. After both sides had put so much time and resources into getting this far, Kang and his team all wanted to see it through.

Noh again, I thought. The issue kept coming back to the director general. His boss had to go around him to make anything happen. Now his subordinates wanted us to go around him as well. The deal was being supported by the negotiating party on the other side, the chairman of the FSC, and the president of the country, but we couldn't make any progress because the man who occupied a critical position in the bureaucracy was either unwilling or incapable of pushing it forward. No wonder everyone was frustrated with him. It seemed he only knew how to say no.

Another piece of useful information brought back by Cho from his dinner was Kang's confirmation that HSBC had put its own deal in a holding pattern, waiting to see what was going to happen with the KFB deal. According to Kang, because the HSBC deal was worse for the investor than the Newbridge deal, HSBC would like to use the KFB deal as a benchmark.

★ ★ ★

By the middle of 1999, the economic outlook for South Korea had begun to brighten considerably. This was good for the country but did not bode well for our deal. The government was on the verge of officially revising its projected growth rate for the year to a higher-than-expected 6 percent. The Korea Asset Management Corporation, the government-owned bad bank, was selling nonperforming loans to foreign investors at more than 50 cents on the dollar, up from about 20 cents just a few months earlier, reflecting a surge in investor confidence. The stock market was rising. And all of that meant there was much less motivation on the part of the Korean government to close the Newbridge deal.

On June 23, the *Wall Street Journal* carried an interview with Korea's new finance minister, Bong-kyun Kang. As if to confirm my fears, Kang said, "The terms for the now-delayed sale of two banks to foreign investors should reflect improvements in Korea's economic outlook since the deals were first discussed." The next day, the paper published an article entitled "HSBC May Not Buy Stake in Seoul Bank amid Signs of Improvement in Economy." The recent economic growth numbers had prompted a rethink of the FSC's bargaining position, the article noted, "leaving the government to conclude that perhaps there was no need to offer dramatic concessions to lure outside buyers."

For some reason, however, there seemed to be a renewed sense of urgency on the part of the FSC to make progress. The day after I read Kang's interview in the *Journal*, I learned that Chairman Lee wanted to meet with us and had asked his team to give him a report on the status of negotiations as soon as possible. Lee seemed to want to make some sort of decision over the weekend. It seemed that Lee needed us to meet with the FSC team to discuss our latest term sheet.

It was already Thursday, so I left for the airport as soon as I was able to get a flight from Hong Kong to Seoul.

The meeting with the FSC went surprisingly well. The FSC team raised a few questions and made some suggestions that I thought were constructive. They also seemed to have come around to our position on the 95 percent mark on the loan portfolio, which had been a sticking point, although they stopped short of explicitly accepting our proposed mark.

Still, I was cautious. Politically it was a sensitive time in South Korea. The United States had just announced that President Kim would visit President Bill Clinton in the White House in early July, amid a resurgence of tensions between North and South Koreas. Although much of their discussion was expected to revolve around Seoul's belligerent neighbor to the north, it was also well understood that the Clinton administration was dissatisfied with the pace of South Korea's economic reforms. It was possible that the overtures from the FSC were just an attempt to buy President Kim some good publicity. "If so," I wrote to my colleagues, "then today's meeting does feel too good to be real."

★ ★ ★

Regardless of what was driving this new sense of urgency, I felt encouraged that the FSC and Chairman Lee himself were actively engaging with us. I had always thought our deal was good for the government. All it took was the political will to get it done. But the political opposition within the government could not be underestimated. There was always a force pulling in the other direction.

That Sunday, back in Hong Kong, I learned that Lee had no major issues with the deal on the table, but he wanted three things. First, he wanted Newbridge to accept the Korean standard for assessing whether a loan was in default. We had specified a 90-day delinquency period, while Lee wanted 180 days. Second, Lee wanted us to improve the mark on the loans. Third, he wanted to cap the return on equity KFB could make at 25 percent.

I called Bonderman to discuss the proposal. This was one of those times when a fax wouldn't do.

Both of us thought that the first issue was an easy give.

On the second issue, initially Bonderman did not agree to improve the loan mark. I persuaded him that we could improve the mark from 95 percent to 96 percent, provided that if the loan was put to the government, KFB would get to keep the 3.5 percent loan reserves. This would effectively reduce the mark to closer to where we wanted it to be.

Bonderman also agreed to cap the return on equity at 25 percent for KFB. Even though he conceded this point, in my heart, I did not like it. I considered it unfair, and I planned to not yield on it unless absolutely necessary. However, the return on equity for the bank was not the same thing as the rate of return on equity for Newbridge. If KFB made an ROE of 25 percent, which was considered exceedingly high, we would be able to sell the bank for multiples of our investment cost. Still, did the FSC understand that distinction? I wasn't sure. The best strategy, in my view, was not to agree to the notion at all.

I flew back to Seoul the next day, Monday, June 28. On the flight, I drafted a note to the FSC. In the note I emphasized that we had already given the government 5 percent warrants in accordance with the MOU, which would allow it to capture more upside than its shareholding, more than what Newbridge would get. Therefore, we would not agree to cap the return on equity or on sharing any further upside with the government.

The next day, I went to the office of Kim & Chang, and met with Ambassador Hyun and two of his partners, Byung-moo "BM" Park and Kye-Sung "KS" Chung, both of whom would also work with us on the deal. Since seeing my memo of the day before, Hyun had already been in discussions with Lee, who thought that, as the warrant was already in the MOU, it should not be considered a concession. Furthermore, he wanted to cap the return on equity to about 16 to 17 percent and wanted no markdown on the loans, although he agreed that the government would provide reserves for the loans and would take over any loans in default.

June 30 was a day of intensive negotiations. Ambassador Hyun negotiated with Chairman Lee by phone on our behalf, and Lee had to call back three or four times as he was interrupted by other matters of urgency. President Kim was scheduled to visit the United States on July 1 and 2. The FSC had already leaked to the press that the Newbridge/KFB deal would be concluded before the visit. Lee was personally involved in all our negotiations, and he had also spoken with the press to send a few signals that the deal was imminent. It was now or never, I thought to myself. We had to seize the moment.

Lee proposed that Newbridge invest $600 million over the next two years in exchange for a greater percentage of shares, which I had no problem with. He pushed for us to accept no markdown on the loans but eventually relented, although he insisted that the mark should be 96.5 percent, no less. And he offered that we did not have to accept his mark until all other issues were resolved. At the end of the day, though, those other issues were still outstanding.

Thursday, July 1, was a holiday in Hong Kong, and my family had escaped the city's muggy summer heat with a vacation to the United States while I stayed behind. I could not tear myself away from the negotiations in Korea, so I decided to stay in Seoul to continue the negotiations, as did my colleague Paul Chen.

We all felt it was critical to get a deal done before the end of the day on July 1. President Kim and President Clinton were scheduled to meet on that day in Washington, DC, which was 13 hours behind Seoul, and it was clear that Chairman Lee wanted the deal done before the two leaders shook hands. We were afraid if we could not reach a deal by then, there would be no political pressure on the part of the FSC to do a deal any time soon.

Bonderman faxed me a memo overnight, which I received the first thing in the morning on July 1. "It is time to get this done now, if it is going to get done," he wrote. Now there were four issues left to resolve— and we had one day left to pull something off.

I went over Bonderman's memo, which included his thoughts on the four remaining issues:

1. *Mark. I think we can live with 96.5 if you agree that it is time to hit the bid tomorrow if Lee does not move.*
2. *Capital Contribution. I think your proposal works.*
3. *Government Support. You have to continue to adhere to our position. I would trade Lee [points] one and two for this one.*
4. *Upside sharing. I gather this is off the table, which is good.*

To summarize, you should try very hard to reach a deal with Lee tomorrow. Four is off the table, stand fast on three and hit his bid on 1 and 2 if you have to.

We were ready and we were in gear. The moment we had been working so hard for had arrived.

$$\star \quad \star \quad \star$$

I spent all morning of July 1 negotiating with Chairman Lee through Ambassador Hyun again, by phone. We reached agreement on the capital contribution of $600 million over the next two years. As for the markdown figure, I told Hyun it should be 94 percent now, because the capital base was now bigger. However, I would accept 96 percent. I thought I would hold out on this point until all other issues were resolved. Lee no longer insisted on the cap on the return on equity or upside sharing, nor was there any further argument on issues related to the government support. I felt a deal was in striking distance. I called Daniel Poon, who had left for holiday, and asked him to cut short his trip and join us in anticipation of working overnight to finalize the term sheet.

In the afternoon, I continued to negotiate with Chairman Lee until all major issues were resolved. Meanwhile, Paul Chen and the rest of our team were at the FSC office, negotiating with Director Kang. Much to my surprise and dismay, the more they negotiated, the more issues popped up. With the sun setting in Seoul and about to rise in Washington, the team reported there were 18 unresolved issues between them.

I was still with Ambassador Hyun at Kim & Chang's offices, but I hurried over to the FSC to join our team, arriving at around 6 pm. I was surprised again by how smooth the negotiation progressed after I got there. In slightly more than an hour, we were able to reach agreement on all the remaining issues. Seeing the deal was in hand, all of us, including the FSC team, were visibly delighted.

I rushed back to Kim & Chang to update Ambassador Hyun. I told him that I could agree to Lee's proposed mark of 96.5 percent. Lee had said earlier that I did not have to agree to that figure until I was satisfied that all other issues were resolved. Now that they seemed to be resolved, I was ready to hit his bid on the 96.5 percent, as Bonderman had suggested.

That evening I sent Bonderman a memo that said "Verbally, we have a deal."

I had asked Ambassador Hyun to relay a message to Chairman Lee that we would not agree to make an official statement before a binding term sheet was signed. Now we were in a rush to produce that sheet, incorporating all the agreed-upon terms, and send it to the FSC team. "The hope is that we can sign it tomorrow. But I do not know if it is possible," I wrote to Bonderman. "Details will be in the draft term sheet which will be faxed to you overnight. I will write tomorrow."

Although we had told Chairman Lee in no uncertain terms that we would not agree to a deal announcement without a signed term sheet, all the major Korean newspapers reported on July 2 that Newbridge had reached agreement with the government on the KFB deal, in time for President Kim's meeting with President Clinton. Lee was quoted as saying that the two parties had reached agreement on all major issues. He also said many kind words about Newbridge.

For the first time, the FSC team moved faster than we did. They sent us their version of the term sheet in the morning. We weren't able to send ours out until that afternoon. I had a quick phone conversation with one of the FSC's Morgan Stanley advisors to tell him where our version of the term sheet and the FSC's version disagreed. After we sent over our term sheet, I called him again to say that we could meet in Kim & Chang's office in an hour to discuss the final proposal.

Just when I thought we were down to the short strokes, I received a call from Ambassador Hyun.

"We have a problem," he said.

Chapter 8

The Chairman
Takes Charge

Director General Noh had thrown a tantrum.

Ambassador Hyun was being characteristically understated when he
called me on the afternoon of July 2. Noh had complained to Chairman
Lee, saying that Newbridge was insulting the government by issuing an
ultimatum, which was how he characterized my suggestion for a meeting in an hour. He was also upset with some legal terms our lawyers put
in the term sheet and accused us of imposing such terms on the government. Hearing this, Chairman Lee flew into a rage at Newbridge.

As Ambassador Hyun explained what had happened, I was stunned.
I thought both Lee's and Noh's reactions were completely unreasonable.
We had not pushed them to meet with us or issued anything close to an
ultimatum. We had suggested a meeting in a respectful manner, which
seemed a logical next step. Especially when we were both working toward
a deadline. I did not know if Noh was simply being capricious or if he was
using this as an excuse to scuttle our deal.

In any case, Noh still wanted to meet, and it was a disaster from
the start. Suddenly, the attitude of the FSC team had totally changed.

Noh used the occasion to dress us down, repeatedly accusing us of "distorting" the words of their chairman. Throughout the meeting, Noh ranted and refused to discuss anything substantive. I was hoping he would calm down after venting and get back to business. But he never did, and went on grandstanding until abruptly declaring the meeting adjourned around midnight. He requested that we reconvene at 9:30 the next morning.

Blum, Bonderman, and the rest of our team were expecting word that we had signed a binding term sheet. Mystified at the unfortunate turn of events, I scribbled a note of what had transpired before going to bed, shortly before 2 am.

The next day, we met with Noh and his team again. But Noh was not interested in discussing any substantive issues. Instead, he only made statements, without suggesting anything constructive. While making these grand pronouncements he would stare toward the ceiling, his eyes rolled up in his head, "like those of a dead fish," I scribbled down in my notes. I felt we were wasting our time.

As if that were not enough, other members of the FSC team began to raise issues with the terms they'd agreed to the evening before. They challenged the basic premise and terms of the MOU. The gap between our two sides rapidly grew larger and larger. As the morning session came to an end, we counted 20 new issues raised by the FSC team.

We all felt frustrated. We did not know if the FSC was playing a game or if it was serious. Regardless, reaching an agreement looked unlikely now. Ambassador Hyun explained to Chairman Lee that what Noh had reported to him was simply not true. After that, Lee purportedly calmed down, but I did not know what to do next, because I felt it was impossible to negotiate anything with Noh. The gap between our two sides that had nearly closed just a few days ago was now so wide that we could hardly see the other side.

On July 4, we received an update on the U.S.-South Korea summit meeting in Washington. President Kim had informed President Clinton that the KFB deal was concluded, and the two had congratulated each other. It seemed that the die was cast, at least politically; this transaction *had* to happen. But that was not the situation on the ground. Paradoxically, with the presidential meeting behind us, we had lost a major impetus to move things forward.

Our team prepared another copy of the term sheet overnight, taking into consideration the latest issues raised by the FSC. We wanted to get the document ready before our 2 pm meeting.

However, the FSC repeatedly postponed the meeting. A little after 7 pm, I went to go to meet with Ambassador Hyun in his office to let him know what had happened and to discuss our next move.

While I was there, the FSC summoned our team to its office. My colleagues went without me. Sometime after 10 pm Paul Chen called me from the FSC, to tell me that, once again, there was a new issue. The FSC was now demanding that *the government* retain control of the bank after the sale.

This was a preposterous and shocking suggestion, under the circumstances. It ran counter to the basic premise of the deal, which was that the foreign investor would control the bank and introduce a new credit culture to the Korean financial system. This new demand was as absurd as if a car dealer sold you a car and then insisted that he drive it. I thought Noh had finally lost his mind.

The director general had apparently been driving his own team crazy all day with new demands and was now asking that Newbridge accept a whole swath of new conditions on the deal, including the government's equal representation on the board, participation in management appointments, and approval for all loans over 5 billion won (about $4 million). I instructed Chen that the whole team should walk out of the meeting in a polite, calm, and measured manner. There was nothing left to negotiate.

Chen informed the FSC team that their new proposed changes altered the fundamental premise of this transaction, and that we had to go back to speak with our chairmen to think about the whole deal anew. Astonishingly, Noh was shocked at this reaction and tried strenuously to prevent our team from leaving.

"It seems that Mr. Noh is making an ever-stronger effort for us not to take him seriously," I noted in an update to Bonderman later that night.

★ ★ ★

I was out for my morning run the next day when Bonderman called. I briefly discussed with him what actions to take under the circumstances.

By the time I'd returned to my hotel room, Bonderman had sent me a draft letter addressed to Chairman Lee, requesting in strong terms that Lee remove Noh from the negotiations. When I showed it to Ambassador Hyun, he told me delicately that he did not think it would be helpful, and proceeded to modify it until it didn't sound like Bonderman anymore. But I decided to accept his more diplomatic approach.

The ambassador met with Chairman Lee. The chairman did not get into any of the new issues raised by Noh; nor did he respond to Bonderman's request to remove Noh. Lee had two major requests of his own. The first was that Newbridge increase the amount of its investment to a total of $700 million, from $600 million he had previously proposed, consisting of an initial $500 million, followed by $100 million in each of the two years following. The second was that the government not be required to provide three-year protection for loans that would mature after two years.

To his first point, I decided to write the chairman a letter explaining that we could consider such investments, but there had to be conditions. To the second point, BM Park of Kim & Chang suggested that we could follow the same arrangement we'd established for the work-out loans in our earlier term sheet, which was to subject them to a buy/sell process at maturity. I concurred.

★ ★ ★

"There is good and bad news today," I wrote to the team after the ambassador had met with Chairman Lee and his team that Wednesday, July 7. A number of the issues that remained on the table were resolved, and on several, Lee accepted our position against the objections of his team. On other issues, however, Lee appeared to have had second thoughts.

The main one was the issue of "due care." The FSC side wanted to insert a clause into our agreement that Newbridge would be obliged to "exercise due care" in its management of the bank. There was, of course, no question that we would, as would any prudent shareholder. In fact, the commercial code of South Korea required it. But our lawyers objected to having this written in as a contractual obligation to another party. They worried that it exposed us to legal risk. If we left it up to the government to rule on due care in this case, they might arbitrarily decide that we'd failed to exercise it.

We were comfortable adding a due care clause as a nonbinding side letter accompanying the agreement, since that would just entail our following the law, and any disputes would be resolved in court. A day earlier, Chairman Lee said he would be happy with a side letter. But Noh, supported by the FSC's White & Case lawyer, Eric Yoon, objected. They claimed, falsely, that Newbridge had a bad track record on due care. They alleged that there had been a dispute over a lack of due care involving Bonderman's previous deal for American Savings Bank. (There had not been.) "Lee, having been convinced by his team, now seems to go back to the inclusion of the due care clause in the term sheet," I wrote in my update. "This is obviously unacceptable to us."

Another serious issue was Chairman Lee's request to increase our share of the capital contribution. His terms from the day before still stood, with the minor alteration that he had changed currencies and was now asking us to invest 500 billion won initially and an additional 100 billion won in each of the following two years (approximately $500 million and $100 million respectively). Our concern, however, was that the bank's balance sheet had shrunk so much after its failure and nationalization that this was far more capital than it required. If we overinvested, it would reduce the rate of return we could generate on that capital.

It was a matter of economics. If a bank with a capital base of $1 billion generates $120 million in profits, the return on capital is 12 percent. If the capital base is increased to $1.2 billion but the profit remains $120 million, the return on capital drops to 10 percent.

After some discussion, Lee agreed to drop his request that Newbridge contribute an additional 100 billion won in each of the following two years. But he remained adamant on the initial 500 billion, and he would not consider any measure that would dilute the government's ownership of the bank below 49 percent in exchange for Newbridge's increased payment. "Newbridge has pointed out a number of deal breakers over the course of our negotiations," the chairman told Ambassador Hyun. "This is the only deal breaker from me."

O'Hanlon and his team at Lehman Brothers came up with a number of potential solutions to address the issue, such as putting the excess capital in the form of a preferred stock that would pay a special dividend or using it to buy back the stock in KFB from the government. But those were unlikely to fly with Chairman Lee. Ultimately, however, I did not think the issue was insurmountable. If the bank could increase its total assets fast, making more new loans in an environment of economic recovery, we would be able to literally grow our way out of this problem. The bank's profit would grow in tandem with its total assets. However, if we increased the amount of capital contribution for our 51 percent, the government would have to increase its capital contribution for its 49 percent. If Newbridge alone increased its capital contribution, then our ownership would have to increase and the government's ownership would have to be diluted. What I would not agree to was to unilaterally increase our capital contribution without getting anything in return.

★ ★ ★

We let Chairman Lee know that we were willing to consider the incremental investment he requested but no other issues. We also informed him that I had to leave the country on Sunday, for Europe on a business trip, so we hoped we could finalize the term sheet before then.

Late Saturday evening, I spoke with Director Kang of the FSC. He was in the middle of negotiating with our lawyers from Kim & Chang, and told me he was extremely tired from the endless meetings and work. The FSC team was working as hard as we were, and I really felt for him. I learned later that his meeting with our lawyers lasted until about 2:30 am.

The next morning, I awoke to a fine, sunny day. It was a welcome change after several days of clouds and heavy rain. We had been working so hard and had spent so much of our days in office buildings and hotel conference rooms that I had hardly noticed the change of seasons, I realized. The fine weather of early spring was long gone, and Seoul in July was hot and humid. Korean business etiquette required that I wear a formal suit and tie to every meeting, which was uncomfortable in the midsummer heat. When meetings went long and things did not go well for us, it was unbearable.

A voicemail from Ambassador Hyun was awaiting me. After Chairman Lee learned I planned to leave town, he called to ask Hyun to hold me back. Lee said that the deal should be done by Monday or Tuesday at the latest. The subtext, we both knew, was that if negotiations broke off now, the deal might be indefinitely postponed. It was difficult to change my flight, but I managed to postpone my departure by 24 hours in the hope of concluding the deal.

That Sunday, July 11, we marshaled all our forces—including our team from Newbridge, the bankers from Lehman Brothers, and the lawyers from Cleary Gottlieb—and went to Kim & Chang's office for a conference with Ambassador Hyun and his colleagues. KS Chung and BM Park, both partners of Kim & Chang, had been negotiating with BS Kang until 2:30 am, so we were anxious to get an update on what had been agreed to and what remained unresolved.

Once we had determined where we stood on various open issues, KS Chung and BM Park went to meet with Chairman Lee to continue negotiating on our behalf. The rest of us went to a restaurant on a hill behind the Blue House to have dinner. It was in a traditional Korean house with a large terrace and an expansive lawn, affording magnificent views of the mountains, the Blue House, and the city of Seoul. The air was cool and fresh, even though it was midsummer. It was the first time in a long time we had been able to enjoy a relaxed dinner in beautiful surroundings.

I went back to Kim & Chang's office after dinner to meet with Ambassador Hyun, KS Chung, and BM Park. The two lawyers had just returned from their visit with Chairman Lee and reported that he had not changed his position on the issues. He did, however, invite me to meet with him privately at 9:30 the following morning. The chairman still seemed strongly in favor of getting some kind of deal done. "I will do it even if I have to go to hell," he told KS Chung and BM Park.

Although we did not appreciate it at the time, Chairman Lee was under intense pressure. He later recalled in his memoirs that he received a fax from a senior secretary to President DJ Kim in late June saying: "Please cooperate to complete the sale of Korea First Bank before the President's visit to the U.S." President Kim was growing frustrated with the lack of progress on the deal. But the rumors going around the Blue House at that time were that Chairman Lee himself was the reason for the delay and that his officials at the FSC were deliberately sabotaging the sale. The pressure was on him to make sure the deal happened. However, overseeing the KFB sale exposed Lee to the risk of political ruin. Even if he cut the best deal he could, would anyone remember how grave the crisis was once the bank turned around?

"People would soon ask, 'Why was a functioning bank sold at a fire-sale price?'" he recounted in his memoir, fearing "The person responsible for the sale would be labeled an unpatriotic traitor." Still, the international community was watching. If the KFB talks collapsed, so would the market. Korea's economic reform efforts would lose all credibility. "If I sell the bank, I will be finished," he told his closest staff members. "If I don't, the country will be in a shambles."

★ ★ ★

I slept for a fitful five hours and rose before dawn on Monday, July 12, to get ready for my meeting with Chairman Lee. To do so, I reviewed materials our team, including those from Lehman and Cleary, had worked through the night to prepare. I had a call with Bonderman before going for a half-hour run to clear my head.

After breakfast, I left the hotel for Kim & Chang's office, where I met up with Ambassador Hyun and KS Chung. After a brief discussion, Hyun and I went to meet Chairman Lee in the Korea Federation of Banks Building located in Myeong-dong in the center of the city's business district. Myeong-dong's architecture was a mix of nondescript concrete high-rises and commercial low-rises. Most of the buildings were relatively new and modest in their appearance, with little that distinguished one from another. But the Korea Federation of Banks Building stood out. It was older, constructed in a Western style with an imposing façade. We walked through grand heavy doors like those in old banks, built to impress customers. The lobby was spacious, and the meeting rooms gave the impression of a bygone era. We got there to find Chairman Lee already waiting in what looked like a small reception room.

The room was relatively dark. Lee sat cross-legged in a big chair, with his feet tucked up beneath him. Although he wore a serious expression, he seemed at ease, and I was happy to see him assume such a casual pose. Koreans can be among the world's most formal people in business settings. Their posture is often ramrod straight. Junior staff will not even cross their legs in front of their superiors. Seeing Lee relaxed meant he felt comfortable and was not going to treat me as an outsider.

There were only three of us in the room. I sat facing Lee in an armchair to his left. Ambassador Hyun took the seat on Lee's right. We immediately proceeded to talk through the open issues, which I read off one by one from a document I had brought with me. Once we dealt with one issue, we moved on to another.

We kept going like that, without interruption, for about five hours, with a quick pause for lunch. I was impressed that the chairman seemed to have a better understanding of certain issues than the FSC staff members we had been negotiating with. It seemed to me that the chairman was making an effort to get the deal done. As we ticked off one item after another, he occasionally chatted in Korean with the ambassador, who told me later that the chairman lamented, several times, that he did not have a competent staff to help him.

I soon discovered a pattern: The chairman was more concerned about issues with regulatory implications than monetary ones. In sharp contrast with Noh, Lee listened to my arguments and explained his own rationale. The two of us could persuade each other with reason and logic. It was such a pleasure to negotiate with a counterparty whom I could reason with—and make progress with—especially after several months of stonewalling by the FSC team. Together, Lee and I managed to reach a tentative agreement on several major issues. These included the selection of initial assets before closing, how to treat and define payment defaults, and the handling of long-term loans.

On the last point Lee impressed me by volunteering that the problem with financial institution loans was that essentially bankrupt financial institutions could survive by continuing to pay interest even if they were not able to pay principal, which was exactly our side's point when Noh insisted such loans should be treated as normal. Now, without being asked, he suggested that any financial institution loans with maturities of more than two years should be treated like work-out loans, meaning they would be subject to three-year protection by the government.

Before we were able to finish my issue list, Lee said he had to leave for another meeting. During our discussion, as we resolved one issue after another, I took notes, but he did not; neither did Ambassador Hyun. For five hours Lee never took out a single piece of paper to look at or to write on. Before we adjourned I said, "Chairman Lee, how do you remember all the things we have discussed to inform your own team of what we have agreed?"

"Just give a copy of your notes to them and ask them to follow what we have agreed," he said, looking straight into my eyes. There was no hesitation in his facial expression.

I was quite surprised. While I appreciated his trust, I was afraid my shorthand might be illegible to anyone else. Also, I remembered the meeting between Lee and our co-chairmen in Hong Kong, after which he disavowed what they had agreed to even though it was recorded in Bonderman's minutes. I did not want to take any chances.

"How about if I read my notes back to you to see if your understanding is the same?" I asked.

He agreed. After I finished reading my notes, he said, "Good. Ambassador Hyun, please make sure my team receives a copy of these notes."

I was impressed by how Chairman Lee conducted this meeting.

★ ★ ★

There was no closure or agreement on the term sheet at the end of the 24-hour extension of my stay. There was no telling when the FSC team would get back to us to confirm agreement on all the issues I had discussed with Chairman Lee. The next day, July 13, I left Seoul for Europe empty-handed, other than my bags, that is.

While traveling I wrote to my colleagues, updating them on yet another round of changes from the FSC and their lawyers: "We have witnessed a disturbing pattern of reaching a business agreement with the chairman only to have White & Case reject our language." In order to keep things moving smoothly, the ambassador agreed to speak with Chairman Lee and encourage him to instruct Eric Yoon of White & Case to make comments based only on the business understanding rather than what Yoon believed the terms should be.

Wondering if my presence might make a difference, I offered to fly back to Seoul to meet with Chairman Lee to resolve all the remaining issues. A couple of times during my trip Lee requested that I return to Seoul immediately, but each time, shortly before I was about to get onto a flight, he called back to say it was unnecessary. I was puzzled about what the FSC was up to. The tempo of our engagement had noticeably slowed down. It seemed that the pressure on the FSC to do a deal had cooled off now that the presidential visit to America was concluded. I thought we had to find another way to push them.

While on the road, I received yet another letter from the FSC complaining that the language of our draft document did not reflect the understanding reached between the parties. It was signed by BS Kang, but I could tell from the tone that the letter had been drafted by Eric Yoon. I responded with my own on July 16, in which I tried to be both blunt and restrained, as I knew it would be read by both of them.

> *Dear Mr. Kang:*
>
> *We received at 10:53 p.m. on July 15 your facsimile dated that date, which, among other things, claimed that the riders provided to the FSC on the morning of July 15 do not reflect compromises agreed to with the FSC and indeed constitute steps backward. To the contrary, our proposed riders reflect not only our but also our various advisors' understanding of the business agreement that had been reached between the two sides. In fact, we are the ones who are quite surprised and disturbed to learn from our advisors and your letter that there appear to be signs of backtracking from your previous or agreed-upon positions as well as introductions of entirely new issues at this late date. We hope that this is not the case and that this merely represents a misunderstanding on our part.*

Kang (or, really, Yoon) suggested that in order to resolve all the outstanding issues, we organize a marathon all-parties drafting session, and suggested holding one at the FSC office the next day, Friday, at 2 pm. This, I thought, was a terrible idea, not least because I was still in Europe. "The first priority must be to reach agreement on those terms of the transaction that remain open issues," I wrote back to them. "In the absence of such agreement, it is pointless to try to redraft the document. We continue to be frustrated to find that even when we seem to come to terms, no understanding of that agreement is demonstrated by those on the FSC working team and its counsel who comment on documentation. In light of this, an all-hands meeting would be unproductive." If they had any further questions or needed clarification, I reminded them that our own lawyers, Kim & Chang, were always available and willing to help.

I thought it was best to leave to the lawyers on both sides to work out the specific language.

★ ★ ★

There were signs that Chairman Lee was becoming distracted by other priorities. For much of July, we had been meeting with the chairman or the FSC negotiators practically every day, including weekends. By the end of the month our contacts had become far less frequent. Chang -yuel Lim, a former finance minister who was now governor of Korea's populous Kyonggi Province, had been accused of taking bribes to help stop the government from shutting down the heavily indebted Kyonggi Bank. Chairman Lee had moved to shut the bank anyway. But Lim and Lee were former classmates, and suspicions persisted about possible collusion between them. President DJ Kim had fired two cabinet ministers in the past two months over ethics scandals, and I heard Lee was fretting that he might be next as, like Lim, he wasn't really "DJ's man."

Adding to his woes, on July 20, the day before I flew back to Seoul, it was announced that Daewoo Group, one of KFB's biggest borrowers, was going to need an extension on 7 trillion won in short-term loans—about $7 billion. The embattled *chaebol* had agreed to pledge collateral to its creditor banks and restructure its motor vehicle division. The Daewoo mess was a major surprise for the Blue House, and Lee was being held responsible for not having done much to force the restructuring of this group. Confidentially, I learned, the banks were unhappy with the extension of credit. Most viewed the arrangement as a temporary stopgap measure that would do nothing about the *chaebol*'s fundamental problems.

Amid all these distractions, Ambassador Hyun and I thought it would be useful to set up another chairman-to-chairman meeting. On July 21, I sent Bonderman a memo updating him on the situation and asking whether he would be able to come to Seoul in the next couple weeks. Bonderman, as usual, responded promptly, "Shan, if it is necessary to conclude a deal, I am sure that Dick or myself can make ourselves available in Korea for a day. However, I am absolutely unwilling to do this unless it is clear that we will sign a document while we are there."

"This deal seems to be the only potential good news for [Lee] amidst the trouble happening around him," I wrote to Blum and

Bonderman. "But I think that we have to exert maximum pressure to push him to move."

We decided that Blum and Bonderman should first send a letter to President DJ Kim, drafted by Tall Guy and Short Guy, and also that Bonderman should send a letter to Chairman Lee. Both letters urged the government to reengage.

There is a Chinese saying, "If the night is long, dreams are many." It can also be applied to nightmares. The specific problems distracting Chairman Lee were unexpected, but there were bound to be problems jumping out in this troubled chapter in Korea's economic history. That was the reason we were anxious to resolve the remaining issues and sign a binding agreement. There was just no telling what would emerge to scuttle the deal. But it would take two to tango.

Chapter 9

Daewoo Crisis

The FSC was clearly stalling us, and we didn't know why. We attributed it to a change of heart on their side, or the loss of political will. All of our internal discussions were focused on finding ways to push the government forward on our deal. Had we known what was really behind the delay, we might have taken a different tack.

The crisis at Daewoo, it turned out, was starting to look worse than the FSC had feared. But until it knew just how bad it was, it did not want to finalize the deal for Korea First Bank. KFB was the *chaebol's* main creditor, and there was no way to gauge the delinquency level of its loan book without resolving the Daewoo scandal first. Chairman Lee, I discovered much later, was intent on stalling until the Daewoo exposure was fully revealed.

In addition, the chairman had made a personal request to Seung-won Han, the chairman of the Board of Audit and Inspection of Korea, to conduct a full audit of the FSC's restructuring efforts. "It was probably the first time that the head of a government body had requested to be audited," he recalled later in his memoirs. But

the crisis called for special measures. The decisions that we made now under crisis conditions should not be evaluated later under a new

post-recovery set of standards. History can be unkind once the market
recovers, so I wanted a fair evaluation before it was too late and stale.

Had I known this at the time, I would have found Chairman Lee's
attitude understandable and, in fact, quite far-sighted. History, no doubt, is
full of actors who were crucified by later commentators, second-guessing
their decisions in the moment. But I had no idea. Had Chairman Lee or
anyone on the government side explained to us that they needed time to
work out the Daewoo debacle or to complete the special audit, we would
have understood and we would have waited more patiently.

But the FSC kept us in the dark, leaving us wondering if it had changed
its mind. Consequently, we spent much time and energy coming up with
different ways to push them along. Sometimes our tactics were effective;
at other times they backfired. In the end, both sides were frustrated.

★ ★ ★

On July 22, all hell broke loose. Again.

To keep Tall Guy and Short Guy up to date with the latest developments in our negotiations, my colleague Paul Chen had drafted a confidential briefing memorandum outlining our current negotiating position
and how we saw various scenarios playing out. The memo had three parts.
The first part provided the background of the latest negotiations, clarifying
the agreement we'd reached with Chairman Lee on July 2, describing
how Noh had stalled the transaction, and concluding by noting that Lee
was now personally involved in discussions and had reached agreement
with Newbridge on most major issues.

The second part of the memorandum laid out the recent issues raised
by the FSC team and described our less-than-favorable response. "The
FSC's working team has been unable even to agree to proposals that the
working team itself made, has raised some 30 new issues in the last few
weeks after more than six months of negotiations and seems to be unable
or unwilling to bring this matter to conclusion," a particularly direct
passage read.

The third part discussed potential "consequences of a collapsed deal,"
which included embarrassment for President Kim, loss of opportunity for

South Korea, the potential collapse of KFB, and the negative repercussions for South Korea in the international community.

We expected this memo would be used by our advisors as background information and possible talking points when they met with various constituencies. It was unaddressed and unsigned, and was not meant for outside consumption. Unfortunately, our advisors must have accidentally left a copy of the memo behind after a meeting, and, the next thing we knew, it was leaked to a Korean newspaper, which sensationally reported it as Newbridge's "ultimatum" to the government.

The leak caused an uproar. The "threatening document," as the *Daehan Mail* called it, allegedly insinuated that "unless KFB is sold, negative effects on Korea's credit rating and the Korean government's structural adjustment are inevitable."

Understandably, Chairman Lee and others at the FSC were upset. Apparently, they suspected that we'd leaked the document in a bid to improve our bargaining position. I moved to send out a statement of clarification to the press. Usually, we would go through the public relations department at KFB. But this time, KFB executives refused to help us, presumably because they were upset as well. We had to fax our statement to the Korean newspapers by ourselves.

The memo debacle had suddenly put us on the defensive. Our advisors and the FSC's advisors at Morgan Stanley urged us to write a letter to Chairman Lee explaining the leak. Frustratingly, there was nothing wrong with the memorandum itself; every word in it was correct and accurate. But when presented as an attempt to strong-arm the government, it sounded different, and the coverage touched a raw patriotic nerve among the Korean public. As a result, our negotiations stopped.

Following the advice of Ambassador Hyun, we sent a letter signed by Blum and Bonderman to Chairman Lee, expressing our regret and reassuring him of our commitment to the KFB transaction. "We share your exasperation with reports last week in the Korean media regarding a memorandum on the KFB transaction," the letter read. "The document was not authorized by us and we regret the misunderstanding and confusion it has caused. As stated in Weijian Shan's correspondence with you, we can assure you that Newbridge has always and will continue to negotiate this transaction in good faith."

The letter aimed to quash the market speculation that Newbridge might be having second thoughts because of KFB's large exposure to the troubled Daewoo Group. "While Daewoo's difficulties serve to highlight the potential risks inherent in the acquisition of KFB," it went on to say, "we wish to assure you that Newbridge remains committed to completing the proposed transaction."

We hoped that the letter would mollify the FSC somewhat, but we also urgently needed to get moving on the deal. It did not seem likely. Chairman Lee was due to go on holiday the following week. After that, the Newbridge leadership was scheduled to go to Aspen, Colorado, for a two-week conference. "I suppose the term sheet may not get signed until possibly September," I noted in a memo of mine. "A very depressing thought."

What we hadn't anticipated was that the FSC would react by telling the press about Blum and Bonderman's letter or that they would describe it as a "letter of apology." This would be interpreted as a tacit admission that we had indeed sent them an ultimatum. While we badly wanted this episode to pass and be forgotten, we could not let it stand that we apologized for something we did not do. In particular, I was concerned that the FSC would use this as an excuse to back away from the deal.

I sent a letter to Ambassador Hyun on July 29 to express my frustration and to seek his advice. "Some Korean reporter called me to tell me that they heard from the FSC that Newbridge had sent an apology letter to Chairman Lee," I began. "Needless to say, this is quite disturbing." "We sent the letter," I said, "in the belief that it would calm down Chairman Lee and in the hope that both sides would forget about this so we could concentrate on closing the deal, not to give the FSC an excuse not to do a deal."

★ ★ ★

Meanwhile, the reports we were hearing about the situation at Daewoo were getting worse and worse. On July 28, Standard & Poor's downgraded Daewoo's debt from B– to CCC, reflecting deteriorating investor sentiment. Meanwhile, the FSC was asking the *chaebol*'s foreign creditors, in addition to its domestic ones, to roll over their loans to the struggling firm. Daewoo at this point needed an emergency extension on more than 20 trillion won ($16.7 billion) of debt maturing that year and 4 trillion won ($3.3 billion) of new capital to avoid collapse. It was becoming clear that Chairman Lee was completely preoccupied by Daewoo. We learned that the FSC negotiating team had prepared a final position paper for the KFB deal and was recommending to Lee that these positions be given to us on a take-it-or-leave-it basis. However, the next time Ambassador Hyun spoke with Lee, Lee said that he needed to mull over the internal report for a couple of days. He also said that he would not accept his team's take-it-or-leave-it recommendation, which was good news. But it still left us waiting on the chairman. The FSC team could not make any move without his leadership.

It seemed that the chairman wanted to keep us warm by getting the FSC's advisors to deal with us instead. On July 30, Lee instructed Morgan Stanley to meet with us to "clarify the remaining issues." However, it quickly became clear that the bankers were not authorized to do anything other than understand open issues; there was no movement forward.

We also heard that a stock offering by another Korean bank, Hanvit Bank, the second-largest bank in Korea, had collapsed due to lack of investor interest. Our advisors at Lehman Brothers had also been working on the Hanvit offering. That news was quite relevant to our KFB deal. The sale was to be a test of investor confidence in the Korean banking industry, and it revealed that investor interest was flagging. Combined with the Daewoo debt crisis, the Hanvit collapse raised questions about the firmness of Korea's economic recovery.

What was bad for Hanvit helped us, however. If its attempt to raise $1 billion of new capital had been successful, it might have made it more difficult for the FSC to agree to our terms. Its failure might have breathed new life into the FSC's interest in our transaction.

Through other channels, we were hearing optimistic reports on our deal's progress. One of Tall Guy's contacts had a meeting with Director General Noh, who informed him that the deal was pretty much done. And an article summarizing all the events since the "threatening document" in the *Daehan Mail* concluded by saying that the "incident was resolved" between Newbridge and the government and that "all agree that the negotiation will soon conclude."

Despite the rife speculation, I was not optimistic. We had been in similar positions many times before, and I couldn't see how this would end any differently.

★ ★ ★

As the summer wore on, Seoul got hotter and steamier by the day. Yet the deal seemed relegated to the deep freeze by the FSC. Lee was scheduled to go on vacation on August 1. The Newbridge team was heading to Aspen for its offsite meeting for about two weeks. As it seemed the FSC was not talking to us anymore, there was no reason for us not to go. The prospect of a deal any time soon looked remote.

I left for Toronto on Monday, August 2, to meet with my family, whom I had not seen in two months. We were all going to Aspen for the Newbridge meeting, and I was looking forward to being together as a family.

As soon as I got into Toronto, I learned that Chairman Lee was still tied up with the Daewoo situation. He was also heard complaining about Morgan Stanley not doing its job. Harrison Young, the Hong Kong–based managing director who had been deeply involved in the early stages of the sale process, apparently got a dressing-down from the chairman. The chairman requested that Morgan Stanley analyze the remaining issues and prepare a report to the FSC by August 5 or 6.

The next day, we learned that Chairman Lee had postponed his vacation, which we took as an encouraging sign. Through our Kim & Chang lawyers, Lee specifically raised five issues pertaining to the transaction.

The first issue concerned the put right. While the MOU provided Newbridge with an unlimited put right to transfer bad assets to the government pre-close, Lee now took the stance that Newbridge should not be afforded such a right. He claimed that buyers in typical mergers and acquisitions assume all the assets of the acquired company. Lee indicated that he would allow Newbridge some latitude in asset selection, presenting this as a "concession" rather than as something that the government had already agreed to. Ambassador Hyun assumed that the parameters surrounding the selection would be far more stringent than what the chairman had agreed to regarding asset selection in our July 12 meeting.

I asked Hyun to send Lee another copy of my note from that meeting, which I had read to the chairman, who had signed off on it.

The second issue concerned risk weighting and the government's guarantee of KFB's loans. This determined how much capital KFB would need to hold in order to offset the risk posed by its loans. Rules established by the Bank for International Settlements (BIS) required that a bank maintain a certain amount of capital against its loan book, expressed as a percentage called a *capital adequacy ratio* or *BIS ratio*. For example, if the capital adequacy ratio was 10 percent, a bank would need to have at least $100 of capital on hand for every $1,000 worth of loan. This could be adjusted by risk weight. Naturally, the riskier the asset, the higher the risk weight and capital requirement. If a bank set the risk weight of a loan at 100 percent, it would need to hold the full $100 in capital. If it judged the loan to be less risky, it could set the risk weighting lower; a risk weighting of 80 percent would require the bank to hold $80 in capital.

Typically, local-currency government debt was considered to carry zero risk weight. The rationale behind this was that the government could always print money, so the chances of a default were assumed to be zero. Despite this, Chairman Lee wanted us to apply normal risk weighting to these loans, meaning that he wanted us to assign full risk-weight to KFB's loans, treating them as if they were not guaranteed by the government. This meant we would have to put more capital into the bank to be capital adequate even though capital against zero-risk assets, such as those fully guaranteed by the government, is not necessary.

I didn't think the chairman was unreasonable on this point. A regulator always wants more capital in a bank, not less, because it makes the bank safer. It also would bring more capital into the country, which was another benefit from the chairman's perspective. From our point of view, the more overcapitalized the bank, the lower our expected return on investment, but this wasn't a major issue for Newbridge. We had already agreed to invest 500 billion won into the bank, which would give the bank a capital adequacy ratio of no less than 10 percent, which was a full 2 percentage points higher than the 8 percent BIS requirement at the time, even after assigning a full risk weight to the government-guaranteed loans. Chairman Lee's emphasis on this point underscored his political concern that Newbridge should not be perceived as unduly benefitting from government assistance. I was optimistic that we would be able to easily come to an agreement on this point, based on what had already been negotiated.

Chairman Lee's third point of concern regarded KFB's staff head-count. Lee indicated that any employee reductions should be completed prior to closing to avoid further political fallout after the close. Lee also implied that no indemnification would be provided post-close for actions associated with layoffs. This was a more difficult gap to bridge. We could not rule out a voluntary workforce reduction program that would occur after closing. Such an action could be necessary to give new management the opportunity to carefully evaluate employees and terminate any low performers or redundant positions. Since staff redundancy, the extent to which we had not yet fully identified, was a legacy problem, we wanted the government to indemnify us against the costs and risks associated with cutting laden redundancies. Regardless of the timing of any such action, indemnification would be necessary to address any lawsuits or other liabilities that would arise from potential staff reductions.

The fourth issue Lee raised concerned the government's upside. Lee's comments to Hyun indicated that he needed to be able to explain to the public how the government would benefit from our deal. Lee was vague about what exactly he wanted on this issue, but I made it clear to Hyun that we were not open to renegotiating the price again. If that was the chairman's intention, Newbridge had to be prepared to walk away from the deal.

Lee's final issue concerned a request for the government to have the option to buy any loan if any disagreement about its provisioning arose. Since provisions for a loan would be determined by the management under Newbridge's control but would be paid for by the government, Lee wanted the government to have the option to simply buy the loan at book value plus accrued interest, instead of paying the provision, regardless of whether the loan was still under the government's guarantee. Previously, we had agreed that if the government did not agree to the provisioning determined by management, the dispute would be submitted to a third party for adjudication. Now Lee wanted to have the option to buy the loan if the government did not like the adjudication result. I thought the government should have the right either to ask for adjudication, the results of which would be binding on both parties, or to buy any loan under dispute, but not to have both rights, because it would be unfair for one party to an adjudication process not to be bound by the results—then what would be the point of adjudication?

Lee did not specifically address any of the other open issues, which meant that even once they were negotiated other sticking points would remain. It was especially frustrating to me that he seemed to ignore the agreements he and I had reached in July, which we had asked to be the starting point for future discussion. It felt like we were going in circles, rehashing topics that had already been resolved—in some cases more than once. It was also difficult to tell how seriously to take Lee's remarks because he supposedly had not had time to review his team's report and was still waiting to hear from Morgan Stanley. It was possible— if not likely—that this list would change again after Lee had consulted Morgan Stanley.

Chairman Lee discussed with our K&C advisors how negotiations were to proceed. First, he would review all the information, including the recommendations of the FSC working team, then he would ask us for comments. Around Wednesday, August 11, he would likely make a final decision on whatever issues remained open. Our window to get the deal done would be between August 11 and August 20. After that, Lee would be involved in the implementation of a new restructuring plan for Daewoo so he would not have much time for anything else.

I wasn't sure if I should take all the feedback at face value. Lee's actions seemed consistent with intelligence from Short Guy that the FSC chairman was trying to stonewall the deal. According to Short Guy, Lee believed that KFB would be able to recover on its own and therefore should not be sold to Newbridge. But with the Blue House still in favor of the deal, Lee was attempting to stall. He had already asked President DJ Kim for three additional months to conclude negotiations, trying to buy as much time as possible for KFB to show improvement in its performance. If and when that happened, Lee could then try to convince the president that KFB should not be sold.

Chen and I outlined our own plan to move things forward. We thought we could use the slowdown to our advantage if, in our public communication strategy, we shaped our deal's success as a sign of confidence in Korea's reform policies and economy. Daewoo's plight had been a major setback in the nation's recovery, which put us back in a situation similar to when we negotiated the original MOU. Korea badly needed the endorsement of a foreign investor.

We considered pointing out that the collapse of our transaction at the height of Daewoo's problems could badly damage the already fragile investor confidence toward Korea, cast further doubt on whether Daewoo would survive any restructuring efforts, and result in a run on the stock market that could cause irreparable damage. Chen and I drafted a memo to Blum and Bonderman and proposed that over the next few days, our political advisors should communicate this to their contacts in the National Assembly, Blue House, and elsewhere to continue to pressure Lee to complete the deal on our terms.

Bonderman responded the next day and agreed. It was clear that he and Blum were frustrated with the constant stalling and had run out of patience with Chairman Lee. They were prepared to take a hard line and be clear that "if the deal isn't done by August 20 we will take whatever actions we think appropriate."

★ ★ ★

Working through backchannels, Short Guy had been in touch with a Mr. Kwoon, who was said to be a close political advisor to President DJ Kim. On August 4, an opportunity arose. Our political advisors wrote to say that the president had instructed Kwoon to meet with Short Guy and me to discuss our deal's outstanding issues and resolve them as quickly as possible. When I questioned how we could conclude the transaction without Chairman Lee's involvement, Kwoon had relayed a message to me through Short Guy: "Internal Korean matters are of no concern to you. We are discussing the matter with Chairman Lee."

Short Guy advised that if we wanted him to meet with Kwoon, we should let him know immediately. "At this point I have no opinion on the matter than to agree with David Bonderman's memo that if this transaction is to be completed, it will only be done with direct involvement from the Blue House," he wrote. "I would not venture to guess at this late date whether we will be successful or not but should Newbridge be willing to pursue this opportunity I would make myself available to arrive in Seoul on Monday."

Short Guy's memo was followed by another almost immediately, this one with the subject "Dick Blum Conversation." It read as follows:

Subsequent to drafting my memo to you I received a call from Dick Blum. He expressed his feeling that a meeting with Mr. Kwoon should not be accepted without confirmation that Mr. Kwoon is authorized to speak about the KFB transaction by the President.

He also believes that the proposed meeting should be discussed with Ambassador Hyun and that Chairman Lee's acceptance of our discussing the transaction with Mr. Kwoon be obtained.

Following Dick's instruction, I will ask Mr. Kwoon for his bona fides from the President. It may or may not end discussions through this channel. You know well the Korean mentality.

Blum was the most politically astute, sensitive, and cautious among us, and he had an unerring knack for keeping us out of trouble. Obviously, if whatever we or our advisors did was authorized by the president, we could do no wrong, but sometimes it was difficult to tell if our political advisors were speaking with authorized people. Many people claimed to have the ear of the president or to have influence over the government's decision making. With the exception of Chairman Lee, it was very difficult for us to tell who in the government could or could not make a difference in our situation. The memory of the leak of our confidential briefing memo was still fresh. While we wanted to put pressure on Chairman Lee to act, we did not want to antagonize the FSC, which was both our counterparty for the transaction and our partner if the deal got done.

★ ★ ★

Things went quiet for about 10 days, while Chairman Lee was on vacation and we were all in Aspen for internal meetings. A number of my colleagues at TPG questioned why we had not walked away from the KFB deal when it appeared to be a hopeless situation. Many thought we were wasting our time. Indeed, the opportunity costs were rising; each day we spent waiting for the KFB deal to happen was a day we could not spend on some other transactions elsewhere. I was not ready to give up in spite of the skepticism, including my own. I thought if there was any hope at all, we should persevere.

Dan Carroll was more sanguine about it. He said that, considering all the dramatic ups and downs, twists and turns in the deal process, "at least we have earned the right to make a movie out of it."

★ ★ ★

My family and I returned to Hong Kong on Saturday, August 15. The next day, I received a fax from Ambassador Hyun, who had apparently been trying to track me down since I'd left Aspen. The memo was rather formal and was signed simply "Kim & Chang," as was customary for formal correspondence from the firm. I read it eagerly since I had not heard anything from the battlefront in nearly two weeks.

In a fairly roundabout way, the memo informed me that the timeline for our deal conclusion would likely be pushed back again, this time by a week and a half. Chairman Lee had been called to appear before various committees of the National Assembly to answer questions on the Daewoo crisis, and the coming week was already filling up with Daewoo-related meetings and conferences, including a public announcement that the *chaebol* had reached a restructuring agreement on its debt.

Chairman Lee, the memo continued, also wanted to make sure we were taking the five points he had raised on August 2 seriously. "Chairman Lee requested that we convey his wish that Newbridge give serious thought to these issues, as he explained that it would put him in a difficult political position with the public and other interested parties in Korea if his concerns are not resolved."

★ ★ ★

Ambassador Hyun had been accurate in his reading of the demands of the Daewoo situation. Lee had a full plate. The news was making headlines far beyond Korea. Even Hong Kong's newspapers carried stories of the Korean government's financial and political woes. For example, on August 16, the AFP, a global press agency, ran multiple stories on the latest news out of Seoul, including headlines "Seoul to sink US$8.3 billion into financial markets," "Final talks on sell-off details, Daewoo set to announce restructure," "Samsung seeks dialogue as it urges creditors to delay sanctions," and "Battling President vows to stamp out graft."

That same day, I received a fax from Jihong Kim in Seoul. His take on the situation was that President DJ Kim was still in our corner. While the Daewoo issues were getting the most attention, recent articles seemed to indicate increasing concern about the slow process of selling KFB and Seoul Bank. During one meeting with a junior official at the Blue House, Jihong was told that the Blue House wanted to close the deals for both banks. Jihong wrote that the official "personally believes the gap between Newbridge and the FSC is very narrow, and a senior level meeting is necessary."

Through our conversations with various contacts we also learned quite a bit about what was going on behind the scenes. A *Korea Times* reporter told me that Chairman Lee was seen to be the root of many problems, including the Daewoo crisis, and would likely be removed from his position before the end of the year. I confided in him that we were running out of patience, but he encouraged us to stay the course because the Blue House was still very serious about the deal.

While some of these developments seemed to be in our favor, the Korean economy improved slightly as the Daewoo situation seemed to come under control. Bank of Korea reported Korea's GDP quarterly growth of 9.8 percent, which I supposed would make the Koreans less willing to compromise to sign a deal for our takeover of KFB. Other deals like ours were also struggling. A recent bid by Carlyle Group and AIG for Korea Life Insurance fell through after the seller insisted on changing the price, despite having signed a binding MOU. It seemed that everyone was having similar experiences to Newbridge's.

Now we were just waiting for the FSC to reengage with us when it was willing and ready. I returned home to Hong Kong late on Saturday, August 21, to find a voice message from Ambassador Hyun. I returned his call the next morning. He opened with "Lee appears serious about doing a deal." But, he added, since the economic and political conditions had changed, if we still wanted to do a deal, several deal terms had to change. Hyun proposed flying to Hong Kong or San Francisco to have a conversation with Blum and Bonderman.

The last time Hyun had suggested a face-to-face meeting like this had resulted in our June 8 meeting with Chairman Lee in Hong Kong, when we'd come close to what we had thought was a breakthrough. Now, with far fewer issues to resolve, all we needed was Lee's political will to ink the deal. It felt as if we were on the brink of a final agreement—and the anticipation filled me with excitement. I also wondered if Hyun had told me everything he knew, or if there was something he wanted to tell me, Blum, and Bonderman all at the same time.

I immediately agreed that he would fly to Hong Kong the next day to meet with me in person and then have a phone call with Blum and Bonderman.

Chapter 10

Black Rain

Hong Kong Island is situated in a well-worn typhoon path on the southern tip of China's eastern coast. The period between July and September is the peak season for these massive storms, which draw energy from the warm Pacific Ocean and move northwest toward the Asian landmass. The city has grown accustomed to these typhoons, though, and literally pulls down its shutters and battens the doors when one approaches.

As luck would have it, a typhoon was bearing down on Hong Kong on Sunday, August 22, the day before Ambassador Hyun's scheduled visit. The Hong Kong Observatory, the official government weather service, measures typhoons on a scale of intensity: 1, 3, 8, 9, and 10, with 10 being the strongest. The number 3 signal was hoisted that morning. Dark clouds were gathering, and the wind was strong. I hurried to go out on my daily 10-kilometer run before it was too late. A major storm hit almost as soon as I got back home. By then, the number 8 typhoon signal had been raised. I felt lucky to have missed the worst of the storm, but I was worried that if the weather did not let up soon, Ambassador Hyun might not make it to Hong Kong the next day.

The weather wreaked worse havoc than I imagined. Typhoon Sam, as it was called, brought torrents of rain bucketing down on the city along with high winds that ripped branches from trees. At Hong Kong's new

Chek Lap Kok airport, a China Airlines (Taiwan's flagship airline) jet flipped over while attempting to land during the storm, skidding across the runway median and catching fire. Three passengers were killed in the crash. The next morning, the storm had abated somewhat but the observatory maintained its black rain warning, and most offices were closed. To say the very least, I expected Ambassador Hyun's arrival to be delayed.

This was frustrating, as our various conversations over the preceding days had been interesting, if not entirely productive. Chairman Lee was now "serious" about doing a deal before the end of the month, Hyun told me, although candidly, I didn't think any of us took his seriousness seriously anymore. However, he felt the recent uptick in the Korean economy had strengthened his bargaining position, and he was still insisting that we resolve the five issues he had raised on August 2.

In a strategy memo to Blum and Bonderman, I outlined my plan for discussions with the ambassador. As far as the economic situation was concerned, I was in agreement with Chairman Lee: Things had changed. But not for the better, given what was going on with Daewoo. And while Newbridge was honorable enough to be willing to keep our part of the bargain, the patience of our chairmen was wearing thin. We needed to bring this transaction to a close by Labor Day in the United States—or else. I intended to leave our actions to Chairman Lee's imagination if the deadline wasn't met. The more we left things ambiguous, I reasoned, the more threatened our counterparty was likely to feel. Regardless, the message was the same: Storm clouds were gathering.

Ambassador Hyun did make the trip to Hong Kong, but his flight was delayed by several hours and he did not arrive until very late. We agreed to meet the next morning in his hotel.

The next day, August 24, the black rain continued. The clouds were so dark and the rain was so heavy that day looked like night. The traffic was snarled by the flooding and felled trees. It took me three times longer than usual to drive from my home in the Mid-Levels to the Shangri-La Hotel, where the ambassador was staying. I met with him at about 9:30 am.

After the drama of his arrival and my anticipation of a new message, I felt quite let down when, in our meeting, Hyun simply urged us to seriously consider Chairman Lee's five points and revealed nothing new. Hyun explained that Lee was sticking to his position on the points because economic conditions had changed so deal conditions needed to change.

After hearing this, I wondered why the ambassador thought it was necessary to make a special trip at all. After thanking him for taking the trouble to come all the way from Seoul in such dreadful weather, I said, "Ambassador Hyun, candidly, I have written this project off. In our view, the economic situation is not getting better, it has worsened, but we have kept our word. I regret that Chairman Lee did not keep his. At this stage, I think there is nothing further to discuss with him."

At about 11:30 am, Hyun and I called Blum and Bonderman. Without having consulted with me, their response echoed mine. Bonderman bluntly said Chairman Lee had been less than straight with us. After some discussion, Hyun agreed that we should send Lee a final position paper and term sheet. If Lee agreed to use it as a basis for further negotiation, I would go to Seoul for a final round of talks. If Lee did not agree, we would terminate the negotiation.

Hyun left that afternoon for Seoul. I felt so sorry for him having traveled all that way in the middle of a major typhoon without being able to achieve the intended results.

I went home to draft our position paper. My children were there, happy because schools were closed for the third straight day due to the weather. The next morning, I got up at 5 to begin revising our term sheet. By noon, I had it ready to fax to Hyun, who was back in Seoul.

Our position paper was three pages long and accompanied our revised Terms of Investment document, which now ran to 25 pages. The paper reviewed our stance on all the major issues raised by the government and indicated where we could accommodate the government and where we could not. We also addressed Chairman Lee's points to the extent we felt was necessary to communicate that we were serious. We didn't respond directly to Lee's request for upside participation for the government, but we noted that the MOU and subsequent agreement already included a 5 percent warrant. Therefore, the government would have more upside than its pro rata share of ownership.

Regarding the call option for the impaired loans if the government disputed the provisioning amount, I had earlier agreed with Chairman Lee that if the government did not wish to pay for the impairment determined by KFB's management, it had the right to submit such disagreement to an adjudication process. I pointed out that it would be unfair to give the government a call option after it lost in the adjudication process whereas we had to accept the ruling one way or another. I suggested we could accept either adjudication or a call option by the government but not both.

We stuck to our guns on the issue of capital ratio and risk weight. Loans needed to be assigned risk weights commensurate with their risks in accordance with internationally accepted banking regulations. As for the capital ratio, the FSC wanted KFB to maintain a capital ratio of no less than 10 percent, as opposed to the regulatory requirement of 8 percent. We thought KFB's BIS ratio would be above 10 percent anyway, but we could not accept a capital ratio requirement that was different from that of other banks.

Addressing Lee's concern over asset selection. We repeated, again, that we would provide a list of the assets we would not want to keep a month after the term sheets were signed, and any disagreement as to initial asset selection would be liquidated as agreed upon in the MOU.

Finally, we addressed the topic of staff reduction and the associated indemnification. We were willing to concede to the government's request to notify it with a list of employees subject to reduction before closing.

These were the main points at issue, but there were several others, including a few of our own that we wanted to make sure everyone was clear on before proceeding.

The first pertained to the drag-along right. This referred to Newbridge's right to sell the shares owned by the government when we sold our own shares, and it was critical if we were ever going to exit this investment. No matter how good a job we did turning around the bank, nobody was going to want to buy it if they had to negotiate separately for both halves. The drag-along language had been agreed to in the MOU, and we weren't going to revisit it.

Our lawyers were also unequivocal on not including the phrase "due care" in the contract, as requested by the FSC. Newbridge was willing to address the issue with a side letter, per our earlier agreement, but we could not make any further commitment above and beyond what was required by law.

Finally, we explained why we would require that all payments made to KFB by the government in exchange for carved-out bad assets be in the form of interest-bearing government bonds. This was consistent with the MOU, and our rationale was the same as it had been throughout negotiations. It would be too costly for the bank to hold a large amount of cash that would not earn any yield and that, under current market conditions, would take time to turn into loans and other interest-earning assets.

Before passing the terms and position paper along to Ambassador Hyun, I faxed them to Blum and Bonderman for their review, along with a cover memo in which I also shared a few other pieces of news. It seemed that Chairman Lee was being sued, along with the FSC, by a U.S. firm called Panacom, which had tried to bid for Korea Life Insurance but had been eliminated from the process—unfairly and illegally, Panacom claimed.

Separately, I'd heard from a friend about a similar suit. Leslie Koo, a Taiwanese businessman, told me that his company, Taiwan Cement, had served notice of potential litigation on a Korean firm for breaching an MOU for the acquisition of a black carbon business. He said that the Koreans had stopped talking with him prior to the notice. Afterward, he said, they became anxious to strike a deal with him.

"I think that we should similarly consider threatening to sue the FSC for our losses and expenses in the event Lee refuses to do the deal based on the term sheet we will send him," I wrote.

"I can see no reason why we, too, should not sue the FSC if the deal falls apart here," Bonderman faxed back. Blum agreed.

We sent both the position paper and the revised Terms of Investment document, which both parties would refer to as the TOI, to Ambassador Hyun to discuss with Chairman Lee on our behalf on August 25.

Hyun met with Lee the following morning and called me at 10:30 am to give me an update. The meeting had lasted for more than an hour, with Hyun going through the position paper point by point. Lee reacted rather strongly to the idea that the government would be dragged along into whatever sale Newbridge decided to make, Hyun told me, although the ambassador took pains to explain to Chairman Lee that Newbridge was a reputable long-term investor and there was no reason to assume it would do anything other than what was in the best interest of all shareholders. When they were discussing the upside participation issue, Lee asked again if Newbridge was committed to investing 500 billion won initially and another 100 billion won a year for the next two years. Hyun replied yes, if all other conditions were met, which wasn't entirely correct. I had to remind the ambassador that when we agreed to the 500 billion

won number, Lee had already dropped any request for subsequent investments of dividends. Hyun agreed to remind Lee and clarify this point with
him again.

Chairman Lee had either explicitly or implicitly accepted a number of
Newbridge's requests. For example, he thought our position of "either call
option or adjudication" for impaired loans seemed to be fair. He agreed to
our right to select assets before close and asked only that we provide the
list of what we would not take one month before close. He thought that
Newbridge had a good argument that KFB should not follow a different
standard for capital ratio. And he did not argue against our position on
indemnification for employee reduction.

Aside from those issues, Chairman Lee did not have much of a reaction one way or another to the points raised in our position paper. After
going through it item by item, Hyun moved on to the message I had given
him in Hong Kong. Support for this deal within Newbridge was wearing
thin, he said. Newbridge was losing confidence and trust in Chairman
Lee, and his own reputation was at stake.

On the bright side, Hyun continued, "If you do this deal, Newbridge
will bring in world-class management. They are good corporate citizens
with a reputation to protect." The international response, he reminded
Chairman Lee, was going to be positive. Whatever domestic political
problems might arise could be handled.

Chairman Lee listened attentively. At the end of the meeting, he said
that he would need some time to think about it and get back to us.

★ ★ ★

The next day, however, we were surprised by a Bloomberg report
with the headline "Korea First Bank Sale Will Take Several Months, FSC
says." It quoted Chairman Lee as saying "The talks are only at the stage
of drawing up terms of investment, and it will take several more months
to complete."

I was quite disturbed by these remarks. What did Lee mean, the KFB
deal would take several more months to complete? Was he stalling for
time? Why did he indicate a willingness to reengage with us and then turn
around and give this statement to the media?

The press was eager to hear our side. I spoke with both Bloomberg and Bridge News expressing our displeasure, but I asked them to hold off printing my comments, because I wanted to hear first what Lee's real intent was. I called Ambassador Hyun to say that in view of the fact that the FSC was clearly walking away from the deal, we needed to demand compensation for our costs and damages.

Hyun had not yet seen the Bloomberg article and was quite alarmed by it. He called Lee right away. The chairman claimed to have been quoted out of context. The reporter had asked if the troubles at Daewoo would affect the KFB transaction with Newbridge, Lee explained. His answer was that by the time definitive documents were signed, the Daewoo situation would have become clear and therefore there would be no effect. He insisted he was referring to the time it would take to sign the definitive documents concluding the sale, not the signing of the terms of investment. He said he understood fully the negative impact on the financial community if the deal collapsed.

It being a Friday, Lee promised Ambassador Hyun he would have a definitive answer on our term sheet by Monday. Over the weekend, he would formally discuss the deal with both the finance minister and the Chief Secretary for Economic Affairs of the Blue House. He might have to obtain the approval from the president as well.

"Do you think Lee is serious?" I asked Hyun. I had to report back to both Blum and Bonderman, and the ambassador's thoughts would influence our internal decision making. I also repeated that we had to draw this process to a conclusion, one way or the other, by Labor Day, September 6.

The ambassador replied that, in his view, Lee was serious but he wanted to do the deal with a minimum amount of criticism. The upcoming meetings with the finance minister and the chief secretary were crucial.

★ ★ ★

In spite of Chairman Lee's promises that he would get back to us after his weekend meetings, we heard nothing from him for days. We could only guess why there was no response. He had plenty to say to reporters, though. On Monday, Bloomberg ran an article reporting that the

HSBC/Seoul Bank deal was on the rocks. The headline read "HSBC, Korea Reach Impasse on Seoul Bank Sale, Regulator Says." The article opened with a quote from Chairman Lee that the government was "no longer talking" to HSBC about the Seoul Bank sale after HSBC and the FSC couldn't agree on how to define bad loans. "It is very difficult to reduce the gap," Lee told reporters.

The article mentioned that the FSC was still in talks with Newbridge over the sale of Korea First Bank and quoted Lee as saying that the government was "still working very hard to narrow the differences with Newbridge." However, he went on to say that even if the terms of sale were agreed upon soon, completion of the transaction would take two to three months.

Often, it was hard to tell what spin Chairman Lee was putting on the stories he fed the press. It would be quite significant for us if the FSC was really having trouble reaching an agreement with HSBC. I knew Lee would not have publicly broadcast this if the terms and conditions HSBC was offering were more favorable than ours were. What I was not sure of, however, was if this was actually the situation between the two parties or just more posturing. I did not know if Lee was using the press to put pressure on HSBC to sweeten its terms, or if their deal was really dead.

Jihong Kim wrote me a memo the next day, saying that Korean newspapers were running similar stories, describing the negotiations with Newbridge as on track while saying the HSBC deal for Seoul Bank was likely to fail. Lee again went on the record, blaming the impasse on HSBC's insistence on using forward-looking international criteria for evaluating loans, despite its earlier agreement to use the Korean standard. By the end of the day, the FSC and HSBC made an announcement that they had mutually agreed to terminate negotiations for Seoul Bank. The breakup was now official. At this point, I could not tell if it was good or bad for us. If the government felt it had to do one of the two bank deals, then it was good news. If the termination reflected a stiffened stance adopted by the government or its unwillingness to sell either of the banks, then it was bad news. In any case, there was no word from Lee.

★ ★ ★

Given the lack of communication from the other side, I made plans to return to Hong Kong because there was nothing for me to do in Seoul. But on September 1, the day before I was scheduled to fly out, Hyun called to say that Lee had contacted him. Lee wanted me to meet with him the following afternoon, so we made plans to meet at 3 pm.

In the meantime, we received a position paper from the FSC. I didn't know whether this was a result of my letter, but it was a start, at least. On reviewing the paper, however, I realized we were still far apart on a number of issues. Lee still felt strongly about the drag-along clause, despite the fact that we had already addressed and dismissed the concerns of the FSC during previous rounds of debate. In addition, we were still no closer to an agreement on risk weighting, compliance, the form of government payment, and a host of other issues.

Even though there appeared to be some movement on the FSC's part, we felt that this might be yet another false start. We were still looking into the possibility of filing a lawsuit against the FSC in the event that it decided to walk away from the deal. Panacom, the U.S. company, had recently won a critical court victory in its battle to take control of Korea Life. The success of this court challenge against the FSC was an encouraging sign that the Korean judicial system could be counted on to be impartial, even in lawsuits against the government. Bonderman was looking into who was representing Panacom to get a sense of how strong Newbridge's case could be, should we need to walk away.

★ ★ ★

Hyun and I went to meet with Chairman Lee on September 2 in the same Korea Federation of Banks Building in Myeong-dong. Obviously, Lee preferred to meet there rather than in his own FSC office building. I assumed there were two reasons for his choice of the meeting place. One was to avoid the reporters camped out at the FSC. The other was that he did not want to invite Director General Noh and his team but wanted to avoid the overt snub of excluding them from a meeting in their own building. I thought it was a good sign that Noh was not invited.

We walked into the meeting room to see Lee seated in his usual seat. He did not look good, and seemed to have a bad cold.

The meeting turned out to be both encouraging and frustrating. All the issues that I had expected to be sticky ones turned out not to be very difficult. Some issues that I had thought would be easy ones turned out to be very difficult indeed.

We made considerable progress around the size of the investment, the way we would handle impaired loans, indemnification, and initial asset selection.

As far as the size of Newbridge's investment, Lee wanted to have a larger number for public relations purposes. I showed him a copy of a side letter that we had sent to the FSC on July 11, which made clear that Newbridge would consider making an additional investment of 100 billion won in each of the next two years but would be under no obligation to do so. If we did invest more, our share of equity would increase accordingly. He had no problem with such a formulation.

On impaired loans, Lee agreed to treat all loans the same way: KFB would determine the necessary provision (impairment amount); the government had the option to fund it, call the loan (buy it at book value), or go for adjudication. If it chose adjudication, the result would be binding on both parties, and the government would have no more call right.

Regarding our initial selection of assets and liabilities, we agreed to provide a list of those assets that we would not keep within a month after signing of the new terms of investment. I confirmed that we would keep the head office building at its book value.

We even managed to reach an agreement on the drag-along right. After we'd spent a considerable amount of time on the issue, the ambassador suggested that we put in language to say that the purpose of the drag-along right was to maximize shareholder value, which was the argument I had been making all along. Surprisingly, that was okay with Lee, as he thought that would satisfy any possible public inquiry. He only asked that we share information with the government, on a confidential basis, when we were negotiating to sell our and the government's shares.

Employee reductions, however, proved to be an area where we could not reach an agreement. Lee agreed to a reduction of "senior management employees" and to indemnify the new KFB for such reductions, but he insisted that the government would have nothing to do with any reductions among KFB's unionized workers. It was a political issue more than

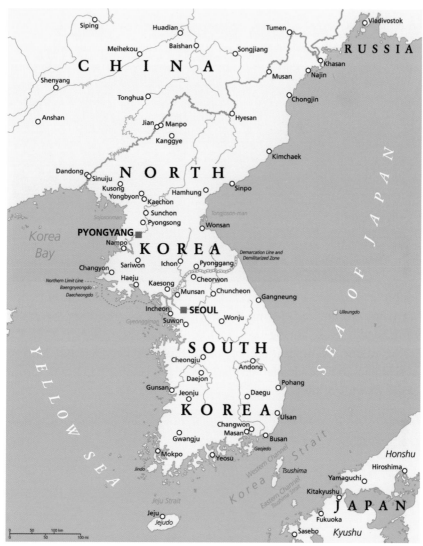

Exhibit 1: Korea occupies the entire Korean Peninsula, which borders China and Russia on land in the north. The Korean Peninsula is separated from Japan to its east by the Sea of Japan and from China to its west by the Yellow Sea. The 38th Parallel divides North Korea and South Korea. Seoul, the capital of South Korea, is situated about 40 miles (60 kilometers) south of the North Korean border.

Source: Peter Hermes Furian/Alamy Stock Photo

Exhibit 2: Hun-Jai Lee (center), Chairman of the Financial Supervisory Commission, introducing the author (right), with Dong-soo Chin sitting in the back, during the press conference immediately after the signing of the Memorandum of Understanding between the Korean government and Newbridge Capital, Seoul, December 31, 1998. (Photo Credit: JoongAng Ilbo)

Exhibit 3: Cartoon in Maeil Kyongje Economy, May 26, 1999 depicting KFB as an ugly girl (sitting in the middle) who could not find a husband, and Newbridge, shown as the Western man, walking away on the right. The bubbles over the heads of the two women on the left read: "They tried cosmetic surgery to marry her off quickly . . ." "I heard she needs another 3 trillion to finish the job." The bubble over the head of the Western man, representing Newbridge, reads "She doesn't look anything like her photos!" The original caption reads: "It is so hard to marry her off." (Photo Credit: Maekyung Economy)

Exhibit 4: Cartoon in *Korea Economic Daily*, May 15, 1999. The man holding a blood transfusion bag is supposed to be President Dae-jung Kim and the wobbly woman is KFB. The label at the bottom of the bridge (that symbolizes Newbridge) reads "Rejection" and the man on the bridge is shouting: "We don't want to have a funeral . . ." (Photo Credit: Korea Economic Daily)

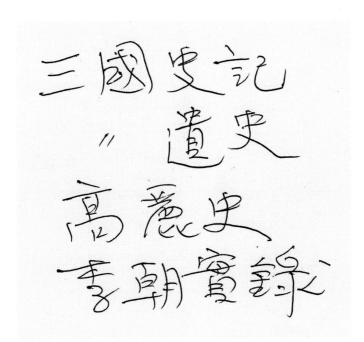

Exhibit 5: Like most educated men of his generation, Ambassador Hong-choo Hyun could write beautiful Chinese calligraphy. On September 9, 1999, he wrote down a list of ancient books for the author: *The History of Three Kingdoms, The Saved History of Three Kingdoms, The History of Goryeo,* and *The Annals of the Joseon Dynasty*.

Source: Weijian Shan

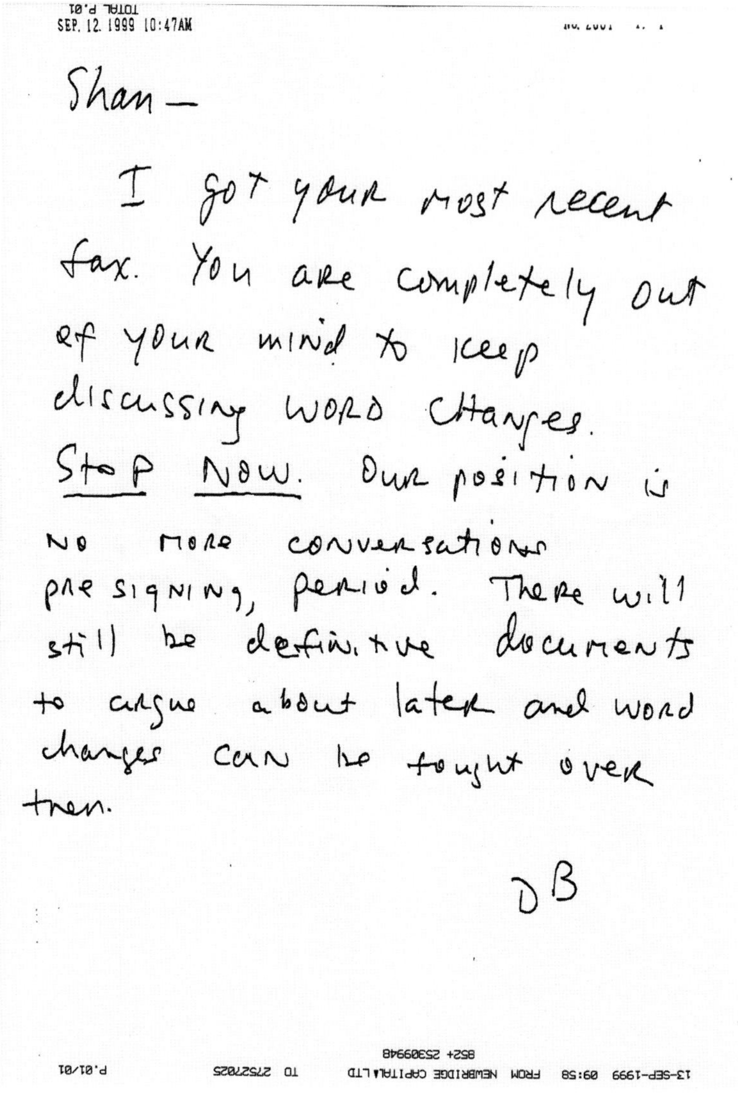
SEP. 12. 1999 10:47AM

Shan –

I got your most recent fax. You are completely out of your mind to keep discussing word changes. Stop Now. Our position is no more conversations pre signing, period. There will still be definitive documents to argue about later and word changes can be fought over then.

DB

13-SEP-1999 09:58 FROM NEWBRIDGE CAPITAL LTD P.01/01

Exhibit 6: A note by fax from David Bonderman to the author, September 13, 1999.

Source: Weijian Shan

Exhibit 7: Early morning, December 23, 1999, in the Business Center of the Shilla Hotel, Seoul. In the foreground are Philip Gilligan (left) of White & Case and BM Park (right) of Kim & Chang. In the background are members of the KDIC team and their lawyers.

Source: Weijian Shan

Exhibit 8: Paul Chen (left) and BM Park (right) signing the final documents in the Business Center of the Shilla Hotel in Seoul, December 23, 1999.

Source: Weijian Shan

Exhibit 9: Daniel Poon working on the final documents, morning of December 23, 1999, the Business Center of the Shilla Hotel.

Source: Weijian Shan

Exhibit 10: Cartoon in *Korea Economic Daily*, July 3, 1999 upon the false rumor that the KFB deal was concluded. It shows KFB (bride) and Newbridge (groom) taking marriage vows and the bride's mother (left) heaves a sigh: "Finally!". (Photo Credit: Korea Economic Daily)

Exhibit 11: The final signing ceremony, KFB headquarters, December 23, 1999. The author (left) shakes hands with Dong-jun Paeng, Executive Director of the KDIC, with Shee-yul Ryoo (right), Chairman of KFB, looking on. (Photo Credit: JoongAng Ilbo)

Exhibit 12: Dick Blum (left) in meeting with President Dae-jung Kim of South Korea in the Blue House, Seoul, March 15, 2000. (Photo Credit: JoongAng Ilbo)

Exhibit 13: Left to right: Bob Barnum, Wilfred Horie, Dan Carroll, and the author, Seoul, January 2000.

Source: Weijian Shan

Exhibit 14: Members of the Board of Directors of KFB and their spouses visit Tongdosa (Salvation of the World through Mastery of Truth), a Buddhist temple in the South Gyeongsang Province, Korea, after a board meeting in 2002.

Source: Weijian Shan

Exhibit 15: Robert Cohen (left), CEO of KFB, and the author write on the tiles in Tongdosa Temple on a sightseeing tour after a board meeting, 2002. The author writes "Korea First Bank" in hanja.

Source: Weijian Shan

Exhibit 16: The author (left) chatting with Dan Carroll while visiting Tongdosa Temple after a board meeting in 2002. The plaque on top of the temple reads: Sanskrit Bell Tower.

Source: Weijian Shan

Exhibit 17: David Bonderman (left) and Dick Blum at a meeting, Seoul, 2004.

Source: Weijian Shan

Exhibit 18: David Bonderman (second from left) and Dick Blum (middle) present a check representing Newbridge's donation to charities in South Korea, 2005. (Photo Credit: JoongAng Ilbo).

an economic one; the government did not want to be perceived as being involved in those types of layoffs at all.

We also got stuck on the question of risk weight. This was a regulatory concern, Lee said. He noted that other government-owned banks had similar protections but received full risk weight. I argued that injection of capital by the government, as happened with other banks, was not the same as protecting the capital base from loan losses, which was what we would be facing at KFB. In this case, government protection of a loan reduced its risk practically to zero, but my reasoning was to no avail. I got the feeling that Lee was going to continue to be stubborn on the issue.

Fiscal year was another surprising sticking point. We wanted to move the start of KFB's fiscal year from calendar year to the month immediately following the completion of our acquisition of KFB, so there would be a clear break point marked by the change of control. Again, Lee considered it a regulatory issue he absolutely could not give ground on. All banks must use the calendar year as the fiscal year, he said.

A final, confounding issue was the binding nature of the Terms of Investment document that we were negotiating. I had not expected it to be a stumbling block. We spent over an hour discussing it, but Lee would not agree to use the term "binding." Lee's own team had advised that Eric Yoon, their White & Case counsel, told them that a binding TOI was unusual in international contract law and that to include the term would open them up to potential damages greater than a breakup fee.

Although the latter might be true, I responded, it would go both ways. Newbridge would be exposed to the same risk as the government. Furthermore, I said, it would be meaningless to sign a nonbinding TOI document. We adjourned without an agreement on the issue.

Lee had to leave, but he reiterated that half of the government payment to KFB (to fill the hole left after the bad loans were carved out) be in cash and half in the government note. He suggested that we meet again the next afternoon to resume negotiations.

Overall, while I was reasonably pleased that we had managed to make headway on some difficult issues, I was concerned that this too might prove fleeting. We had been here before, having reached an agreement only to see the FSC change its mind again.

For example, we had agreed on the binding nature of the terms of investment before, but now Lee was being advised by his lawyer not to accept this. From our point of view, another MOU-type term sheet without any binding effect would be meaningless. If the MOU could be ignored, there was no reason another piece of paper could not be treated the same way. Lee was asking us to trust that the government would abide by the term sheet, even if it was nonbinding. In view of our experiences so far, all of us on the Newbridge side were adamant that if we signed anything at all, it had to be binding on both parties.

I had dinner that evening with Ambassador Hyun at the Japanese restaurant in the Chosun Hotel. Although he was always careful with what he had to say, Hyun seemed pleased with the outcome of the day's meeting. He was cautiously optimistic.

So was Bonderman. "It looks like there is actually some progress being made," he noted wryly in response to my memo updating him on the latest developments. He thought we might be able to agree to the government's position on unionized employees, as long as there wouldn't be many terminations at that staff level. As to the risk weighting, Bonderman suggested that we recalibrate our model to see how much the change would affect the results. His response to the binding nature of the terms surprised me a little. Bonderman was willing to consider a nonbinding term sheet as long as there was a breakup fee and that all of our team's expenses would be paid by the government if it did not proceed. He thought a breakup fee would at least improve our position over where we had been, which was that we might end up with neither a deal nor any compensation for our expenses.

I didn't think I could accept a breakup fee or anything short of a legally binding obligation on both parties. At that point, my biggest regret was having agreed to an MOU without any legally binding effect. That was what had put us in such a difficult position. We could still end up with no deal, even having spent so much time, effort, and resources on it. I was determined not to repeat the mistake. Bonderman was right that the breakup fee would be better than nothing, because we had no intention of walking away. I felt such a fee would both deter the government from walking and compensate us for our considerable efforts and expense. Even so, it was a suboptimal solution. I was especially mindful of the fact that politicians tended to change their minds when political winds shift, and I did not want to give them an easy way out after all this work.

I met with Chairman Lee again on the afternoon of September 3 at the same Federation of Banks Building. I could tell immediately that he was in a foul mood. He began to complain as soon as we sat down. "You claim to have a world-class management," he said. "Why can't you take half cash and half government note?" What he meant was that with a world-class management, we ought to be able to turn cash into loans or earning assets quickly, so he didn't see why we were resisting accepting cash which the government would pay KFB for the carved-out bad loans before closing. He said the FSC could opt to pay cash, in lieu of the government note.

On the government note, he took issue with how we would calculate the basis to set the interest rate. We had planned to use the average funding cost, or the average cost of liabilities, of the bank. He pointed to our position paper and said that the government had never agreed to "this condition," meaning the basis of calculating funding costs to exclude non-interest-bearing liabilities. I disagreed and pointed out that we actually took the exact language of the FSC's own term sheet of July 2 on the government note. After much discussion in English and Korean, Lee looked confused and told me several times that was not how his people had reported the situation to him.

"Mr. Noh must have hidden the truth from you," I said, half joking. I recommended he call BS Kang. He did and confirmed that his team did agree.

Nonetheless, he offered me two alternatives: (a) a 100 percent government note from the Korea Deposit Insurance Corporation, but the cost basis had to include non-interest-bearing liabilities; or (b) 50 percent notes and 50 percent cash if the cost basis excludes non-interest-bearing liabilities.

The interest rate on the government note was to be set at a spread over the average funding cost of the bank. If non-interest-bearing liabilities, which were part of the bank's funding sources, were included, the average funding cost would be lower; therefore, the interest rate on the government note would also be lower. We could not agree with each other but simply noted our differences.

The rest of the conversation was similarly frustrating. It turned out that the Newbridge side had erred, based on the analysis by our consultants,

Bain & Company, in asserting that the reductions would concentrate more on nonunion labor; the opposite was true. "We goofed on this subject," I admitted to Blum and Bonderman in a memo. We'd have to go back to Bain to do further analysis to see what our alternatives were.

Just as the meeting was getting ready to wind up, however, we had what seemed to be a breakthrough on the binding nature of the terms of investment. Lee said that while he could accept the document as binding, he objected to the word "binding," which was potentially offensive in Korean.

After consulting with out lawyer, Rich Lincer of Cleary, we came up with some new language, which read, in part, "the parties hereby agree to abide by these terms of investment as the basis for definitive agreement." Lee seemed satisfied with the new language but said he would need to reconfirm. It seemed clear that the form was more important than the substance in this case. On other issues, though, we remained far apart. One new concern was how KFB and the government would handle yield maintenance for work-out loans, such as the massive new work-outs the bank was dealing with from Daewoo. If a bad loan was restructured into a work-out loan, usually the loan maturity would be much extended and interest payments would be either frozen or forgiven to give the borrower time to work out its problems and to get back on its financial feet. The government was fine with paying for provisions for the loans but considered yield maintenance—essentially, guaranteeing the expected interest payments on the loan—off the table.

Because loan and interest payments froze during work-outs, this put us in a bad position. In the case of a default or bankruptcy, the bank could always put the loan back to the government. But a long-term work-out would deprive KFB of sorely needed interest income without the government's yield maintenance. As we could not agree with each other, for now, I noted my strong objection to Lee's position on the issue.

Lee proposed to meet again on Sunday at 5 pm at the Shilla Hotel.

I didn't know what to make of Chairman Lee's transformation between one meeting and the next. On one hand, just by devoting so much time to it, it seemed that he wanted a deal, and our progress in the first meeting was promising. On the other, the second meeting brought new issues on which the chairman refused to budge. I hoped that a third meeting would lead things to finally break in our favor.

Chapter 11

Ultimatum

September 4 was a Saturday. I thought I could take a short break, but it turned out to be impossible. To prepare for the next day's meeting with Chairman Lee at the Shilla Hotel, Hyun and I checked out the hotel's meeting facilities. Eventually, we decided to use the conference room in its business center.

I went to the office of Kim & Chang and wrote a three-page briefing outlining our stance on various issues. The intended audience was not only the FSC but also the Blue House, which had requested an update on Newbridge's position. Kim & Chang was in a unique position. It was Newbridge's legal counsel, but it was also trusted by the government, which, knowing Kim & Chang was our counsel, also often requested help from the firm. This arrangement suited us, as we trusted Kim & Chang's professional integrity—especially that of Ambassador Hyun—and were comfortable its lawyers would keep our confidence. We had come to see the firm as an important bridge between the government and Newbridge.

On Sunday, at 1 pm Seoul time, all the members of our team had a conference call to discuss the remaining issues in preparation for my meeting with Chairman Lee later that afternoon. Many thorny issues had been resolved by then, including the agreement, on July 1, on the markdown of 96.5 percent on the retained loan portfolio. The remaining issues were few but no less important. After much internal debate and analysis, Bonderman decided to accept Lee's proposal on the government note: half the payment would be in the form of a government note and half would be in cash. This would be a major and costly compromise. KFB needed interest-earning assets to match its interest-paying liabilities; it would lose money until the cash could be lent out to creditworthy borrowers, which were scarce in an economic crisis. We also accepted Lee's position on the risk weight of the government-guaranteed loans. But on employee reduction, Bonderman insisted that we stick to our guns.

At 4:15 pm, Lee called Ambassador Hyun. Eric Yoon, the White & Case lawyer, strongly objected to the language on indemnification, binding effect, drag-along, and God knew what else. Given the fact that the gap on the remaining issues was so large, Lee did not think it worthwhile for him to meet with me. He asked that I meet with Noh and Yoon instead.

I could not believe that Lee had gone back on his word again, just as I thought a deal was within reach. I considered his suggestion to meet with Noh and Yoon a pussy-footed way to say no, because he knew all too well it was impossible for us to make any progress with those two. I refused.

Perplexed, Hyun went to meet with Chairman Lee at his FSC office to urge him to keep the meeting. Lee relented and called me in to discuss. We met for about two and a half hours, but given the bad start, the meeting was tense. Meanwhile, our lawyers from Kim & Chang met with the FSC negotiators, including Noh and Yoon, in another conference room on a different floor.

Based on my earlier call with Bonderman, I offered up our two major concessions. On risk weight, I told Lee that it was in the government's best interest that KFB's loans carry the appropriate risk weight and that the risk weighting of government-guaranteed loans should be zero since they were risk-free. In spite of that argument, I said we would not insist, and we would concede to his wishes.

On the government note, I accepted Lee's position that KFB would be paid half in the government note and half in cash. Incredibly, instead of being pleased, Lee retorted that he would consider it. I replied that we were accepting *his* proposal and it was a major concession on our part. At the end of the meeting, we agreed that Newbridge would prepare yet another draft of the terms of investment, which Lee wanted to receive by midday on Monday.

Before we could ready that draft, Noh's team sent its comments on a paper, "Agreed-Upon Issues," which the Kim & Chang lawyers had prepared at Lee's request. Eric Yoon's response was titled "So-Called Agreed-Upon Issues by K&C." In it, Yoon basically contradicted everything Lee and I had agreed upon. According to Yoon's version of events, we did not have an agreement on the language for drag-along right, or indemnification (he clearly wanted none), the investment amount (he wanted us to commit to additional investments), due care (he rejected our side letter), and a host of other issues. While I doubted Lee and Newbridge would ever agree on everything, I was convinced that we could have no deal if the FSC continued to accept advice from Yoon on commercial, as opposed to legal, issues.

"Although we have very few open issues left, my feeling is that we are further apart than ever before," I wrote Bonderman that evening. "It seems whatever Lee agrees is subject to subversion by Yoon, his team, and himself. Therefore, I have no idea if what we consider open issues are the only ones."

The next morning, I talked with Bonderman by phone. He questioned whether the deal was still worth it, in view of all the changes and concessions we had made.

"Let's take a step back to look at the big picture," he said. "This might be death by a thousand cuts."

I called Mike O'Hanlon of Lehman and asked him to run our model again using the latest terms, to see if the deal still worked for us economically. My feeling was that fundamentally, it did, even with the recent concessions, but we had to verify this by looking at the numbers.

Based on the outcome of my negotiation with Lee, Linda Matlack at Cleary had worked the whole night to revise the terms.

During this process we discovered a bit of good news: The question of employee reduction, which was a major remaining issue, turned out, upon closer examination, not to be a major issue after all. Our consultant, Bain & Company, which was examining KFB's operations and management for us, had estimated the cost of these headcount reductions to be anywhere between $55 million and $70 million, and we were at loggerheads with the government over who would cover these costs.

However, every company in Korea was legally required to maintain a funded pension, earmarked for each individual employee. On September 6, BM Park at Kim & Chang pointed out that the "legal severance package" was in fact the same thing as "the funded reserves" already on the bank's balance sheet—thereby eliminating the need for either the government or Newbridge to fund severance anew, except if we wished to pay more than legally required. I thought we definitely should pay more than legally required to better take care of these employees who had sacrificed a lot during the financial crisis. Such generosity would also help build goodwill with the employees we retained.

The last time KFB had implemented a voluntary reduction program like the one we'd hoped to use, it had paid out an extra eight months' salary, which had averaged out to less than $10,000 per person. Running the numbers, even if we tripled the payout (which Bain recommended, and was considered extraordinarily generous), we would only be talking about $9 million, which was far less than our working assumption. Just in case, I suggested that we go back to the FSC and ask it to provide KFB with approximately $20 million in additional reserves to pay for the 300 Class 4 employee reductions we had in mind. It seemed that the last major issue between us and the FSC had become manageable.

BM Park proved to be a major force on the Kim & Chang team, and it was insights like this that had made him so. Only 38 years old, he was already a partner at the largest and most renowned law firm in South Korea.

Square-jawed and bespectacled, BM always appeared to be relaxed, but he was meticulous and worked at a relentless pace. Not only was he familiar with the law, but he was also a good and effective problem solver.

★ ★ ★

The next day, I went to the Blue House to meet with the president's Senior Secretary for Policy and Planning, Han-gil Kim. Kunho Cho of Lehman helped translate. Kim listened carefully to my report and requested that I provide a position paper. He said that he would review it, report it to the president, and get instructions from the Blue House to pass along to the FSC. He said that the official communication channel remained to the FSC but President Kim and the Blue House were very committed to this deal. To my remark that we had 24 hours to bring this process to a conclusion, he asked for more time. I said that I would so report to our chairmen and thanked him for his support.

I was quite encouraged by this meeting, and went back immediately to start putting together the position paper the senior secretary had requested. I felt we had to push every button we could to move the process forward, including applying political pressure. I felt that Chairman Lee needed not only political pressure but also political support to make up his mind to do the deal with us. As the process had dragged on endlessly, I would have been more than happy to stop the political campaign if he would move to complete the deal with us.

Meanwhile, Ambassador Hyun met on our behalf with Lee for an hour, followed by several phone conversations. Lee again raised questions about the language on drag-along, indemnity, the binding effect of the TOI document, and the investment amount, because his lawyer Yoon had raised them. But to me those issues were closed. Another meeting was scheduled for Chairman Lee and me at 9 am the next day. Before our meeting, I learned from our sources that he had expressed some anger over my Blue House meeting, complaining it was distracting at this critical juncture, but he was not so upset that he changed our plans to meet as scheduled. It now seemed to me that Lee was making a serious effort.

The next morning, September 7, I met with Chairman Lee again, but only for five minutes. Ambassador Hyun, his partner KS Chung, and I had gone to meet with him at the Federation of Banks building, but Lee met only with the ambassador, while Chung and I waited in an adjacent room. The lawyers at Kim & Chang had prepared a folder of documents, which included copies of contracts for other American banking deals showing that indemnification was a common feature. Hyun told me afterward that Lee had called the FSC director, BS Kang, to say that he thought our indemnification clause looked logical and reasonable and challenged his team to give reasons for their objection. Kang replied with something about hidden liabilities, and Lee retorted that was exactly why investors wanted this. In spite of his siding with us on this issue, however, Lee did not immediately agree with our indemnification language. I was sure his lawyer would object strenuously.

Lee remained firm on the employee issue, insisting that the government could be responsible for management reduction of only up to 100 people (this was down from the 150 he had suggested on Sunday). He seemed to be receptive to the idea of additional reserves to pay for extra severance, however. His stance on the language of drag-along and binding effect seemed to have become ambiguous.

Lee came out to meet with me briefly and appeared to be much more relaxed than he had been for the past week or so. He said he wanted to get the deal done that day. He also complained about my meeting at the Blue House the day before and reminded me that he, Lee, was the only one who could make a decision on this deal. Nobody, not even the president, could influence him. I replied that I definitely respected his authority and would very much like to concentrate on completing the deal with him.

BM Park and KS Chung of Kim & Chang went to talk with the government side at 2:30 pm and called later that afternoon to say that they were making slow progress. Meanwhile, I went to the Blue House for the second time in as many days to meet with President Kim's senior press secretary. He listened carefully and asked me a couple of questions. He assured us that the president was very committed to doing this deal.

At about ten that night, Chung and Park returned to the Shilla Hotel, where the ambassador, Chen, Poon, David Kim, and I were waiting for them. The deal was 99 percent negotiated, they told us triumphantly.

However, as they laid out what had been negotiated, we realized that a number of unresolved issues remained. Soon, Chen and the lawyers were arguing with each other over what had and hadn't been decided.

Around one o'clock in the morning, Hyun and I adjourned the meeting. There were just too many issues to be resolved that night.

After we got up, Chen, Poon, and I went to Kim & Chang's offices to go over the remaining issues that Chung and Park had brought back from their meeting with the government side. We spent the whole morning formulating our position on the various points, all of which were technical but critical in the context of the deal.

Bonderman, a lawyer by training, was careful with language. When Ambassador Hyun persuaded Chairman Lee to accept our drag-along right, it was understood that such a right would allow us to maximize shareholders' value—to extract the best price from a buyer seeking to acquire 100 percent ownership of the bank. The government side wanted the language to read that the drag-along right's "purpose is to maximize shareholders' value." Bonderman insisted that the language should be changed to say that its "purpose is to enable the maximization of share-holders' value."

The difference was subtle but important. We did not want to give the government an excuse to argue in the future that Newbridge had failed to meet an obligation to maximize shareholders' value, since there was no objective measurement as to what "maximize" meant. If I had said "The purpose of wearing shoes is to run at my top speed," someone might argue I wasn't running fast enough. But if I said "The purpose of wearing shoes is to *enable me* to run at my top speed," the purpose was only to enable me, but not necessarily to obligate me, to do so. Given the dynamics of the negotiations, we had to be extremely careful with every word in an agreement so as not to leave room for misinterpretation in the future.

On the afternoon of September 8, Chung and Park went back to negotiate with the government side on our behalf. Ambassador Hyun and I waited in his office for their return. After several hours, they called to report: no progress. Toward evening, I received a call from a senior presidential aide I knew well. He admonished me for visiting with senior officials of the Blue House. He asked me to stop my lobbying with the Blue House, as it was distracting. I respected him and his advice highly, but at that juncture, I was determined to remain annoying until we had signed a binding document, although I kept this thought to myself. While the negotiations dragged on, the ambassador remained optimistic. He suggested that I prepare a draft announcement for the signing of the legally binding TOI with the government. I was skeptical but did as he requested.

The next day, Hyun went to meet with Chairman Lee at about 10 am, spending about an hour there. Lee raised only three issues. First was regarding the initial investment. Our language was "Newbridge intends, but is not obligated, to invest 500 billion won." He asked that we remove "but is not obligated" from the sentence. Second, regarding the drag-along right, he wanted us to remove the words "to enable" from the sentence stating that "the purpose is *to enable* maximization of shareholders' value." Third, the government would provide 30 billion won for the purpose of employee reduction, but Newbridge would be responsible for its implementation.

I called Bonderman to get his views. He was agreeable to the first and third points but would not yield on the second. On the third point, although Bonderman was agreeable to Lee's position, I thought the sum of 30 billion won might be insufficient and we needed 40 billion won. After much back-and-forth, Lee agreed to 38 billion won, which was close enough to my goal.

Resolving the question of that single word, "enable," proved much tougher than I had anticipated. Incredibly, I spent three or four hours arguing with the government side over the retention or removal of the word. Finally, around 6 pm Seoul time, I proposed a compromise that the government could live with. We would keep the word "enable," saying "the purpose is to *enable* maximization of shareholders' value," but add "and in exercising this right, the investors will seek to achieve this purpose." My thinking was that "seek" meant to make an effort, but it was not an obligation.

Since this was a point on which Bonderman was insistent, I called him, at what must have been 5 am in New York City, where he was, to check if he was agreeable to my proposed wording. Bonderman had an amazing ability to take a call at any hour. Even if awoken from a deep sleep, he talked and thought with total clarity, as if he were on standby and had been waiting for the call. The only time he would not answer in the middle of the night was when he was at home. I usually called at odd hours only when necessary and when I knew he was traveling.

Usually, Bonderman would give quick, unhesitating answers. This time he was silent for almost a full minute. If I had not known him better, I would have thought he had gone back to sleep. I knew it was an important point, so I waited patiently for him to think through the implications of my proposed language. Finally, he said, "I am okay with it" and rang off.

Bonderman once told me that he was able to go right back to sleep after taking a call. I am a light sleeper. If someone wakes me in the middle of the night, my sleep is ruined. I could not believe it was so easy for him.

It had been another long day. At about eleven-thirty that night, I finally left Kim & Chang's offices and returned to the hotel. I was about to brush my teeth and dive into bed, feeling pleased for having made some progress, when the phone rang. Ambassador Hyun said that he, Chung, and Park wanted to come to the hotel to meet with me. I hung up the phone and closed my eyes for a catnap before their arrival, sensing this would be a long night. No sooner did I fall asleep than the ambassador called to let me know he was en route, and Chung and Park were on their way as well. I went to meet with Hyun in the business center. While waiting for Chung and Park, Hyun and I chatted to pass time.

Like most educated men of his generation, Hyun could write beautiful Chinese calligraphy (Exhibit 5). That night, as our wide-ranging conversation wandered to Korea's history and I lamented not being able to find good Korean history books, he wrote down a list of ancient books for me: *The History of Three Kingdoms [of Korea]*, *The Saved History of Three Kingdoms [of Korea]*, *The History of Goryeo ("Goryeo" is the name that "Korea" is derived from)*, and *The Annals of the Joseon Dynasty*. All the ancient books of Korea were written in Chinese, and therefore I would have no trouble reading them, although unfortunately the younger generation of Koreans no longer can, because the teaching of hanja, or Chinese characters, had been phased out in South Korea since the early 1970s.

The night wore on without word from Chung and Park, who had been painstakingly negotiating with a senior government official designated by Chairman Lee at a location inside the Blue House. Ambassador Hyun and I were both exhausted. Eventually, he fell asleep on a sofa. I lay on another sofa but could not sleep a wink. Chung and Park finally showed up at 4 am. I woke up Daniel Poon in his hotel room and asked him to come downstairs to join the debriefing.

The Blue House official wanted to revise the language on a number of terms, some of which I found acceptable but others not. It was too early to wake up our legal and financial advisors in Seoul to consult with them, so I called Linda Matlack of Cleary in Washington, DC, and David Jackson of Lehman in New York, to discuss the proposed changes with them. We decided to accept some but pushed back on others. With some back-and-forth between the Kim & Chang lawyers and the Blue House official, the gap between us was narrowing.

By daybreak, it seemed we had almost closed the gap entirely, until Ambassador Hyun received a call from Chairman Lee. The chairman expressed surprise about the binding nature of the TOI and said he was disturbed about the absence of a mutual breakup fee. The ambassador became uncharacteristically upset, because we all knew the binding nature of this document had been agreed to, after a long and strenuous negotiation process. The last-minute change came as a shock. We flatly refused to negotiate further on this point. Half an hour later, Lee's office called the ambassador's office twice to request an "all-hands" meeting at 4 pm.

I refused to attend it unless there was some assurance that the document would be signed, but instructed Kim & Chang to deliver three copies of the final document and side letters with a cover letter reading "Enclosed for your signature." The ambassador did not attend either.

Shortly after the meeting began, Lee called the ambassador and apologized for having "forgotten" about the discussion on the binding nature of the TOI. At this, Hyun agreed to attend the meeting, joining Chung and Park. On the other side were Lee, the Blue House official, Director General Noh, and Yoon the lawyer. Lee presided over the meeting and asked everyone to raise issues or be silent from then on. Yoon immediately took issue with the "binding" issue, Hyun told me later, and Lee told him to "forget about it." As the Kim & Chang lawyers went through the TOI, explaining our positions on whatever points they had raised, Noh said nothing.

Afterward, Lee met with Ambassador Hyun to say that the decision was to have the TOI signed on either Monday or Tuesday, when President DJ Kim would be flying back to Korea from the APEC summit meeting in New Zealand, where he and President Clinton were scheduled to meet again. The idea was not to make an announcement prior to the meeting, fearing the public would criticize the administration for having buckled under pressure in advance of the meeting with Clinton.

★ ★ ★

It was a Friday, so I was heading to Hong Kong to spend a weekend with my family. On my way to the airport, Bonderman called and I updated him on where things stood. "Well, if it doesn't happen, it isn't your fault," he said. "If it does happen, it's your fault." I laughed and said it would be my fault either way.

I was relieved to be home. The next morning, I went for a run and came home in time to see my daughter, LeeAnn, just waking up. But I did not get to spend much quality time with her as we were soon interrupted by repeated phone calls from Seoul. BS Kang, the FSC director, had called Kunho Cho at Lehman early that morning with big news.

"It's a done deal," Kang had told Cho. The TOI would be signed early next week. Major local newspapers were also reporting that the deal was imminent. Ambassador Hyun called me that afternoon to say that the

FSC wanted the signing to take place on either Tuesday or Wednesday. Lee and his team raised a couple of minor issues, but we made it clear that Newbridge would not negotiate any more.

The ambassador said that Lee had requested a meeting with me as soon as possible, suggesting Monday afternoon, which Hyun expected would largely be ceremonial, a coda to the negotiation on the TOI.

I spent the rest of the day drafting an official announcement with the Lehman team. They wanted to make a big deal of it, and I agreed. We needed to impress upon the Korean public that this was a done deal, so that no one, either within or outside the government, would second-guess us as we negotiated the definitive documents.

We arranged for our advisor, Bob Barnum, and my partner, Dan Carroll, who would be traveling in Asia that week, to join the rest of our team in Seoul for the official announcement. We intended a show of force, to make an impression on the Koreans.

"It ain't over until it is over," I wrote to Blum and Bonderman on Saturday evening. "This deal has seen enough ups and downs. I am now cautiously optimistic. Let us keep our fingers crossed."

Even though I was trying not to get anyone's hopes up, most of all my own, I was relieved that there was finally light at the end of the tunnel. I had not slept well for a long time, although I did not feel tired. Now that it seemed all was set, I must have subconsciously let myself relax. My daughter's bed was on a raised platform, half of which was for her bedding and the other half a play area. That Sunday morning, I was lying on her bed to play with her as she sat beside me. Usually, I cannot sleep if there is the slightest noise, but I fell into a deep slumber, despite the noise my daughter was making playing right by me. When I woke up, the room was quiet and it was already two-thirty in the afternoon. I could not believe that I had slept for two and a half hours in broad daylight.

On Monday morning, September 13, I took the first Cathay Pacific flight to Seoul and went straight to the offices of Kim & Chang to meet with Ambassador Hyun, Chung, and Park. Hyun said that he met with Chairman Lee earlier in the day and that Lee still had five issues. Over lunch, we discussed them and decided that Hyun should meet with Lee to explain that Newbridge would not entertain any further changes. Lee could either accept the last version of the TOI or the negotiations were finished. Coincidentally, a fax from Bonderman had arrived while I was en route to Seoul. It was a short, handwritten note that read:

Shan —

I got your most recent fax. You are completely out of your mind to keep discussing word changes. Stop Now. Our position is no more conversations pre-signing, period. There will still be definitive documents to argue about later and word changes can be fought over then.

His note (Exhibit 6) reminded me of a Chinese saying, "The tree wants to be motionless, but the wind just doesn't stop." I too wanted to stop. But I could not stymie every attempt by the government side, and I could not refuse to speak with them.

The next day, Barnum, Carroll, and James Chang, another Newbridge colleague, arrived in Seoul early in the morning. Paul Chen and Daniel Poon had flown in the night before. They were all here to take part in the signing. We went to Lehman's office to review the Lehman team's financial analysis of KFB, based on the negotiated terms of the deal. I knew that Ambassador Hyun was meeting Chairman Lee at 10 am, and I was restless waiting to hear from him. At about noon, Hyun called and asked me to meet him at his office.

He told me that Lee would not yield on the issues he had raised the day before. In addition, Lee did not feel comfortable with a number of other items in the current document. I was very disturbed by this last-minute turn of events, and I informed Hyun I had no desire to negotiate further. It seemed to me that Lee still had no intention of bringing the negotiation to a close, even though earlier he had indicated that signing was imminent. I said I would immediately return to Hong Kong if there was no deal.

I went back to the hotel and briefed our team, most of whom agreed that the best course of action was to decamp from Seoul. Now that there was nothing left to do, I went to my room and fell asleep, since I had slept very little the previous night. I woke up at about five in the afternoon, to a voice message from Hyun. He said that Lee decided to give up most of the issues on his earlier list, although he was still insisting on two technical ones.

Now that Chairman Lee had shown a willingness to compromise, we decided to make another effort to accommodate him, and discussed our response amongst ourselves until about 2 am, when I called Bonderman to discuss the changes and get his consent.

I went to bed at 3:30 am but, after a grand total of two and a half hours of sleep, was up again at about 6. I felt like death warmed over. I reviewed the revised TOI and then drafted a note to explain where we made changes and why. Dated September 15, the note was addressed to Ambassador Hyun:

Dear Ambassador,

I note the message from Chairman Lee on the various issues yesterday. As indicated, we would be willing to make one more effort to close the deal on the basis of the communication. After working with my team until 3:30 am today, we have been able to accommodate most of the requests. However, there are other issues [on which] we cannot change our positions because we believe our positions are fair, reasonable and logical. We have tried our very best, again, in the hope of closing the deal. To avoid any misunderstanding, I am writing this note to explain the various changes (or non-changes). Please share this note with Chairman Lee. . . .

I wrote in conclusion:

This list is as complete as I can tell. Please let me know if I have missed anything. As you are aware, I have truly and completely exhausted all the efforts to be accommodative and will not be in a position to concede any further.

It was Wednesday, September 15. Since this was the day on which we expected to mark the signing of the TOI, every member of our team except me was in a suit and a tie. I hadn't gotten much sleep, nor did I think there was any hope of signing on that day, so I wore shorts and must have looked totally disheveled.

The night before, Bonderman had made a request. He wanted us to sign the revised TOI unilaterally and send it over to the FSC chairman with a cover letter, giving the government 24 hours to sign it or we would withdraw from the transaction.

His request put me in a bind. I thought if we sent a signed TOI to Chairman Lee, he would view it as an ultimatum. Even if he wanted to do the deal, he probably would not be able to, lest he be perceived as having caved in to foreign investors under duress. Even in the best-case scenario, he would be forced to wait until after the ultimatum expired to respond. I was afraid such a letter would be counterproductive. Yet all of us had run out of patience, and there was no way I could persuade Bonderman to change his mind. I called Hyun.

"Ambassador Hyun," I said, "I have a letter from David Bonderman to Chairman Lee to give him 24 hours to sign the TOI or we would walk."

Hyun responded with alarm. "Mr. Shan, that would be disastrous," he warned. "The government can't be perceived to cave to an ultimatum. It's really not necessary."

"Ambassador, I fully understand, and I'm on the same page," I said. "But I don't think David can be persuaded at this point. Nor do we have time. I'll send you his letter, but I'll leave it to you to decide what to do with it."

The ambassador immediately got it. "You think you can ignore Bonderman's instruction?" he asked.

"I am not ignoring it," I answered. "I am faxing the letter to you." Then I added, "When the general is out in the battlefield, the emperor's decree need not be followed." It was a well-known ancient Chinese adage, which the ambassador would be familiar with and would understand.

My colleague Paul Chen, ever alert, knew I had reservations about Bonderman's ultimatum and suspected I might be plotting some way of evading his instructions. At that point, not only Bonderman, but everyone on our team thought enough was enough. To avoid needless internal argument, I asked Chen to fax Bonderman's letter to the ambassador.

Ambassador Hyun never forwarded Bonderman's letter. But I was sure that, in his own diplomatic way, he conveyed to Chairman Lee the message that it was now or never.

We waited and waited. There was no response from the FSC; they fell completely silent. It was getting late and nothing was likely to happen. It appeared that Chairman Lee had changed his mind again.

In the afternoon, after having waited long enough, Carroll and the rest of our team left Seoul in Blum's private plane. They had come all the way to Seoul for the signing, only to leave empty-handed. I decided to stay to see what would happen next. But nothing did, and all was quiet for the rest of September 15.

By that time, all emotions seemed drained from me. I knew we had done everything humanly possible. I thought, "Man proposes, God disposes," as the saying goes. There was nothing more I could do. Therefore, I was totally relaxed as I waited to see what would happen next.

At about midnight, just when I was about to go to bed, I learned that the Korean government still had some issues with our revised TOI. That call ruined my sleep for yet another night.

The next day, Thursday, September 16, I wrote a memo entitled "Safe: What is going on. . . ." After apologizing to the team for radio silence over the past few days, I provided a summary of the events since last Saturday. Then I reported:

> *Ambassador called me around midnight last night to say that Lee was "disappointed and discouraged" after having reviewed our final TOI and Mr. Chin of the Blue House expressed similar sentiment. I said that was too bad but there was nothing we could do about it. I asked Ambassador to urge Mr. Lee to look at the big picture, how far he has come from the MOU, do not be a prisoner of himself focusing on a few minor issues, behave like a statesman for a change and make a final decision.*

Despite the continued silence from the FSC, I was relaxed. I felt that we had done everything we could, and it was up to Chairman Lee to make the final decision. That afternoon, I took a nap and then met with a reporter, Sue Chang of Bridge News, who visited with me at the hotel. I had built a good relationship with a number of journalists during this deal, and she was one of them. Typically, I stayed at the Shilla Hotel, but this time I could only get a room at Seoul's Grand Hyatt. We sat by the pool chatting, but it was not an interview and I did not give any indication of where we were in our negotiation with the FSC. I still had no idea what the FSC would do, even at this late stage, in view of repeated disappointments in the past months.

By 5:30 pm, there was still no word. I had spent another day waiting in vain. There was nothing further I could do in Seoul. I could not bear to wait around anymore, not knowing what to expect. If Chairman Lee wanted to do the deal, I would have already heard from him by now.

I decided to leave town. But Hong Kong was in the grip of another typhoon. The number 10 signal, the strongest level, had been hoisted, and all flights in and out of the city were canceled. I decided to go to Beijing, only about a two-hour flight away, to attend to some business there. If necessary, I could return to Seoul on short notice.

It was 6 pm when I checked out of the hotel. Leaning back and closing my eyes in the backseat of the car as it pulled out of the hotel's driveway, I felt a tinge of regret that we had come such a long way but the deal remained elusive. I took out my mobile phone to dial Ambassador Hyun's number, to tell him I was leaving town. At that exact moment, my phone rang, quite loudly, startling me. It was him.

"Ambassador Hyun. I was just about to call you," I said. "I am on my way to the airport to take the next flight out."

"Mr. Shan, you must not go to the airport. Please don't leave," he said. I could sense some anxiety in his voice. "Please come to my office immediately. I will debrief you when you get here."

Chapter 12

Sign It or Forget It

I directed the driver to take me to the Kim & Chang office in Jongno-gu District in downtown Seoul. On the short drive from the Grand Hyatt, I passed Gwanghwamun Square; at its center is a statue of Admiral Yi Sun-sin, the sixteenth-century naval hero who repeatedly defeated Japanese invaders. It marks the center of Seoul. So much of the Korean identity was wrapped up in the idea of keeping foreigners out that Korea has been called the "Hermit Kingdom." The economic crisis was forcing South Korea to open up its market more than ever for foreign investments. Little wonder that Koreans viewed foreign investors with suspicion and distrust.

The car moved slowly through Seoul's evening rush-hour traffic, taking me much longer than usual to get to the office. Hyun and his colleagues were waiting for me. He got right to the point: "I think we have been able to resolve all the issues except one. We need to talk with you about it."

I let out a barely audible groan. Hashing out deal terms with the FSC was like playing Whac-A-Mole: As soon as we agreed on one issue, another would pop up.

Hyun told me he and his colleagues had spent more than two hours that day negotiating with Chairman Lee. In addition to my explanatory note on our position on various issues and terms, they had also prepared a lengthy note in Korean to argue our case with Lee. In it, they carefully reviewed the FSC's "remaining issues." Referring to my memo, Hyun pointed out to Lee that Newbridge could be trusted, as we respected prior commitments, reason, and logic. Finally, Lee said that he would drop all other issues but one.

"If you will agree to restore Newbridge's original language for adjudication related to 'involuntary bankruptcy,' I will be ready to sign the TOI," said Lee.

"Involuntary bankruptcy" referred to bankruptcies initiated by creditors, usually banks, but not by the borrowers themselves. For example, a bank might refuse to honor or cash a check issued by a borrower, effectively denying it credit, which legally could lead the borrower into bankruptcy.

I was surprised, because the language on involuntary bankruptcy had been changed at the FSC's request only the day before, after much argument between the parties. Now they wanted to revert to our original language?

Without any hesitation I said, "I am fine with it."

Ambassador Hyun and his colleagues looked at each other, relieved.

I called Rich Lincer and Linda Matlack, our Cleary lawyers who had drafted the TOI, asking them to make the change. To my surprise, they objected to the change and to restoring our old language.

They explained that the old language was fine if applied to all cases of disputes, as we had it. But we had moved away from that construct after conceding to FSC's request. If we used the old language only for "involuntary bankruptcy," it would imply that this particular situation would be treated differently from all other cases and other types of disputes.

Ah, that was the catch. It was like an insurance policy having a specific sentence to say fire damage to a desk would be covered. That sentence itself would not be a problem, but the implication was that there would be no coverage for other pieces of office furniture.

I did not want to deny the FSC's new request outright, so I asked the lawyers to craft some language they felt comfortable with. After much back-and-forth, we agreed among ourselves to add a sentence to the restored original language to ensure that other cases would not be excluded. It was already midnight when we submitted the new language to the other side.

Soon word came from the government side that they felt the added language was too rambling, and they would no longer insist on any change at all. They requested that our lawyers prepare a final version of the TOI to be delivered to the FSC at eight the next morning.

The next morning, September 17, Chung called me and said that the FSC insisted on adding some language that all transfer events could be referred to the court in addition to a well-defined adjudication process. Nor would they agree to make payments, subject to refund, before adjudication was concluded. I went back and forth with Lee's team through our lawyers on these issues until we reached a compromise. It was already three in the afternoon.

I did not send these revisions to our team members because I did not consider the changes substantive, nor did I want our team members to know I was still negotiating with the FSC, as the collective view was that further negotiations were off. I had received a note from Bonderman:

Shan,

I have gotten a thick red line draft of the TOI from Linda Matlack. My view is that I am not going to read another draft because we are making a mistake by proceeding further. Tell Lee to sign it or forget it.

David Bonderman

Later that afternoon, Ambassador Hyun told me that the FSC was ready to sign, and the signing was scheduled for 8 pm. Only then did I realize we had been so busy that I had completely forgotten the lunch I had ordered and left on the table. But there was no time to eat; I had to prepare a press announcement. While Bonderman had refused to review the TOI, he was happy to be woken up to help edit the press release.

I had been wearing my suit the whole day in anticipation of signing the TOI. I left my hotel at 7 pm and headed for the FSC, where I was the sole representative from Newbridge, as none of my team members were still in Seoul. I arrived at 7:45 pm and went up to the 15th floor, to a conference room not far from Director General Noh's office. Then I realized that, in my haste, I had not brought a pen to sign the papers.

BM Park had arrived before me, to do a final review of the documents, and he let me borrow his burgundy-colored Montblanc.

Shortly after I arrived, Noh entered the room without a word of greeting, followed by BS Kang and other members of the FSC team. They lined up in single file, according to their rank. Noh wore his usual frozen-fish expression, pale and cold. He was angry, no doubt, that the TOI had been negotiated without him. He did not spare me a glance. I was not surprised that he was unhappy, because it seemed he had been completely cut out of the negotiation process in the last couple of months. I had not seen him since early July. I reckoned he may not have known until the last minute that the TOI was to be signed.

Noh sat down across the table from me and immediately proceeded to sign the documents laid out in front of him. This was unusual; typically, two parties at such a signing ceremony would sit on the same side of the table. I proceeded to sit down on my side of the table to sign the documents in front of me. After we finished signing the papers before us, Park exchanged the documents between us for countersigning.

There was complete silence in the room, other than the rustle of paper. And after we finished there was no applause and no congratulations. There was no exchange of signed copies. We both just left the documents on the table. I knew Park would collect my copy. Although the atmosphere was tense, I kept my cool. I might have looked serious, but I was happy that we had finally come to this point. With this legally binding term sheet, the deal was locked down, even though there was still a long way to go to complete it.

Contractually, a legally binding term sheet is not the final agreement. But if the parties fail to reach the final and definitive agreements, they are legally obligated to go through the transaction on the basis of the TOI. Therefore, I knew completing the definitive documentation would just be a matter of time from this point on. The deal was locked up.

The major terms of the TOI had been agreed. The government would equalize assets and liabilities of KFB by filling the hole left by carved-out bad assets with an interest-bearing government note. Then Newbridge and the government would contribute equity capital for 51 percent and 49 percent of the common stock, respectively. The portion of Newbridge's investment would be 500 billion won. The government would receive warrants representing 5 percent of common stock. Newbridge would select the assets for KFB to retain. The loan portfolio retained by KFB would effectively be marked at 96.5 percent of the original book value by KFB keeping 3.5 percent of already funded loan loss reserves. The retained loans would be protected by the government in the next 2 to 3 years depending on the loan type in such a manner that the management of KFB would periodically determine additional loan loss reserves and the government would fund such reserves with a government note. There was a mechanism to resolve disputes over the impaired amount. Newbridge would have 100 percent voting control of new KFB.

The deal in the TOI was a significant improvement for the government from the MOU, especially in that the 96.5 percent mark on the retained loans was substantially lower than anticipated if they had been marked to market as contemplated in the MOU. But Newbridge would take over a clean bank whose legacy assets would be fully protected by the government, and would no longer pose risks to the bank.

I stood up and extended my hand to shake Mr. Noh's. Still without looking at me, he took my hand, shook it lightly, and let it go. Then he turned and left the room without saying a word. Boy, he was angry!

Mr. Chun, who was seconded from KFB to the FSC and was a member of the FSC team, shook my hand and broke the silence. Looking into my eyes, he said, "Congratulations." He was the only person from the FSC team who had even a trace of smile on his face. I knew others were friendly, but none of them wanted to show it in the presence of Mr. Noh. I did not blame them. It would only invite trouble with Noh if they appeared too friendly with me.

A group of reporters were waiting in an adjacent room. When Chairman Lee and I signed the MOU nine months ago, we held a joint press conference. Noh did not seem to want to be seen with me, so he did his own press briefing. I waited for about half an hour for my turn to meet the press with Park, who kindly volunteered to act as my interpreter. I spent about 45 minutes talking and taking questions. My message was simple. I said that we were happy to reach this stage and that the deal was good for all parties, including the government, the bank, and Newbridge. I said that, although we had work to do to finalize the definitive documents, both the government and Newbridge were now legally committed to completing the transaction under the terms and conditions of the TOI.

The general sense I got was that the journalists were surprised that we had reached this stage. They had already heard from Noh about the basic terms of the TOI, especially how much capital we would invest in KFB. But they had a number of questions left for me:

"How much control does Newbridge have of the bank?" asked one reporter.

I answered, "Newbridge will have full control of the bank, regardless of how much the government owns. Newbridge will have 100 percent of the voting rights. This is what the government wants too. It doesn't want to renationalize the bank. The idea is for us to bring in world-class management, so it would be counterproductive if we didn't have full control."

Another reporter began a more complex inquiry. "The government will acquire all the nonperforming loans of KFB by the closing of the sale, and will give KFB the put right to transfer loans that become nonperforming in the next two years. For loans to financial institutions, the term of the put will be three years. Why?"

I explained that it was important to make sure the bank would be clean to begin with. We didn't want to inherit previous mistakes.

"Who will determine whether a loan is good or bad if it is subject to the put right?" asked another reporter.

"The management of KFB, appointed by Newbridge, will make all loan classifications. The management will make the provisions for nonperforming loans and the government will fund the provisions. If the government disputes the loan value or the provision determined by KFB, it has the option to buy the loan at face value and sell it to a third party at a better price. It's very fair," I explained.

There was one more important question: "What are your immediate objectives for KFB after taking control?"

I said, "We would like to return the bank to profitability as soon as possible. This will almost definitely happen in the next two years, hopefully sooner."

On my way back to the hotel, I called Daniel Poon, who was still in the office in Hong Kong at that late hour. I said, "Daniel, we finally signed the TOI."

There was a pause on the other side of the line. Then with a tone of incredulity, he said, "Really? Are you serious?"

I flew back to Hong Kong on Saturday, September 18, 1999, the day after signing the TOI. When I landed that afternoon, I saw that media, including Bloomberg and the *South China Morning Post*, had already reported the story. I was so happy to be home, with the deal finally locked down. I spent all my time with our children over the weekend. During my past visits home, I had spent so much time working or on the phone that I felt I had hardly seen them. I had missed them a lot. LeeAnn, my seven-year-old, told me that she had learned some big words by over-hearing me on these calls, such as "loan," "agreement," "idiosyncrasy," and "xenophobia." That day, I fell asleep before she did, while I was lying next to her reading her a bedtime story. It was the best sleep I had had in months.

★ ★ ★

The Terms of Investment, signed on September 17, 1999, was only 22 pages long, not counting the signature page. But it more than doubled the 10-page MOU of December 31, 1998. The legally binding TOI superseded the MOU and incorporated terms that the MOU had not contemplated. Whereas the MOU was an agreement at a conceptual level, the TOI contained operational details, which would need to be covered even more deeply in the pending, fully fledged final documents.

★ ★ ★

I was back in Seoul with my team members on Monday. Even with the signed TOI, we were still a long way away from closing the transaction. There were numerous details left to work out. For example, we needed to inform the government side what KFB assets we would not want. Although we already had some good ideas based on our preliminary due diligence, we had not wanted to expend resources on digging deeper before we knew there was a deal. There was a lot of work to be done before we could confirm our initial conclusions. Additionally, we had to negotiate and finalize the definitive documents—essentially, the final contract—that would incorporate the terms of the TOI and then expand them into operational details that could be executed.

I circulated a memo titled "Next Steps" on September 19, including a list of things that we needed to get started on immediately:

- *Prepare a list of overseas [KFB] branches and subsidiaries we will not retain ([to be completed by] Cleary, Bain, K&C, Newbridge). By the TOI, this needs to be done within a month.*
- *Prepare a list of facilities we will not retain ([to be completed by] Bain, K&C, NB) within a month.*
- *Revise and deliver draft definitive documents (Cleary).*
- *Form a transition team to work within the KFB: S.H. Lee and Won-kyu Choi (of the KFB) and discuss with the FSC. Among other things, this team is necessary to ensure correct classification of loans by the closing time, the proper use of overdraft facilities so the balance will not significantly decline at the closing, and responsible credit and loan policy.*
- *Recruit management team.*
- *Establish timetable with the FSC.*
- *Update financials (E&Y and Lehman).*
- *Sources of capital.*
- *PR issues.*

I sent a similar letter to Ambassador Hyun, entitled "Next Steps," so that we could align our next steps and timetable in the next phase of the transaction. There was one thing I was keen to find out from the government side, which was exactly who we would be working with to finalize the deal. "As you know, we have reason to be concerned about who would lead this process," I wrote.

In view of the hostility that Noh exhibited at the signing and how difficult it had been for us to work with him, I dreaded a repeat of past experiences even though a binding term sheet had already been signed. I was also slightly concerned that the White & Case lawyers would continue to make life difficult for us.

We soon found out. At breakfast Monday morning with the Kim & Chang lawyers, I was delighted to hear that we would be dealing with a different team on the government side. The FSC would hand over the rest of the transaction process to another government agency, the Korea Deposit Insurance Corporation, or KDIC. The team would report to Chairman Lee of the FSC, in addition to its usual boss, the Minister of Finance and Economy. I learned from Ambassador Hyun that the government side had decided that Noh could not handle the transaction. The head of the KDIC team had joined the Lehman Brothers roadshow for the aborted Hanvit offering, and our friends at Lehman told us he was a very reasonable man.

Meanwhile, we carefully monitored the Korean press to see how the deal announcement was being received. The local reaction was mixed, as I reported in a memo to Blum and Bonderman:

> *It applauds the deal but criticizes the FSC for having sold "too cheap."*
> *Lee had to come out to defend the transaction. The international reaction, as expected, is all positive, as is the stock market. Korea Exchange Bank went up 12% yesterday, the first day of trading since the announcement and bank stocks went up 3% in general. The KFB deal has become a national pastime and we also need to help the other side to continuously sell the deal to the public.*

The fact that we would be working with the KDIC was a welcome change. The KDIC had been modeled after the U.S. Federal Deposit Insurance Corporation (FDIC), which was created by the 1933 Banking Act during the Great Depression, to restore trust in the American banking system. Like the FDIC, the KDIC insured retail deposits so that people who kept their money in the bank could get it back, within certain limits, even if the bank failed. When the KDIC bailed out retail depositors of a failed bank, it effectively became the bank's new owner. KDIC was 100 percent owned by the Korean government and therefore was regarded as a government agency. The head of KDIC reported to the Minister of Finance and Economy.

The KDIC had been founded in 1996 with a mandate to protect depositors and maintain the stability of the financial system. It began its operations as a deposit insurer on January 1, 1997, collecting its first deposit insurance premiums only on April 30 that year. That summer, the Asian Financial Crisis hit, and many banks failed, including, of course, KFB. For KDIC's finances, the timing of its birth could not have been unluckier. All the money KDIC had to dole out came from taxpayers, as KDIC was called upon to start paying out before it had collected meaningful amounts of deposit insurance premiums. It was like a new insurance company starting up business and writing a policy to cover all future hurricane damages for the entire nation, the day before the storm of the century hit.

★ ★ ★

It was only after the signing of the TOI that I noticed the change of weather. The summer heat had dissipated, giving way to the cool breeze of the autumn. It was the best season to run in the mountains, as leaves began to change color, presenting a splendid view of green, yellow, and red at every turn.

On September 29, 1999, we held an all-parties meeting at the office of KDIC. I counted 40 participants there, including representatives of KDIC, the FSC, KAMCO, KFB, and the advisors on both sides of the transaction. KAMCO was the Korea Asset Management Company, essentially the government-owned "bad bank," which had been created to buy bad loans and assets. At the meeting, we discussed a timetable and the work required prior to closing the transaction, which we aimed to complete by the end of November.

Both sides agreed to the timetable and promised to work hard to finalize the deal as soon as possible. We briefly discussed the disposal of KFB's New York branch. Under the Bank Holding Act of the United States, a bank holding company was not permitted to engage in non-banking businesses. If Newbridge became owners of KFB while the bank had U.S. branches, we would be considered a bank holding company for the purposes of the U.S. law. But the law prohibited a private equity firm from becoming a bank holding company. For this reason, we had no choice but to shut down or otherwise dispose of KFB's branches in the United States before we closed the deal. Shutting down KFB's New York branch was of little economic consequence to the bank, as the business volume there was insignificant and, if necessary, the bank could turn the branch into a finance subsidiary, which would be permitted by the law. The difference between a bank branch and a finance company owned by a bank is that the branch is licensed to take retail deposits whereas a finance company is not. But by the estimates of our U.S. counsel, disposing of the branch would mostly likely delay the closing of the transaction.

After months of tough negotiations and heated arguments with Noh's FSC team, we were pleased to discover that the KDIC team was friendly and cooperative, even though they were not exactly sure what they were supposed to do at the beginning. BS Kang, who was the only representative from the FSC at the meeting, greeted us, and we chatted with each other like old friends. Eric Yoon of White & Case was also there. Many times over the course of the deal, I had felt like reaching across the table and strangling him. He had acted in ways we thought were unreasonable and at times seemed to be forcefully pulling his client away from the table. But now that the binding TOI was behind us, he seemed a different person. He made a point of approaching me after the meeting. "Shan, I've got my marching orders to get the deal done," he told me. We held no grudges against him, as we knew he was trying to be protective of his clients, even if he wound up being overprotective to the point of obstruction.

I had been trying to discuss the KFB transition plan with Chairman Lee ever since we'd signed the TOI, but after 10 days I was still not successful in setting up a meeting with him. After the all-parties meeting, Kang urged me not to wait for Lee but to discuss the transition plan with the KDIC's executive director, Dong-jun Paeng. He emphasized that the FSC would be supportive. I was delighted that our tough-negotiating counterparty had now turned into an old friend. Everyone on the government side seemed as motivated as we were to get the deal done. What a difference a binding document made!

★ ★ ★

While both sides negotiated, KFB continued to hemorrhage cash. The binding TOI was signed not a moment too soon. The bank lost a staggering 4.23 trillion won, or about $3.5 billion, in 18 months. To put things in perspective, the total assets of the bank had fallen to less than $30 billion by then, and approximately $1 billion of equity was required to recapitalize it. A recap was essential. Without it, the bank was paralyzed and would rapidly lose its franchise value. It needed a quick cleanup of its bad loans and an injection of fresh equity. The opponents who objected to letting us control the bank had missed the larger point: If radical action was not taken, this bank was simply going to disappear.

The National Assembly had begun its session, and a major topic of discussion was the KFB sale. That was why Chairman Lee was too busy to meet with me; he was called before the National Assembly to answer lawmakers' questions about the deal with Newbridge. There continued to be talk in the local press about KFB being sold too cheaply, which seemed to be the journalists' focus.

From the experience of the last several months, we knew that the Korean press would likely criticize and obsess over this deal for a long while. We and the government needed to win them over. We interviewed a number of PR firms in the hope of engaging one as soon as possible to help us, and the government was working hard to explain why the deal would benefit the Korean economy and taxpayers. In an interview with the *Korea Times*, Bong-kyun Kang, the Minister of Finance and Economy, defended the KFB transaction and tried to clarify the misunderstanding regarding the disproportionate injection of capital by the government and by Newbridge: the trillions of won that the government put into the bank had been used to pay back depositors, whereas the new capital invested by Newbridge (and the government) was to recapitalize the bank. Kang also reminded people that the government was going to receive 49 percent of the upside after Newbridge turned the bank around.

Despite this, the Korean press relentlessly compared the amount of capital the government injected into KFB with the amount of capital we would invest. But that was the wrong comparison. Yes, the capital injected by the government dwarfed what we were going to put in, but the critics overlooked the fact that the bank had lost a vast amount of money before Newbridge had come onto the scene. Depositors had entrusted KFB with their money, which had been insured by the government. The public funds were being used to repay those depositors, not to benefit Newbridge. Our investment was like spending $1 million to buy a warehouse that had lost some valuable diamonds for which the insurance company had paid the diamond owners $100 million. The value of the warehouse had no relation to the amount of compensation paid by the insurance company. But many Korean commentators and the public did not understand the difference and focused only on the difference between how much taxpayer money the government used to shore up the bank and how much the foreign investor would invest in the bank itself. They also appeared to ignore the fact that Newbridge was bringing in sound risk management practices, which would prevent similar depository losses in the future.

The public's fixation on the KFB transaction was understandable. After all, the government bailout used taxpayer money, and the public had every right to make sure it was not misused or squandered. We shared this concern and continued to feel that the best way to prevent additional waste was to bring in world-class banking practices, including a strong credit culture, and to restructure and reform Korea's moribund banking system. The significance of the KFB transaction went far beyond the sale of the bank and the foreign capital it brought into the country.

We spent a lot of time managing public relations in the weeks following the signing of the TOI. I met with numerous journalists, both Korean and Western, to get our message across. In early October, at the request of the Blue House, I held a press conference to explain the deal and answer questions from the media. Before a roomful of reporters, I addressed a few major issues of concern, including the transaction timetable, the new management team, and the question of whether there would be layoffs.

"We are working very closely with the Korean regulatory authorities to finish up the documentation," I said, adding that the process was expected to be completed by the last week of November, although it might take longer. As for management, I explained that we intended to put together a team of foreign and Korean executives from among the best in the banking industry. For KFB's CEO, I hinted that we had someone in mind, a Westerner with long experience in banking and "a strong comprehension of Korean business and culture," but I couldn't disclose the name before the transaction was completed.

On the question of layoffs, I told the reporters that they would be up to KFB's new management, although I tried to downplay the possibility of major employee reductions. "We think the size of this bank is just about right," I said.

Finally I reiterated that Newbridge's primary goal was to turn KFB into the best player in the domestic banking industry once again, and I tried to dismiss the criticism that the government had sold the bank at too low a price. "Korea made a good deal," I said.

The press coverage of my briefing was uniformly positive, which also pleased the Blue House, according to the ambassador. It seems that the press, at least some of them, accepted my explanation for why the deal was a fair and good one for Korea. Meanwhile, Chairman Lee and the head of the KFB, Shee-yul Ryoo, were also making a forceful defense of the deal. What a difference it felt to have the government behind us!

Bonderman, however, was more cautious. He sent me a note on October 8 that read:

> Shan,
>
> I saw the newspaper article and I understand why we need to take an affirmative campaign to the press, however, I think it is quite risky to say that we are going to close by any specific date since it is not within our control and even riskier to speculate on the new CEO since we don't have a clue who that will be. I think you need to be more cautious on this stuff.

I understood his concern, but under the circumstances, I could not respond to reporters' questions with a terse "no comment" if we wanted to achieve our PR objectives. The purpose of the press conference was to address reporters' inquiries as best I could so I made sure to answer questions to the extent of my knowledge without being specific about the things yet to be finalized.

It was true that both parties agreed to target closing at the end of November, although I also cautioned the audience that the date might slip due to technical reasons, including the disposal of KFB's U.S. branch. It was also true that we had a CEO candidate in mind, a senior executive at GE Capital, and we were conducting a broad search for other potential candidates. I was quite certain we had to bring in a CEO from outside of Korea. If I had evaded these two questions, there would be endless speculation and we would risk looking either somewhat clueless or too secretive about our plans.

★ ★ ★

The announcement of the binding TOI greatly boosted KFB employees' morale. They now had hope for a bright new future. Ryoo, the bank's chairman and president, sent an upbeat and motivating message to all employees on September 20, 1999. After thanking them for their hard work restoring the bank's business through difficult times, he shared his optimism about the bank's future and reassured his team that with an injection of new capital and the arrival of a skilled new management team, better days were ahead for KFB.

I really liked and respected Ryoo, who had done his best to stabilize the bank and its workforce and took tough measures to restore its health under extremely difficult circumstances. The bank continued to suffer huge losses from its historical bad loans, but Ryoo did what he could, and all of our team members who had met him were impressed with him. Another person might have sat on his hands and waited for the government bailout, as it was hopeless trying to dig the bank out of this hole on his own.

I thought we should retain him as chairman, even though everyone within the bank, in the government, and in the market expected us to replace him. When I floated the idea with my partners, they all agreed with me.

On October 5, I sat down with Ryoo and informed him that Newbridge would like him to stay on as chairman. Ryoo was surprised—although pleasantly so, I thought. He noted that the public would expect a new face at KFB. I explained that we would, of course, appoint a new CEO, who would have ultimate control and responsibility for the bank, but we hoped that Ryoo would be willing to stay on to help manage the internal and external relationships. Ryoo responded that he would need time to think before accepting the offer.

We also discussed a few other transition matters. I informed him that Newbridge would be sending in a transition team, headed by a transition CEO. In addition to members selected by Newbridge, the team would have representatives from the FSC and the KDIC. I also asked Ryoo to have the bank set up a special task force of its own, which would report directly to the transition team and the chairman.

For the special task force, I recommended that we put Won-kyu Choi in charge. During our initial campaign to get the MOU signed a year before, Choi had impressed me with his intelligence and integrity. He spoke fluent English and had been very supportive of the deal. I thought he was a good conduit for communication between the transition team and the bank's employees. However, he had fallen out of favor within the bank during our heated negotiations over the summer, and I suspected it was because of his support for the deal. Formerly the head of KFB's privatization team, Choi had been demoted and was now toiling as the manager of a seven-person bank branch. I wanted him reinstated to a corporate-level position where his skills would be put to good use.

Thankfully, Ryoo did not object to putting Choi in charge of the task force. Quite to the contrary; he immediately instructed his executive vice president to notify Choi to form the special task force. Ryoo also gave me a frank and succinct summary of his views on the rest of the senior management team. I told him that I would be happy to share ideas with the new CEO, who would be responsible for forming a management team of his own.

Later that day, my colleague Steve Lim and I went to meet with Dong-jun Paeng, the executive director of the KDIC and head of the organization's group working on the KFB deal. After an hour's discussion we tentatively agreed on the transition team's marching orders. Newbridge would appoint two or three members to the team, including the transition CEO and a head of credit. The KDIC would also appoint two or three people, while the FSC would send an observer. We expected that the team would be given some level of control over operations within the bank, primarily regarding lending and credit. In most cases, this would mainly be *negative control*, or oversight—for example, deciding not to approve a particular loan, so there would be no argument about loans made before close being subject to the government guarantee. At least nominally, major decisions would be made by the joint team. This was both to minimize Newbridge's liability and to avoid legal complications if we were to be viewed as having taken control of KFB before we'd been able to dispose of the New York branch.

★ ★ ★

It had been agreed to by the parties at the time of the MOU that our side would draft the transaction documents. There were three major ones. The first was the assistance agreement, which would detail the assistance provided by the government to KFB as part of the transaction.

This included, among other things, our right to put bad assets back to the government and the government's payment in terms of government notes to the bank for the bad assets and loans to be transferred to the government. The second was the acquisition agreement, which set forth the terms and conditions under which Newbridge would invest in and acquire a majority ownership of KFB. The third was the shareholders' agreement, which would govern the relationship between Newbridge and the various government agencies, including the KDIC, the FSC, and the Ministry of Finance and Economy, which would all be shareholders of KFB.

These agreements would be written on the basis of the TOI. Where the TOI was only a couple of dozen pages, the definitive documents were expected to be hundreds of pages in length. It took almost a month for our lawyers at Cleary Gottlieb to draft them with the help of Kim & Chang and for the Newbridge team to review the drafts before we delivered them to KDIC. The Newbridge team, including me, reviewed every page, word by word, to make sure all our terms were accurately reflected. After we had sent the documents to the KDIC team, we expected them to do the same.

I was also quite satisfied with how our search for a transition leader was shaping up. Bob Barnum and I had spoken with Steve Hajtun, the CEO of GE Capital Finance, about coming on as the transition team leader, and both he and GE Capital Asia Pacific were very supportive of the arrangement, although he hadn't yet given us a firm answer. Meanwhile, Barnum had been spending a lot of time speaking with different KFB team members and advisors about their work. Chairman Ryoo had also decided to accept our offer to stay on as KFB chairman, although he asked us to keep that confidential until we had announced the new CEO. It seemed that everyone was united in our efforts to revamp KFB and make it an internationally respected institution.

Unfortunately, some legal issues soon arose to complicate matters. About a week after my last transition update to the team, I had to write again to say that it looked as if we might not need a transition team leader after all. Doing so could lead U.S. regulators to consider Newbridge as having crossed from a role of oversight to one of direct control. Even the idea of adding a new credit officer, our lawyers feared, would be an indication, from a legal perspective, that Newbridge had taken control of the bank. "We probably cannot begin to implement anything before the close," I reported. But this didn't stop me from thinking ahead. I thought that Hatjun would make a great interim CEO, in case we didn't have a permanent CEO in place by the time the definitive documents were signed.

This was followed by more bad news. Ryoo informed me that he would not be remaining as chairman after all. He had been elected chairman of the Korea Federation of Banks, which was a full-time job that prohibited him from holding another position. Ryoo expressed his regret, and we contacted our headhunters to let them know that we would also be searching for a chairman.

★ ★ ★

Of all the work streams, the most important was the documentation of definitive agreements. This was a massive amount of work, involving negotiations between representatives of the KDIC and Newbridge and also between the lawyers on both sides. Even though the TOI served as a basis for the final agreements, the documentation process was like turning a book outline into a real book. Imagine the thorny process of two proud co-authors who must agree with each other on every word. Now imagine if each author also had to consult a team of editors and assistants who also had to agree. That was quite a bit what our discussions were like.

The transaction was extraordinarily complex because it involved not just a sales and purchase agreement between two parties but a complex government assistance program that had to treat various classes of the bank's assets differently and also anticipate every possible contingency.

To do this, both sides were assisted by a large team of lawyers and advisors. There were four law firms involved: Cleary Gottlieb and Kim & Chang on the Newbridge side, and White & Case and Lee & Ko, another well-known Korean firm, on the government side.

We received the KDIC's changes to the draft documents about three weeks after we had delivered them. While the government's markups weren't as bad as I'd feared, there were a number of issues we would need to contend with. A few days later, Paul Chen and I went to Kim & Chang to meet with our lawyers there, as well as Rich Lincer of Cleary Gottlieb. After five hours discussing the KDIC's requested changes, we came away with the impression that their requests were "largely manageable."

Five days later, on November 14, Lincer sent through a memo that made me think otherwise. He sent me a list of issues identified at a meeting between all four law firms, and he included notes on each side's responses. It was 28 pages long, which was a grim sign. Lincer's message also predicted that we would once again return to an arduous negotiation process:

> Overall, I would observe that, while the discussions were generally cordial and constructive in tone, it is clear from them that the lawyers are going to have to check back with the KDIC before making concessions on even the most minor of issues and that, in addition to some very fundamental business issues, it is clear that the KDIC is going to read the TOI very strictly and therefore has not been at all receptive where we have tried to introduce provisions to fill in the gaps in the TOI that are consistent with the spirit of the TOI. Therefore, our sessions next week (and undoubtedly thereafter) are going to be quite tedious and progress may be slower than we would like.

It seemed, once again, that we still had a long and difficult road ahead of us.

* * *

Quite unexpectedly, I received an urgent message on Friday, November 12, alerting me to an article in the *Korea Times*. The newspaper had obtained a copy of a study by Bain & Company, our consultant, recommending 1,000 KFB employee layoffs. The report was authentic, but we had long ago decided not to follow its recommendations, which was why in my October 5 press conference, I'd said the size of KFB's workforce was "about right." It would be a blow to our credibility, as well as to the morale of KFB employees, if this layoff number were mistakenly reported as Newbridge's secret plan.

We needed to contain this story before it caused damage that would be nearly impossible to repair. The *Korea Times* article had already been posted to the paper's newswire and was destined for the next day's paper. I felt a rising sense of panic thinking about the consequences of this going to print.

I called Hyung-min Kim, the *Korea Times* reporter who wrote the article, with whom I had a good rapport. I told him the Bain report was old and that we had rejected its suggestion for layoffs, asking him to withdraw the article because it would be misleading. The paper had already typeset the pages, and it would be a hassle to remove and replace the article. But after a long conversation, I was able to persuade him to do so.

Phew, I thought. We had averted a major PR disaster.

However, the *Korea Times* article on the wire caught the immediate attention of KFB employees. In spite of a retraction the paper subsequently issued, the KFB labor union issued a statement denouncing the "planned action" by Newbridge Capital. This was unfortunate and needed to be managed before it spiraled out of control.

I invited Chang-lim Lee, the head of KFB's union, and his deputy, KS Choi, to lunch in the Korean restaurant of the Westin Chosun Hotel on November 18. My colleague Steve Lim went with me to help translate and take notes. Lee and I had met several months earlier, while Newbridge and the FSC were still locked in negotiations over the TOI. Our interview had even been published in the union newsletter. In general, I found the union leader to be a reasonable man with a strong sense of responsibility to his members. But as we talked, it became clear that while my objective was to get him to promise to talk with us before taking any action, his objective was to get me to commit to not laying off any employees. Our conversation went like a tug-of-war, but we managed to find common ground.

"Frankly speaking," I told Lee, "the union's distribution of the recent statement was somewhat irresponsible because it was based on the *Korea Times'* mistake rather than actual facts. The *Korea Times* admitted the mistake and corrected the article in the final version. We had met each other before. If you had talked with me before taking the action, I could have answered your questions with facts."

Lee replied that while he knew my stated policy and had read or heard it several times through the press, he suspected that the *Korea Times* article was not completely groundless. After all, it was based on a report produced by one of our own advisors.

"Our statement was a call for you to clarify, to explain what the facts are and what is really going to happen," he told me. "It is fortunate I can ask you for clarification today."

"It's unfortunate that we weren't able to meet before your statement," I responded. Newbridge considers the union as an equal partner, I told him. "You should have checked with us first. Going forward," I said, "Newbridge and the union have two options: One, ignore each other and we communicate directly with employees. Or two, trust each other and work together as partners."

"I hope we can work as partners," I suggested. "It won't help if you take a confrontational approach."

Lee demurred. The union had never dealt with a foreign party before, he pointed out. "But in our past experience with the management, we have been betrayed many times." The union leader wasn't looking for more words of assurance. What he needed, he said, was a guarantee. "We feel that it is Newbridge's responsibility to show real trustworthiness beyond just words."

"We accept that your statement regarding the need to trust each other is fair," I responded. But trust had to be built over time. I needed them to commit to working with us, at the very least, starting from this moment. "Before discussing further," I said, "the two sides need to agree on what kind of a relationship we are going to have, now and in the future."

Lee appreciated this. But he still pushed for a guarantee. "Talk is just one part of moving toward resolution," he said. "As an example, even if South Korea receives a promise from North Korea that it won't attack, South Korea will still keep up its defenses in the event that the enemy will renege on its word."

"Please don't compare us to North Korea," I said. "We should not regard each other as enemies."

"Between capitalists and labor there are always lines which divide the two," Lee said. Finally, he pointed out: "This has all been caused by the Bain report. If the report is not true, the union needs a kind of guarantee."

"Can you commit to speaking with us before taking any action from now on?" I asked.

Yes, the union leader agreed. He could commit to that.

Then I told him a story of my own experience as a brick maker in China's Gobi Desert. (For details, please see my book *Out of the Gobi: My Story of China and America*, published in 2019 by Wiley.) In order to improve our productivity, I desperately wanted to find capital to alleviate the pain of our hard labor. As a laborer, I would have welcomed the chance to work with capital, I told him. But I was not so fortunate. "Only by capital and labor working together could we maximize each other's value," I said.

The irony was not lost on me that I, a former hard laborer, was now representing capital, negotiating with the leader of a labor union. I had a strong sense of empathy for the union and found it fairly easy to connect and work with it. Much of the money we invested, I told Lee, was on behalf of pension funds for employees of companies and government organizations around the world. Between labor and capital, it was not a zero-sum game. If we did not build a strong bank together, we would lose our capital and they would lose their jobs. But if we did build a strong bank, we would share in the fruits. I knew the union leaders and the employees had already made sacrifices to preserve the institution. I truly believed that we could and should work as partners.

I had to leave in a hurry for a meeting with the KDIC, but Lee and I agreed to meet again. My colleague Steve Lim stayed behind to finish lunch with the two union leaders. He told me later that Lee and his colleague talked between themselves after I left. Before our meeting they had intended to send another strong statement. After our meeting they decided to cancel it. I was glad that I had taken the time to establish trust and build the relationship.

Chapter 13

The Final Sprint

We began the negotiation on the definitive documents with the KDIC at 2 pm on Thursday, November 18, in an all-hands meeting at their offices, exactly one month after our lawyers delivered the first draft to them. By now both parties had outlined the issues that we needed to resolve. Dong-il Kim, a senior officer who reported directly to Executive Director Dong-jun Paeng, was the only representative of the KDIC in the meeting. Eric Yoon of White & Case did most of the talking. Indeed, most of the discussion was between the lawyers representing the two sides. For the most part, the principals just listened. The atmosphere was friendly and the discussion constructive—but it was clear that this would be the first of several meetings needed to get us to the close.

In this first meeting, we went through all the outstanding issues one by one, and for most of them we did not reach a conclusion. The Daewoo loans, which included loans to dozens of subsidiaries of Daewoo Group, were KFB's largest problem loans, so they were a major focus of discussion. Some Daewoo subsidiaries were faring better than others, though credit support for Daewoo as a group had collapsed. What would we do with a Daewoo loan that was still performing but went bad after the closing of our transaction?

213

Our proposal was that if the work-out of a Daewoo loan happened after the closing, we would have the right to transfer it to the government, as we could all other nonperforming loans. However, the government side wanted us to treat Daewoo loans differently from other corporate loans, both because of their total size and because of the company's position in the Korean economy. Yoon proposed categorizing the transfer to the government of Daewoo restructured or work-out loans as "special transfer events," which would be treated differently from all other transfers. But there was much debate, without conclusion, as to how to treat them. We adjourned without agreement at 10:30 pm, after eight and a half hours locked in KDIC's conference room.

The next day, Friday, November 19, we all met again. This time we shifted the venue to a more spacious conference room at KFB's head office. I was pleased to find the atmosphere remained friendly and relaxed even as we worked through our contested points. The two KDIC team leaders, Dong-il Kim and Jong-tae "JT" Kim, were professional, dedicated, and reasonable. We even called each other by our first names, which was unusual in a Korean business setting and had never happened before with the FSC team. They also had a good sense of humor, which made the long negotiation and working session much more bearable. Talking was mixed with laughter as both sides cracked jokes as we went along. What a change from the days of negotiating with the FSC team.

We began the meeting at 9 am and worked late into the evening. There were many issues left to resolve, but the vast majority were technical and legal so they needed to be handled by our respective lawyers. I sat without saying much and, at 10:30 pm, as progress slowed, I suggested we adjourn. To my surprise, many on both sides of the table wanted to continue. I did not see the point of exhausting everyone needlessly now because we were not on a tight deadline, so I convinced the others to call it a night.

"It seems that the KDIC is genuinely interested in completing the process as soon as possible," I wrote in a memo summarizing our two days of discussions. "In making an effort to do so, they try to stick to the TOI. We have more trouble with issues on which the TOI is silent. Where the TOI is not explicit, KDIC people confess that their authority is limited and they need to go back to discuss with the FSC before they can get back to us. As a result, we have tabled a number of issues until Monday next week. However, this will not delay the re-drafting process which has begun." While there were still some major issues, and many smaller technical issues, to resolve, I was confident we'd be able to do so within the next couple of days.

We met again on Saturday, November 20, and devoted the entire day to Daewoo loans, working straight through from 9 am to about 11 pm. But it was not until Sunday, November 21, that we reached agreement on the issue, as I reported in an internal memo "Daewoo Becomes Our Best Credit." It turned out that all the Daewoo loans were either non-performing or restructured to forgive some principal and interest. While Newbridge had the right to put those to the government before closing, we instead agreed to keep them under specific terms.

Under the agreed-upon terms, the KDIC would treat the Daewoo loans like any other nonperforming loans that KFB would keep, and all the nonperforming loans would be protected by the KDIC for potential losses in both principal and interest after closing. I explained:

> The negotiation is conducted in a friendly and business-like manner, alternately tense and relaxed and punctuated by jokes from either side (Eric Yoon's upcoming wedding and honeymoon and how it might interfere with the deal were the main targets). . . . With the government guarantee, these bad loans became good loans because the ultimate credit was the government. Under these conditions, we were happy to keep them.

The arrangement for Daewoo loans would be beneficial for both sides. The hope was that, over time, some of them would work out if the borrowing entities recovered, and therefore the cost to the government would be less than if we had to put them to the government immediately. Under the same principles and conditions, the KDIC asked if we would keep all the work-out or restructured loans that we had the right to put to the government before closing. I explained in the same memo:

> The KDIC wants us to keep work-out loans currently classified as non-performing loans, admitting that the FSC did not know some of the workouts were classified as non-performing loans at the time of negotiating the TOI. I said we would do so provided they were treated the same way as the remainder of Daewoo loans, i.e., the KDIC paying for our provisioning or buying on the first classification date, and [the loans]

*carrying a yield of government note rate plus something around 238
basis points (to cover the opportunity [cost in the form of] "lost interest margin," as we could have re-deployed the capital to create similar
amount of loans in the case of replacing these non-performing loans with
government notes). The KDIC pointed out, correctly, that if it agrees to
our proposal, it might have to buy back all of these if we substantially
over-reserve.*

The Korean government and Newbridge had agreed in the TOI to
the buy/sell arrangement by which KFB would have the right to name the
price of a classified or nonperforming loan and the government side would
have the option to either pay the impairment value (i.e., the difference
between the face value of the loan and the price named by KFB) or buy
the loan at face value plus accrued interest. KFB would set aside reserves,
or provisions, for the impairment value to be paid by the government.
The KDIC's worry was that we might over-reserve for a loan, which
meant we would claim an amount of impairment greater than what it
actually was. If we did so, we would in effect force the government to buy
the loan. For example, if the actual impairment was 30 cents on the dollar
but we claimed it was 40 cents, the government would have no choice
but to buy the loan at 100 cents because it would be better off doing so
and selling it for 70 cents—losing only 30 cents— than paying the 40 cents
we claimed.

This worry was ill founded, though, because there was no economic
reason for KFB to over-reserve any loans. A bank would always want to
keep a good interest-yielding loan and a customer; therefore, it would
have no incentive to lose the loan by forcing the KDIC to buy it. It was as
if we were homeowners buying fire insurance. Most people (most normal
people, anyway) don't take out a policy on their homes intending to burn
them down and collect the insurance money. I was confident that the
KDIC would understand it the same way.

It appeared at that point that the timetable was likely to slip into
December, in spite of the effort by both sides to move as fast as possible,
but I was happy that our counterparts at the KDIC were as anxious to
keep things moving as we were. We worked with the KDIC team for
long hours every day, day after day. Although the work was intensive
and exhausting, we were making good progress. The KDIC team was

reasonable and cooperative, quite unlike our experiences with the FSC team, and we made every effort to accommodate them. But the pace was still slower than any of us desired.

On Wednesday, November 24, we met at KFB for a whole day, from dawn to dusk. Maybe because we had resolved all the easy issues and those remaining were the hard ones, we made no progress, despite best efforts by both sides. Ambassador Hyun suggested that we let BM Park negotiate with the KDIC team in Korean, which he thought would be more efficient, as it would be easier for both parties to understand each other. I thought it was a good idea but said we needed to reach an internal consensus on the issues and mark up the draft documents before Park could negotiate on our behalf.

Reaching consensus internally was a major effort. Because some of our team members and lawyers were based in the United States, we had to hold conference calls at night, Seoul time, to discuss the draft agreements. These calls could go on for hours. On both November 29 and 30, we began the call at about 8:30 or 9 pm and ended in the wee hours of the morning. I was still getting up and going for a run every morning, although sometimes I had to cut my running time in half. Running was the best, and often the only, time in the day for me to think uninterruptedly about various issues and to plot our strategy.

Park spent two days in negotiations with the KDIC team, but there was limited progress. We subsequently had another all-hands meeting, which resolved some issues, but many still remained. Only when Park went out for dinner with the KDIC team that night did we seem to achieve some breakthroughs.

Our team made decisions much faster than the KDIC side. I gathered that our counterparty was taking more time to make up their minds because they were concerned about making costly and irreversible mistakes. I came up with an idea to possibly allay their concerns and to enable them to make decisions more quickly. I suggested to the KDIC team that we would not mind if they retracted their decisions if they later thought they had made a mistake; meanwhile, our side would keep our word for whatever we proposed.

My thinking was based on my own personal experience buying gifts for my wife, Bin. When we lived in the United States, she often returned gifts to the store if she did not like them. But my poor taste never bothered either of us, because in the United States refunds and exchanges were commonplace. I stopped buying her gifts once we moved to Hong Kong, where general store policy seemed to be that every sale was final, with no refund or exchange. It would not bring her much happiness if I bought something she did not like and couldn't return, which happened more often than not.

I thought if we provided the KDIC team with a "full-refund" policy, so it would not have to think too hard about making a decision, our negotiation process would move faster. I explained to the KDIC team that our principle was to be fair, reasonable, and logical with what we proposed. If they accepted any terms we had proposed and later discovered our proposal did not satisfy those tests, they could withdraw their agreement. Full refund.

The full-refund policy seemed to make a difference, but maybe it was the timing. All the issues had now been thoroughly discussed between the parties. Either way, the negotiation process began to pick up pace.

Thursday, December 9, was an unusually nice winter day in Seoul, and I could see bright sunshine through the windows sitting in the conference room in the KDIC's office. We met with the KDIC team for a whole day, from 10 in the morning until about 9 in the evening, and we managed to resolve many issues related to both legal and commercial points.

By the end of the day on Friday, December 10, I thought we were close to resolving all the major issues and expected to sign the documents on December 20.

★ ★ ★

However, as old issues were resolved, new issues popped up.

On the night of December 15, JT Kim of the KDIC and I were locked in a heated debate on the methodology of calculating present value for the purpose of determining the book value of a loan. We spent two hours arguing with each other, as the rest of the teams looked on without being able to chime in. At one point, JT accused me of lecturing. JT was a graduate of the Wharton School, where I was once a professor. If I sounded like I was lecturing, it was out of habit, not intention, as

I thought we were having an equal discussion. But I immediately caught myself and lowered my voice. In the end, I was able to persuade him to accept my methodology.

It was midnight when we adjourned the meeting. On our way back to the hotel, my colleague Daniel Poon, who was also a Wharton grad, told me that my methodology was wrong and JT's was right.

"Really?" I was surprised. "How?" I asked.

I saw where I had erred before Poon had finished his explanation. Poon was smart, and I trusted his judgment, especially when it came to numbers and calculations. When JT Kim and I had been arguing, even though I was listening, my mind was biased against him, which led me to hear him without really listening. When Poon explained, my mind was more receptive, and I immediately saw the logic.

"Why didn't you point it out and correct me during the meeting?" I asked him.

"Well, I didn't want to embarrass the professor," he said.

I wasn't embarrassed, but I did feel regret. If I had given JT Kim the benefit of the doubt, we would not have wasted so much time. In the end he had probably agreed with me out of deference, or maybe exhaustion, as opposed to being really persuaded.

This, however, gave me an opportunity to implement my full-refund policy. When we went back to the meeting the next day, I apologized to JT and accepted his methodology.

I had hoped to go back to Hong Kong on Thursday, December 16. It was the last week before Christmas, and there were many holiday events planned. Newbridge's office Christmas party was scheduled for Friday the 17th, and most importantly, my daughter LeeAnn would be performing in a hand-bell recital that evening. I never wanted to miss any of the major events in our children's lives and desperately wanted to return to Hong Kong, but I could not. There were too many issues remaining, and we had to concentrate our efforts to resolve them. The negotiation ground on slowly.

On Saturday, when we were in heated discussion on what to do with a subsidiary of KFB in China, Doing-il Kim became upset. He abruptly stood up and left the room. But he soon returned, and we found a solution to the issue. That was the only flare-up in our entire negotiating process with the KDIC, but it went as quickly as it came and there were no hurt feelings on either side.

We worked so hard that there was no time to stop and go out for a meal. We had pizza delivered to us in the KDIC office for lunch and dinner three days straight.

★ ★ ★

As one part of our team was intensively working on the definitive documents with the KDIC, Dan Carroll was working with the head-hunters to search for a CEO. A few months back we had identified a qualified candidate who was in Asia, waiting on the sidelines to step into the position, but as the negotiation dragged on, it remained unclear that we would ever succeed in acquiring the bank. He could not wait around for a job that might not materialize and had moved back to the United States with his family in July. Now we had to start again. Through Korn Ferry, a leading global executive search firm, we interviewed many candidates before finally selecting Wilfred Horie.

Horie was a vice president at Associates First Capital Corp. and president of its international operations. Associates was a leading U.S.-based consumer finance company that had been affiliated with Ford Motor Company. Horie had built Associates' business in Japan into the fifth-largest consumer finance business in the country. A third-generation American of Japanese descent, he had grown up in Hawaii and served in the U.S. Army Special Forces. Horie was as red-blooded an American as any I had met, and his extensive experience in consumer finance made him an excellent fit.

KFB was predominantly a corporate bank, with its business concentrated on lending to corporate customers. But that strength had led to its failure, because of the bank's exposure to a few large conglomerates. Our strategy was to transform KFB into a bank with a balanced exposure both to corporate customers and consumers, with more weight on retail banking, which was underdeveloped in South Korea.

Retail banking was the practically virgin territory. Common retail products like checking accounts, which were ubiquitous in the United States, were still almost unheard of in South Korea. People mostly transacted with cash or, rarely, with credit cards. The explosive growth of credit card use did not happen until a few years later. Retail banking also included mortgage or housing loans, which had until then largely been made by only one bank in Korea, the appropriately named Housing and Commercial Bank. In view of our strategy and the market potential, we needed someone who was familiar with retail banking.

Horie was not a traditional commercial banker by training, but his success in the consumer finance business meant he knew how to target retail customers. His expertise and experience aligned with where we wanted the bank to grow its business. We decided to appoint him as both chairman and CEO of the new KFB.

I did have some concern about Horie's Japanese ethnicity, because I was keenly aware of the deeply ambivalent and even hostile feelings many Korean people held toward Japan, which had repeatedly invaded Korea since the late 16th century and occupied it since about the end of the 19th century until 1945, when Japan surrendered to the Allied Forces. The Japanese colonial rule was known to be oppressive and brutal including enlisting or forcing Korean men and women into Japanese military service during World War II.

Many Koreans thought that Japan had never properly atoned for its brutality toward the Korean populace during colonial rule. I was a little worried about how the public might react to our appointment of a CEO with Japanese ancestry. There were, of course, many Japanese businesses operating in Korea, but KFB would be under extra scrutiny because of the bank's high profile. It was, after all, *Korea First* Bank. Also, taxpayers' money was involved. In the end, however, I thought the public, regulators, and KFB employees would probably care a lot more about us appointing the best CEO for the job than about his ethnic background.

The appointment of a bank's CEO required approval by banking regulators. On Wednesday, December 15, we submitted Horie's name to the FSC for its approval; we had planned to keep the name secret until the definitive agreements were signed. However, his name was leaked to the press and, by December 17, the major papers carried the story. All the headlines mentioned his Japanese ethnicity, which was obvious as his family name, Horie, was distinctly Japanese.

I received a call from Won-kyu Choi, now head of KFB's special transition task force. "Mr. Shan, are you guys going to appoint a Japanese to be CEO of Cheil Bank?" he asked in an exasperated voice.

The word *cheil* means "first" in Korean, and many Koreans referred to Korea First Bank as Cheil Bank. Before I was able to reply, he continued, "We are all going to quit! The entire management team will quit and many others will follow if you appoint a Japanese CEO. None of us are going to work for a Japanese." He was almost yelling.

I was shocked. We had unexpectedly triggered a major crisis.

"But he isn't Japanese. He is American!" I protested. "He was born and raised in America, and his family was all American for generations. He served as a member of the Special Forces of the U.S. Army. That is how American he is!"

Choi reluctantly accepted my explanation and acknowledged that his military service might have mitigated his "birth defects," but he warned me before hanging up, "You will have a problem. You will have a lot of explaining to do. You may have a lot of trouble convincing other people. I will have to think about this."

Choi's reaction made me realize that there would be much more trouble than I had anticipated. Thanks to the leak, we had lost the chance to present Horie to the public in the best light and were now in the awkward position of playing defense. We had been fighting xenophobic sentiment toward the acquisition of KFB by a "foreign investor" for over a year now. Appointing Horie was going to be perceived as adding insult to injury. The perception was unfair, but we could not fight it.

I quickly thought of a solution in Bob Barnum. At 53 years of age, Bob was a veteran banker and had served as CFO, COO, and president of American Savings Bank. Tall and distinguished looking, he was a straight talker who did not mince words. He had been an advisor to Newbridge throughout the deal process. We were all impressed with him and his banking knowledge and experience. All of our models and strategies benefited from his extensive input. We would have considered Barnum for the chairman and CEO position, but he was unwilling to relocate to Korea from his home in California. He was willing to serve as a board member, however. If we made Barnum chairman and Horie CEO, I thought, we could present two Americans at the top of the bank, shifting the focus away from Horie's ethnicity.

All the Newbridge team members agreed that we should invite Barnum to be KFB chairman. I called Bob to ask him. He did not say no, but neither did he say yes. He said he had to think about it. I knew it would take Bonderman to persuade him. I felt confident that, given their relationship, which dated back to American Savings Bank, Bonderman would be able to convince him—after all, Bonderman had invited Barnum to advise us on the transaction in the first place.

The next day Barnum called me. As soon as I picked up the phone, he said: "No fair bringing out the big guns!"

I knew Bonderman must have gotten through to him. I laughed and said, "We can't live without you."

★ ★ ★

All of us were keenly aware that Christmas was coming. I knew from the year before that Christmas was a big deal in Korea. It was a big deal in Hong Kong as well, and I was missing the festivities back home for the second year in a row. I did not want to spend another Christmas in Seoul. Our lawyers, advisors, and team members all wanted to go back to their families for Christmas. However, if we could not complete the transaction before the holidays, there would be no telling when we would be able to do it, if ever. Therefore, we were all strongly motivated to complete the work before Christmas. We had worked through many weekends. Now we had to work practically around the clock.

December 19 was a Sunday. The lawyers from both sides jointly produced a list of unresolved issues. During the day, both teams had internal meetings to understand the differences and to form our own positions.

After dinner, at around 8 pm, we resumed our all-hands meeting on the third floor of the Shilla Hotel. There was a strong desire by both sides to iron out our differences on all the remaining issues once and for all. As the clock ticked, I felt that it was not so much a test of endurance but a contest of patience. We almost forgot the time as we focused on our discussions. The KDIC team could win on patience, as it was still taking them much longer to make a decision, while the Newbridge team waited restlessly. But we were tied on endurance, as neither side asked to adjourn the meeting or even take a break. It was not until eight the next morning when we finally finished. We had spent 12 hours in that conference room in a single nonstop meeting, working overnight.

Even though we did not resolve all the issues, the all-nighter was productive. I slept for only three hours and was up again at 11 am on Monday, December 20. There were 10 remaining issues to settle, but I was relaxed. I felt that it would not be so difficult for us to find common ground on them. We met again at 9 pm and, within an hour, we had reached agreement on nine of the 10 issues. The last one was not significant enough for us to bother with at this stage, and I was confident we could compromise on it later.

We largely concluded our negotiations on the definitive documents on the night of December 20. Even though we knew new issues might pop up as the lawyers committed what we had agreed upon to paper, neither side expected any major ones. Now the lawyers had to work to revise the documents while reconciling their differences. They had already been revising the documents in real time as we negotiated. Throughout our discussions the lawyers on both sides were busy writing, without so much as raising their heads. But their work was more than just transcription; they also had to discuss and agree on the specific language on every page in these drafting sessions. That was a massive amount of work, and progress was painfully slow.

All of us from both sides were now camped out in the Shilla Hotel. Even the Koreans who lived in Seoul did not go home. We spent 24 hours a day in that hotel, to the delight, I was sure, of its management. We must have made their sales budget for the entire month that week. Not only did we stay there, we took over the entire business center for our meetings and drafting sessions. We also ate every meal there, ordering room service brought to the conference room.

It felt surreal to me that at any time, around the clock, any kind of food could be ordered just by picking up the phone. The Shilla had at least five restaurants and all sorts of Western and Asian cuisine. I remembered my days working as a hard laborer in China's Gobi Desert as a youth, starving and not knowing when the next meal would be. It was unthinkable to me that food could be so readily available at any time for so many people. I marveled aloud about it again and again. Finally, Paul Chen said to me, to the laughter of all: "Shan, stop. Only you feel this way. The rest of us don't give a damn. You aren't a peasant anymore. Just eat and gain some weight."

So much food, so taken for granted; I could not get over it.

★ ★ ★

Capital raising was one stream of work I had not anticipated. By 1999, we were investing Newbridge Capital's second fund, which had about $450 million to invest. Typically, a private equity fund would not put more than 20 percent of its total fund size into one transaction, to avoid what is called *concentration risk*. The idea is to spread the capital across multiple investments to minimize the downside if any one of them went south. Twenty percent of $450 million gave us about $90 million we could earmark for the KFB deal, which left us well short of the $500 million or so the transaction required. But Newbridge was affiliated with TPG, a much larger firm with a multi-billion-dollar fund, as well as with RCBA, Dick Blum's investment firm. I had never worried about having enough capital for the KFB deal.

For some reason, however, TPG could not invest in KFB, even though we knew many of our limited partners, as our investors were known, would be happy to invest with us. Carroll and TPG's investor relations office had begun to reach out to potential co-investors after we signed the TOI. The co-investors, of course, would have to go through their own due diligence process to evaluate the opportunity. That required much work on our side as well because we had to be ready to answer questions as they went through their own processes.

Our advisor, O'Hanlon, had relocated to Lehman's Tokyo office from New York City. He called to tell me that Masayoshi Son, chairman of SoftBank, might be interested in joining the KFB deal and would like to meet with me. By 1999, SoftBank was a high-flying company, having invested in numerous internet-related businesses, many of which had become worth billions of dollars in the stock market thanks to the dot-com bubble. Son was also interested in banks. Like me, Son was an alumnus of University of California at Berkeley. A mutual friend of ours once told me that Son had developed his long-term business plan while a student at Berkeley.

"Do you know how long his long-term plan was?" the friend asked me.

By the tone of his question, I knew it was very long. I ventured, "Twenty years?"

"No," he replied. "Three hundred years."

Well, Son was certainly longer term in his thinking than any other mortal I knew. It reminded me of a quote by the economist John Maynard Keynes: "In the long run, we are all dead." There is no denying, however, that winners in business are often visionaries.

I met with Son on Monday, December 20, in the Shilla Hotel, where he was also staying. I was happy to talk with him about KFB. I spent some time reviewing the deal and our plans for the bank. After I finished, Son said he was indeed interested in going in with us on the investment.

Knowing SoftBank was a Japanese company, I asked him if he thought there would be a political or public relations problem for us if we invited him to invest in KFB. He said that, to the contrary, his investment would be perceived positively. He gave me two reasons. First, President DJ Kim had invited him to invest in Korea many times, so his entry would be welcomed. Second, he said, he had Korean blood.

Son was Japanese, but he was of Korean descent. His family had adopted a Japanese surname, Yasumoto, but he decided to use his Korean surname upon returning to Japan after finishing his studies in the United States. I imagine he was respected in Korea for his Korean origin and for his success in business. I also thought it was ironic that many Koreans would have an issue with Horie, an American of Japanese descent, but the same people probably felt just fine with Son, a Japanese of Korean descent.

Son gave me a third reason why it would be good for us if he invested. He and his company could bring strategic value to KFB in areas like internet banking. I was persuaded and said to him that we would welcome his co-investment.

Then we proceeded to talk about how much he would invest. He said he had to invest no less than 30 percent of the capital required, or about $150 million, or he would not be interested. I was a little surprised but since I thought he would be a good partner, I said we would consider it. Then I explained that all the investors or limited partners would pay Newbridge, the general partner, a management fee and a share of any future profit, called *carried interest*, for managing the investment. That is how private equity firms make money. We only get paid our carried interest if we make money for investors.

Surprised, he looked at me and said, "People usually pay me for investing in their companies."

This was probably true. SoftBank was hot then. It seemed that whatever Son touched became an overnight success in the stock market, purely on the strength of SoftBank's endorsement. But we were not an internet company, nor did we have a publicly traded stock. We made money the old-fashioned way, by focusing on improving the cash flow and profitability of the companies we invested in.

I did not flinch. I looked at him and said, "I have to make a living."

He laughed. "You are good. You are good," he repeated and then said, "You will be very, very rich."

He then said the reason people paid him to invest with them was because the returns on his investments in the past couple of years had been between 500 and 1,000 percent. I knew he was right. This was the year before the dot-com bubble burst, and internet companies were scaling new heights in the stock market every day. Nonetheless, Son said he would consider making an exception.

I told him that I appreciated it and that he should also know I would be making an exception to charge him a reduced carry. He laughed again and repeated, "You are good."

We spent about two hours together. Before I left, he said he would need a night to think about the carry issue, and we agreed to meet again the next morning at eleven-thirty. The next day, Tuesday, December 21, I was working so intensively on the transaction documents that I completely forgot my appointment with Son until about noon. I am usually punctual and I felt a sense of panic when I realized that I was so late. Fortunately, Son was staying in the same hotel. I rushed upstairs to meet with him. I was relieved that he did not seem to notice my tardiness, probably because he was busy doing other things. We spent about half an hour together, negotiating how much of a discount in the carry we would give him, and we soon reached agreement. Quite unexpectedly, SoftBank became our largest limited partner in our KFB investment.

★ ★ ★

The lawyers worked on the documents nonstop through the night of December 20. They continued to work during the day and into the night of December 21. There were hundreds of pages to write, revise, reconcile, and finalize. There was little I could do to help with the drafting, but all of us were hanging around the conference rooms in the hotel's business center. Whenever issues came up and the lawyers could not resolve them by themselves, the two Kims of the KDIC and our team, sometimes with our respective lawyers, would sit down to resolve them. I met with Eric Yoon of White & Case, who had returned from his three-week honeymoon, and we were able to resolve the last of the 10 issues from the previous day. Whereas before the TOI, I had thought of Yoon as the bane of our existence, ever since the TOI was signed, he had been a delight to work with, now that our objectives were aligned.

I was able to get a few hours of sleep on the night of December 21. I went to the business center early the next morning to discover that, for the second night in a row, the lawyers had worked straight through. They looked exhausted, bent low over their computers, typing, with big stacks of paper by their sides, comparing and discussing drafts with each other. There was no time for a break because we needed to finish before tomorrow, our target day for the signing. But as the day turned dark, I was really worried how long they could continue; they had been at it for three days straight. What they were doing seemed humanly impossible.

As I watched them working away that night, I thought that the lawyers were heroes. They were literally killing themselves to get the work completed to meet our deadline. They were working so carefully and so meticulously, checking every paragraph, every sentence, every phrase, and every word, even though they were horribly sleep-deprived.

Years later, I ran into Rich Lincer, one of our key lawyers from Clearly Gottlieb, at a book party for my last book. We hadn't seen each other in more than 10 years. Rich had lost his full head of hair, although he looked not much older than when I had last seen him. He told me that he had lost his hair after many nights without sleep while working extremely hard on the Obama administration's bailout of General Motors in 2008–2009. His dedication really took a toll on him.

By dinnertime on December 22, lawyers on both sides, led by Lincer on our side and Yoon on their side, called a meeting with Dong-il Kim of the KDIC and me. They needed sleep, the lawyers told us. It would be impossible to get everything done by tomorrow morning. Lincer said that it was absurd to stick to the arbitrary December 23 timetable, as it was impossible to finish the job. The suggestion was to break for Christmas and resume the work afterward.

I felt torn. There was absolutely no question in my mind that the lawyers had reached their physical and mental limits, and actually were way beyond them, but I was also worried. I did not want to spend another Christmas in Seoul, as I had last year. But my main concern was that if we were to break now, we would likely not resume until after New Year's. That would mean lost momentum, and even a risk that if we stopped or slowed down, the deal might fall apart again. That was a risk we could not afford to take.

Of the three documents, the assistance agreement, arguably the most important as it involved the terms of assistance to be provided by the government to KFB, was still a long way from completion. How about if we sign the documents already completed? I suggested. We could leave the rest until after the holidays. That way, we would lock up the deal because at least one or two of the definitive agreements would be signed.

Lincer did not think it was a good idea. He warned me that we would be taking grave risks by signing some, but not all, of the documents. Poon agreed with him. I was not so sure. My prime motivation was to lock the other side into this deal so there could be no unraveling under any circumstances. I was willing to sign just one of the three agreements. I thought it was at least the second-best option if it was impossible to get all the documents done by the next day.

Coincidentally, I was scheduled to meet Horie for the first time for dinner that night. In anticipation of the signing of definitive agreements the next day, Horie had arrived in Seoul, and I was to introduce him to reporters at the signing ceremony. I had to prepare him for the event, but as soon as Paul Chen and I sat down with him in the hotel's Japanese restaurant, I received an urgent call from our colleague, Steve Lim. I was needed at the business center for a meeting with Dong-il Kim and the lawyers.

Dong-il Kim appeared to be more distressed than I was about the potential signing delay. He was deeply worried that tomorrow's sched-uled signing would have to be canceled. Furthermore, he was disturbed by a draft press release prepared by a Mr. Lee at Edelman, our PR firm, which denied that there would be a signing of the final agreements and an announcement tomorrow.

The FSC and MOFE had already leaked the joint press release I had prepared earlier, Dong-il told me, and had already approved the documents that we would sign tomorrow. From the government side, the signing *had* to happen as scheduled. It would be a huge loss of face and credibility if it did not. The draft press release denying that the signing would take place greatly disturbed him, as he thought that it was my official position.

I read through the draft release quickly, then slammed it down on the table and said firmly, to calm his nerves, "I didn't know anything about this denial. It wasn't my idea and we aren't going to use it."

That may have calmed Dong-il Kim, but I also knew we were at the end of our rope. None of us knew how to get the rest of the paperwork done in time for signing tomorrow. There was just no way. The lawyers would go on strike if we pushed them any further. I suggested that we break the meeting and separately think about a solution.

Lincer felt strongly that there was no way to get all the documentation done in time. The problem was that the KDIC's legal team was understaffed. While we had four lawyers from Cleary and three from Kim & Chang—seven in all—they had only three, Lee from Lee & Ko and Yoon and Philip Gilligan from White & Case. Every word in the documents had to be agreed upon by lawyers on both sides. Our team could take turns sleeping, but the KDIC's lawyers could not sleep at all. As of dinnertime, they had not even begun to work on the assistance agreement. Making matters worse, Yoon had been on his honeymoon since November 23 and was just getting up to speed. As the government's key lawyer, he did not know enough about the discussions of the past several weeks.

I took BM Park of Kim & Chang out for a walk around the hotel lobby. I wanted to know if he had any advice for me. He shared my fear that if the deal was not done by tomorrow, there remained a risk that it would fall apart. Lincer and Poon thought that if we signed only part of the agreement, there would be a risk the government could blame us if the deal eventually collapsed. Now my fear was that the government would blame us for the deal's failure if we did not get it done by tomorrow. That was why Dong-il Kim was so upset by the draft press release.

Chatting with Park, a bold and extremely unconventional idea hit me. The bottleneck was the KDIC legal team, which was not only under-staffed but also underinformed about what had been agreed to regarding the assistance agreement. What if we seconded one of our lawyers to work for the KDIC side? Park, standing in front of me, was the ideal candidate. Under normal circumstances, this idea would be considered ludicrous. After all, we were on the opposite side of the negotiating table with the KDIC. The KDIC might think we were proposing to send a fox to guard their henhouse. The idea was risky from our point of view as well. What if Park compromised our interests and suddenly switched sides? In any case, the young lawyer did not seem shocked by my idea. After thinking it over, he said he would be willing to do it if both parties agreed to it.

I thought Dong-il Kim might also be receptive to the idea—not because he was desperate but because he trusted Park to be fair, impartial, and professional. After all, Park only needed to make sure that the final agreement accurately reflected what the parties had already agreed to, and his work would have to stand up to scrutiny even after we had signed the final agreements. Park was unique because we trusted him and his integrity, and I thought the KDIC team did as well. I was gambling, just as Chairman Lee of the FSC had, that the KDIC team would trust the Kim & Chang lawyers to do what was best for Korea.

I brought together Lincer, Chen, and Poon to share my idea with them. Lincer thought I was nuts but he did not have a better suggestion. Chen and Poon also thought the idea was crazy but agreed it was probably the only way to solve our common problem. But this was too unusual an idea and too big a decision to be made in haste.

I took Park to the hotel's Japanese restaurant, where Horie had finished dinner but was still waiting for me to return. I briefed Horie on the difficult situation we were in and apologized again for not being able to have dinner with him. Nor could I spare any time with him at that hour, as I had to think about how to handle the current conundrum. Horie left for his room.

I was so tense that I took a cigarette from Marc Rubinstein of Kim & Chang. I don't smoke, but I wanted to be soothed by the smell of raw tobacco, which always reminded me of my father, who was a chain smoker. I asked Park not to talk for five minutes because I needed complete silence to mull over my idea. Park went out for a smoke himself, but he never returned. I was now alone in the restaurant.

I ordered a steak but, before the waiter went to the kitchen, I called him back and told him to bring me two steaks. He looked at me as if I were out of my mind. When the food came, I quickly ate two generous servings of beef, even though I usually stayed away from red meat. I was worried and desperate, and the food distracted me somewhat.

I made up my mind as I was eating. I went back to the business center to talk with Dong-il Kim and offered him the use of Park for the assistance agreement. I explained to him the history of the TOI negotiations and suggested Park as the only solution to the problem we had. Dong-il looked at me in disbelief, then he walked away thinking. He did not specifically agree but he did not object either. Soon, Park quietly began to work on the other side of the table.

At about 1 am, I received an unexpected visitor: a Mr. Kang of the Korea Development Bank. He wanted to talk with me about selling a forward contract to Newbridge to exchange dollars into Korean won, as we would eventually need to do so in order to close the transaction. He came to see me at this odd hour probably because he had read about the signing of final agreements on December 23 and did not want to be late for a possible deal. He offered me a forward rate of 1,122 won to a dollar, which I thought so ridiculously unfavorable to us that I turned him down. But I had to admire his aggressiveness to pitch a sale at 1 am, without being invited, especially considering the fact he was working for a government-owned bank.

I went back to my hotel room at about 2 am on December 23 to catch some sleep, not sure at all what would transpire in the next few hours.

I woke up at about 5 am wondering about another rather urgent matter on my mind. I had earlier signed a noncompete letter with Masayoshi Son, but I was wondering now if the letter would give us sufficient protection against his getting into competition with us in the future. I called Dan Carroll in San Francisco and we decided to wake up the SoftBank point man on the KFB investment. Carroll was able to persuade him to agree to revise the letter to include some more restrictive language. But I could not stay for the end of the negotiations, because in the middle of those talks Poon called to say Dong-il Kim and his team needed to speak with me about some issues that had come up in my absence.

When I went down to the conference room in the business center, I was pleasantly surprised to find the lawyers had made good progress in the past few hours, and now everyone thought the documents would be ready by 9 am. Seconding Park to the other side turned out to have made a huge difference. I was still skeptical that we could finish by 9 am, but I was tremendously relieved to know the documents would be ready to be signed sometime that day. This renewed hope of finishing on time undoubtedly motivated everyone to work even harder. By then, several lawyers had not slept for three nights straight, but everyone continued to forge on. Their tenacity and fortitude was quite unbelievable.

The government had scheduled a press conference for the signing and announcement to take place at nine that morning at KFB's head office. Dong-il Kim wanted to postpone the press conference. I advised him not to do so at this point, because it looked like we might finish at any moment. The lawyers were getting close, and we were all anxiously waiting and helping them where we could. This event had been so long anticipated by the press that I thought reporters would not mind being kept in suspense a little longer.

At about 9 am, we had a final meeting to discuss a few remaining issues. Dong-il Kim and I agreed without difficulty on the questions that had come up overnight. One major item had to do with the warrants for 5 percent of KFB's equity, which we had offered to give to the government a year ago, at the time of the MOU. At the last minute, we discovered that Korean law did not allow naked warrants, or warrants not attached to any securities. I proposed to change the term "warrants" to "options," which were basically the same thing. But the KDIC side did not think that would work either. Eventually, we agreed to their proposal for KFB to issue a zero-coupon (bearing no interest) bond with warrants to KDIC. That was the final issue to be resolved.

I had bought a disposable camera from the hotel's gift shop and took pictures of people from both teams working together, disheveled and seemingly distraught, in the final hours of completing the definitive documents. I thought the moment was worth recording. (See Exhibits 7 through 9.)

It was nearly 10:45 am when we finished all the documents. The three agreements were marked up, and both parties agreed to their content. They were ready to be sealed, even though we did not have time to produce a clean version, free of markups. Now we knew we could go home in time for Christmas Eve and would be able to enjoy the holiday free of any worry about this deal. We were all so tired but so relieved.

I went back to my room, took a shower, and changed. Then we left for the news conference at KFB headquarters. I rode in the same car as Horie. I called Bonderman on my way, but he was not home. Nor was Blum. I reached Carroll to tell him that we got it done and were on our way to the signing. The moment that all of us had been working so hard for had finally arrived. The union of Newbridge and KFB was complete (Exhibit 10).

I looked at the time. It was 11 am, Thursday, December 23, 1999, the day before Christmas Eve. It had been a long 15 months since Carroll and I had seen that first teaser from Morgan Stanley about buying a Korean bank.

Chapter 14

The Hard Part

I had visited KFB headquarters numerous times, but I had never felt the way I did walking into the building for the official signing of the final deal. Today, I knew the bank was ours. Anyone who has ever bought his or her dream house has felt the same way the first time they crossed the threshold after the closing. The building's broad white façade, its entrance, the spacious lobby, and the customers and employees—it all looked dear and close to me.

The scene contrasted sharply from what had unfolded at the signing of the TOI, when stone-faced Mr. Noh and I had sat on opposite sides of a table in a silent, crowded room, signing documents. Less than an hour earlier, all of us looked disheveled and haggard, having worked through many nights without rest. Now everyone was in their best suit, clean-shaven and radiant. We had all worked so incredibly hard—against all odds, it seemed—in the past few months to cross the finish line. Even though everyone was utterly sleep deprived, no one wanted to miss this moment, which we already knew would go down in Korean banking history.

Executive Director Dong-jun Paeng of the KDIC, Chairman Shee-yul Ryoo of KFB, and I greeted each other warmly before entering the big conference room where the signing was to take place. It was packed with members of the press, both reporters and photographers. On the wall, a large banner with blue lettering read *KFB Definitive Agreement Signing Ceremony* in English and Korean, with the red KFB thumbs-up logo beneath it. On a long table were two blue folders and two pens. The stage was set.

Paeng and I each proceeded to take a seat at the table. Chairman Ryoo stood beside us. Someone opened the folders for us to sign. Inside each folder was a single signature page. I realized then that this was a symbolic signing, for the cameras. The actual documents were hundreds of pages long and would take far too long to sign in a public ceremony. We each signed the signature page, and someone stepped forward to exchange the folders to countersign. Then we stood up, exchanged folders with each other, and shook hands for the cameras, each holding a folder in our left hand. At that point, the room broke into applause and cameras flashed (Exhibit 11). We also both shook hands with Chairman Ryoo.

After the signing, Paeng and I stood side by side and took questions from the press. I took the opportunity to thank the government for working with us as partners and to praise its representatives for their dedication and professionalism. "They have earned our highest respect," I emphasized.

Then I announced Newbridge's appointments of Robert T. Barnum as chairman and Wilfred Horie as CEO of the new Korea First Bank. As Barnum was not in Seoul, I invited only Horie to step forward and introduced him to the reporters. In addition to his experiences in consumer banking, I emphasized his background as a member of the Special Forces of the U.S. Army. I presented him as an experienced, tough, and strong leader, the right kind of leader for the new KFB. Horie presented himself well to the reporters. He came across as humble, confident, and experienced. His first introduction to the Korean public could not have gone better. I was impressed and pleased. It seemed to me that the reporters accepted him warmly.

It was not until the news conference ended that I finally reached Bonderman by phone. He was at home in the United States.

"David, we signed," I said.

"Congratulations," he said. Then, without a pause, he added, "Now the hard part begins."

I laughed, knowing that, of course, he was right. This day marked the beginning of our journey to turn around and rebuild the bank, a task that would prove challenging.

After the news conference, a few of us drove to the office of the KDIC. There, Paeng and I got down to the business of signing the actual documents. The several hundred pages were full of marked-up changes, some handwritten, because there was no time for lawyers to produce a clean copy. Nonetheless, we each signed every page to ensure that the whole set of documents was sealed. That afternoon, I was on a flight back to Hong Kong, to spend Christmas with my family.

★ ★ ★

The New Year was the start of a new millennium. We just barely made it. I closed the year with a final memo, written on the date the clean copies of the deal had been signed:

> *Today is December 31, 1999, the day of official legal closing for the Korea First Bank transaction. The balance sheet is frozen as of today for the old KFB and the new KFB begins its business on January 1, 2000. The funding by Newbridge will occur sometime around mid-January, probably January 20, 2000. But for all practical purposes, the deal is done.*

★ ★ ★

We had assembled a high-powered board for KFB. Barnum would be the chairman, and Chul-su Kim, president of Sejong University and formerly Deputy Minister of Trade, would serve as vice chairman. Four Newbridge partners joined the board: Blum, Bonderman, Carroll, and me. We also invited a number of highly accomplished businessmen and bankers to join the board, including Mickey Kantor, the former U.S. Secretary of Commerce and former Trade Representative; Frank Newman, former Deputy Secretary of the U.S. Treasury Department and former chairman and CEO of Bankers Trust; and Robert Cohen, the former vice chairman of Republic Bank and Head of Americas for the

French bank Crédit Lyonnais. O'Hanlon of Lehman Brothers, an experienced and excellent banker who had been working with us throughout the KFB transaction, also joined. So did Tom Barrack, managing partner of Colony Capital, and Francis Yeo, a professor from Singapore.

In addition, each of the three government agencies—the FSC, MOFE, and the KDIC—nominated a board member. Sung-hwan Oh, the FSC appointee, was a professor of Seoul National University. Representing MOFE was Yoon-jae Lee, a former executive director of Export-Import Bank of Korea. Seung-hee Park represented the KDIC, although he would later be replaced by JT Kim.

We held our first board meeting on the 11th floor of the KFB headquarters building in Seoul on January 21. The boardroom was large, with tables and seats arranged in a wide oval. Only a few board members were there in person. Many called in by phone, as our agenda items were few and mostly a formality for that initial meeting. Barnum presided. The official business included the election of Horie as president and CEO and the formation of the audit, compensation, executive, and risk-management committees. We ratified a number of documents related to the bank's agreement with the KDIC, such as the issuance of the bond with warrants, and appointed E&Y to be the bank's external auditor. The entire meeting lasted for just about one hour. That evening the board members went out to celebrate in a Japanese restaurant (Exhibit 13).

★ ★ ★

If the first board meeting was more form than substance, the second board meeting was all business, with every member attending in person. It took place on March 15, 2000, a fine and sunny day in Seoul. It was springtime and trees were turning green. Everything looked bright under a blue sky.

Before the meeting, at about 8:30 am, Blum, Bonderman, Carroll, and I left the Shilla Hotel to drive to the Blue House to visit with President Dae-jung Kim.

As we approached the Blue House, we could see its blue roof tiles shimmering in the sun. We arrived at about 9:30 am and were led into a large reception room. Soon, President Kim joined us. He had turned

76 in January. With his full head of black hair, he looked much younger than his age, despite walking with a cane. The cane and a slight limp were the scars of an assassination attempt during President Chung-hee Park's rule in 1971, when a truck smashed into Kim's car. As the most well-known political dissident, there was every reason for Chung-hee Park's military regime not to like DJ Kim.

The president greeted us warmly, with a firm handshake. It was the first time I had met him in person, although I had interacted with his staff during the negotiations. Knowing what he had been through, we all had great respect for him. He and Blum took seats side by side in two large sofa chairs in front of a credenza against the wall (Exhibit 12). The rest of us took our seats in a row of chairs on Blum's side. The meeting was ceremonial but everyone was clearly feeling cheerful. I was also filled with overwhelming relief that we had reached such a significant moment.

The president spoke first, expressing his appreciation for the investment Newbridge was making in Korea First Bank. He said the government attached great importance to this transaction and viewed it as a critical step in Korea's banking reforms. "Reforming this bank is at the center of my reform plans," he stressed.

Blum thanked the president and said that Newbridge was committed to turning around the bank and making it a success. He explained that Newbridge had brought in a world-class management team, and we were off to a good start. He also made it clear that we had strong confidence in the growth of the Korean economy under President Kim's leadership, adding that Newbridge was interested in making more investments in Korea.

As we were driving out of the Blue House compound after the meeting, Blum told me, "We helped him and saved his life." I was for a moment puzzled about what he meant until I realized his "we" meant the United States. He told me that Kim, a political dissident under the regime of President Chung-hee Park, was abducted by Korea's CIA agents while in exile in Japan. His captors were about to throw him into the sea, but American agents appeared on the scene from nowhere and rescued him. Kim was exiled in America for more than two years, from December 1982 to February 1985, before his return to South Korea.

Some months after our meeting, DJ Kim would receive the Nobel Peace Prize for his Sunshine Policy of rapprochement with North Korea. He recounted his narrow escape in his acceptance speech for the prize:

I have lived, and continue to live, in the belief that God is always with me. I know this from experience. In August of 1973, while exiled in Japan, I was kidnapped from my hotel room in Tokyo by intelligence agents of the then military government of South Korea. The news of the incident startled the world. The agents took me to their boat at anchor along the seashore. They tied me up, blinded me, and stuffed my mouth. Just when they were about to throw me overboard, Jesus Christ appeared before me with such clarity. I clung to him and begged him to save me. At that very moment, an airplane came down from the sky to rescue me from the moment of death.

Maybe the U.S. government had been doing the bidding of Jesus Christ, or maybe it was the other way around. In any case, DJ Kim was a fighter and survivor. He had other brushes with death, including one in 1980, when he was sentenced to be hanged, on charges of sedition and conspiracy, by President Doo-hwan Chun's government. God intervened again, this time through Pope John Paul II, who sent a letter to President Chun asking for clemency. Kim's sentence was commuted to a jail sentence of 20 years. Though not nearly as divine an intervention, the U.S. government helped secure Kim's release from prison in 1982. A diplomat stationed in Seoul at the time once recounted that President Chun agreed to the release after being offered one of the first audiences with the newly elected president, Ronald Reagan, in exchange.

On the same day as our Blue House visit and board meeting, we visited with Nam-koong Hoon, the new chairman and president of the KDIC, which was now our partner in KFB. We also paid a courtesy visit to Chairman Hun-jai Lee. The FSC chairman had managed to survive the KFB deal with his political career intact and in fact had been appointed the Minister of Finance and Economy in January. (We stopped by to see his successor at the FSC, Yong-keun Lee, as well.) Everyone was friendly and warm, although Chairman Lee still complained about certain Koreans who'd claimed to represent Newbridge during our negotiation process. It seemed that the good work of our political advisors had really annoyed him, even though we did not know who those Koreans were and certainly did not authorize any of them to represent Newbridge.

★ ★ ★

At our second board meeting on the 11th floor of KFB headquarters, the board met with the new management team. In addition to Horie, we had also brought in Duncan Barker, a Scot and veteran banker, as COO, and Ranvir Dewan, an Indian and former Citi banker, as CFO. SH Lee, whom we had sent into the bank back in September of the previous year as part of the transition team to control credit decisions, was made chief credit officer. The management presented the board with a plan and budget for the year 2000. The board members grilled Horie and his team with numerous questions on company operations. It was a tough session, but management did a good job defending its plan and targets for the year. The meeting lasted for more than five hours.

We walked out of Korea First Bank headquarters as twilight was settling in, and we looked around at the bustling foot traffic of people getting off work. Suddenly, Bonderman pointed to a building a short distance away. "Aha, Korea First Chicken!" I looked up to see the bright neon sign of KFC and the smiling face of Colonel Sanders.

That evening, the management of KFB held a reception in the Shilla Hotel ballroom. Several hundred guests attended, including officials from the Blue House and other government agencies. The new chairman of the FSC, Yong-keun Lee, gave a gracious speech congratulating KFB for achieving a great milestone and wishing it a bright future. The room was full of optimism.

The reception was followed by a banquet, on the top floor of the Shilla. In Korean banquets, there are numerous small appetizer dishes, often containing mysterious ingredients. Not all the foreigners found Korean food agreeable with their palates. Bonderman declared, in jest, he would not attend another board meeting in Korea if he were fed Korean food again. He would be perfectly happy with a hamburger or some Korea First Chicken. I had invited Director General Noh and Director

BS Kang to the banquet, but neither showed up. I sent a bottle of whiskey to each of them afterward. Kang sent me a letter in response to tell me that he had not received my invitation. He had left the FSC to become the chairman of a securities firm in Seoul and suspected his invitation had been lost in the mail. Noh returned my bottle with a letter saying that, as a government official, he could not accept my gift.

★ ★ ★

In its first year of operation, the bank made a significant shift toward retail banking, as we had planned. KFB was very much a corporate bank when we first took control, with retail loans, to individuals or households, representing less than 10 percent of the portfolio. By the end of the first year, that figure had jumped to about 40 percent. The change in the loan mix was rapid and significant.

However, not everything worked out to our satisfaction. The size of a bank is typically measured in terms of its total assets. By the time we became owners, KFB's total assets had shrunk to about 29 trillion won (about $25 billion). While our budget called for changes in the asset mix, the bank's total assets were expected to remain largely flat. This was a rather conservative budget, largely because we thought South Korea had not yet fully recovered from the financial crisis, so the economy remained fragile and businesses weak. We did not want to grow our loan books aggressively because doing so would be riskier (except in the retail business, which was both less risky and more profitable). However, management fell short of delivering on total assets by about 10 percent. This resulted in the bank's total assets shrinking further from 29 trillion won to 26 trillion won at the end of the year.

Nevertheless, KFB turned profitable. After two years of multi-billion-dollar losses, the bank generated a net income of about 300 billion won in 2000, the first year under our control. The net profit of the bank in U.S. dollar terms was about $230 million, despite the fact that the won had weakened against the U.S. dollar during the year, eroding the bank's dollar-denominated returns. The return on equity capital, which is the ratio of net earnings as a percentage of book value of our equity capital, was about 25 percent. This was a good achievement and it seemed that all of our efforts were paying off. But Newbridge and the board of directors thought we could do even better.

★ ★ ★

A year later, Bonderman and I were riding in a car together again. This time it was in Tokyo, on a sunny and beautiful day in May 2001. I felt the warmth of the sun on my face as I looked out of the window to take in the view as the car sped by the large open plaza in front of the Imperial Palace. I was tired because I had not slept the previous night. I had taken a 3 am flight from Hong Kong to Osaka and then transited from Osaka to Tokyo to arrive in time to meet with Bonderman. I was fighting to stay awake, while Bonderman read that day's *Wall Street Journal*. Suddenly, he thrust the paper in front of me.

"Did you see this?" he asked, pointing to an article in the paper. "Do you know about this Hynix thing?"

"What Hynix thing?" I asked. Without waiting for his answer, I took the paper to read.

The article was about the financial troubles of Hynix Semiconductor, a major computer chip manufacturer in South Korea and formerly part of the Hyundai Group. Hynix was near bankruptcy, having failed to make payments on its debts. The report noted that many banks had lent to Hynix, including KFB. Now Hynix was in need of a rescue by its creditors. It was negotiating with the banks to restructure its loans. The rescue effort was coordinated by the financial regulator, the Financial Supervisory Services under the FSC, which meant that the lending banks, including KFB, would have little choice but to bail out Hynix. That would involve lending new money to an essentially insolvent firm, and it might lead to a substantial haircut, or reduction, on the value of existing Hynix loans and major losses for lenders.

The news was astounding. It was even more disturbing because we had not known anything about it, despite the biweekly calls between KFB's senior management and the board's Executive Committee, which included Barnum, Blum, Bonderman, Newman, and me. The Risk

Management Committee of the board should have flagged any large and risky loan exposures. But we had been left in the dark about a major exposure to Hynix and the borrower's financial troubles.

I immediately called SH Lee, the chief credit officer of KFB. Lee was a graduate of Yonsei University in Seoul and spoke good English, which he no doubt honed during his 16-year career as a credit officer with Bank of America. He had been working with us since the middle of our process to acquire KFB, first helping us analyze the credit quality of the loan portfolio and then as a credit officer to vet lending decisions. If anything, his reputation was to err on the conservative side, so we wondered how he had missed this.

Bonderman and I were even more surprised when Lee told us that the bank's exposure to Hynix was about 250 billion won, or about $200 million, that the loan was already classified as "substandard," and that the bank had made a 20 percent provision against it. We were shocked, for two reasons. First, if there was one lesson to be drawn from the previous failure of KFB, it was that overexposure to a few large corporate customers was a major risk. To avoid this, the board had established a house limit for all loans. Any exposure of more than 100 billion won to a single customer required board approval. We could not understand how the bank had an exposure of 250 billion won to Hynix, clearly in breach of the house limit, without board members knowing about it.

Second, we hadn't heard anything about it even after Hynix got into financial difficulties, and we only learned the bad news from the newspaper. We should have been kept abreast of all the major issues in the bank by the KFB management.

The matter required immediate attention. I scheduled a conference call with the board's Risk Management Committee to discuss it. The call became an intense grilling of SH Lee, by members of the committee, on how exactly our Hynix exposure had come about and how it had grown so far beyond the house limit.

It turned out that Hynix had been a longstanding customer of KFB, but the bank's credit exposure to it had been managed down to about 100 billion won by November 2000. That same month, Citibank in Seoul led a syndicated loan—a loan made by a group of banks—of 800 billion won to Hynix. Citibank and its investment banking subsidiary, Salomon Smith Barney, pitched the loan to several banks in Seoul, including KFB.

It was a tough sell—all the foreign banks had passed on the deal—but the management of KFB decided to join the syndicate for 100 billion won, which, added to the previous loans and accrued interest, pushed the total credit exposure to Hynix to about 250 billion won.

The problem turned out to be even worse than the headline numbers indicated. Much of KFB's loan exposure was not secured by any collateral. Hynix, it turned out, was going to require more than $4 billion to be bailed out. If the company went under or ceased operation, the entire amount of our unsecured Hynix exposure would be worthless. Whatever value that might be salvaged by selling off Hynix's assets would go to paying off secured debt owners first, likely leaving nothing for holders of unsecured paper.

Hynix got into trouble because of a worldwide collapse in the semiconductor market. The price of dynamic random-access memory chips, or DRAM, had fallen 90 percent in 2001. The semiconductor industry, a highly cyclical business, dived into a down cycle with no respite in sight. Those companies without sufficient cash reserves were at risk of running out of liquidity and failing. At this point, if all lenders or creditor banks had stopped lending to Hynix and called back their loans, the company would go out of business immediately. In fact, if even one of the creditors pulled the plug, the company was likely to fail.

I pictured a group of people about to be crushed by a giant boulder. They were trying to survive by coming together to hold it up with all their collective strength. If one person jumped out of the way, he would probably live, but the rest would surely become meat pies. In this case, even if the banks tried to rescue Hynix by loaning more money to it, there was no telling if the company would survive. It could be throwing good money after bad. The banks had to make a collective decision about what to do or not to do.

Hynix's largest lender, the government-controlled Korea Exchange Bank, requested that all Hynix's creditor banks sign an intercreditor agreement by which if 75 percent of the creditors made a decision to provide new money, all signatories of the agreement would be obligated to follow. We were astonished to learn that KFB had also become a member of this agreement without the board's knowledge. Our management had signed away the bank's autonomy in this matter without notifying the board.

There wasn't anything we could do. Hynix was not yet bankrupt, but we knew it would not survive unless it received another capital injection.

★ ★ ★

I arrived in Seoul on Friday, September 12, 2001, along with some other members of the KFB board. It was still September 11, 2001, in the United States, and I had just learned of the terrorist attacks on the World Trade Center and Pentagon.

My wife, Bin, had just arrived in London on her way to Boston, where she would meet our son, Bo, to fly to Chicago. He was going to start his freshman year at the University of Chicago. Bin did not know about the 9/11 attacks when she called me from London's Heathrow Airport. She hadn't yet seen the news, so at first she thought I was joking when I told her to immediately book a hotel in London because U.S. airspace was closed.

Newbridge had held the grand opening of its office in Tokyo on September 11, before the attacks in New York City happened. The next day, Blum, Carroll, and some others who had been in Tokyo officiating the opening continued on to Seoul. As I prepared for our meeting, the events of the previous day in the United States hung heavily in my mind, and I was not looking forward to discussing the bank's problems in the midst of this tragedy.

It was under such circumstances that we opened the meeting of KFB's board of directors at about 2 pm on September 13. Bonderman called in by phone because he was stuck in Fort Worth, Texas, where it was already midnight his time. The only significant agenda item was the Hynix loan. We board members had been struggling to consider its financial ramifications and how we might get off the hook before the crisis fully unfolded. We were, therefore, all surprised that our CEO, Horie, had invited the CEO of Hynix and a banker from Salomon Smith Barney to join the meeting to make a pitch for new money and to swap our debt into equity. Other Korean banks, led by the government-controlled Korea Exchange Bank, were proposing to do the same.

The CEO of Hynix and the Salomon banker took turns going through their presentation. They argued that Hynix would recover if the semiconductor cycle turned and chip prices began to rise. Their argument struck me as pure tautology. Essentially, they were arguing that if Hynix got out its financial trouble, its debt would be paid. But they managed to deliver their pitch with a straight face, so maybe they had convinced themselves their argument had substance. At this point, Hynix was $6 billion in debt and still losing money. The other Korean banks were contemplating swapping $2.3 billion of debt into equity as part of a $4.4 billion bailout package.

The board listened attentively but was not reassured. It was obvious that the Hynix CEO and the Salomon banker were avoiding talking about the other possibility, that DRAM chip prices would continue to fall and the company would declare bankruptcy after burning through all the new money it aimed to raise. The odds were already stacked against KFB recovering the money it had sunk into Hynix. We were dismayed that our own CEO had the audacity to ask the board to approve even more credit to the troubled firm.

Finally, Bonderman, talking over the speakerphone, cut the Hynix team short. He said that semiconductor prices could fall further or stay depressed and that whatever new money we put into the company could disappear together with the old. Surprisingly, the CEO of Hynix and the Salomon representative had nothing to say in their own defense. It was as if they had never considered that possibility. The board meeting did not adjourn until after 7 pm, which was 5 am for Bonderman. He had stayed up all night to participate in the discussion, as the matter facing us was grave and critical.

KFB would not participate in the Hynix bailout, the board decided, even if it meant it had to sell its Hynix debt to other banks at a steep discount and take a punishingly large haircut on the loans. We thought it was better to lose some of our hair than our head.

Back at the Shilla Hotel, the Newbridge people, Blum, Carroll, Chen, Poon, and I, met with Barnum and Robert Cohen to talk about what to do with the management of KFB. We all agreed that they should be held accountable for the Hynix debacle. Some heads would need to roll. We needed to further improve our system of risk controls and to tighten up the bank's internal processes to prevent this from ever happening again.

We retained a Washington, DC, law firm, Wilmer, Cutler & Pickering (WCP), to conduct an independent inquiry into the events that had led to the Hynix credit decisions.

About a month later, WCP delivered its report. Through a forensic audit of the bank's activities, it found that KFB had gradually been reducing its credit exposure to Hynix, in accordance with the house limit established by the board in September 2000. However, in late November of that year, this trend reversed when KFB management authorized its 100 billion won participation in the Citibank syndicated loan. According to a document the WCP investigation unearthed, the plan was to reduce overall exposure to Hynix from 100 billion won to 61.6 billion won by the end of 2000 and to zero by May 2001—excluding the 100 billion won from the syndicated loan. Why on earth did KFB management authorize participation in the Citibank loan when it wanted to reduce the credit exposure to Hynix simultaneously? "The decision to join the syndication was principally that of the CEO," the WCP report found.

> *Although the CEO recalls that his endorsement of the proposal was expressly stated as being subject to the credit assessment of the CCO [chief credit officer, SH Lee] and the KFB credit team, the CEO's enthusiasm was clear and, sensing that, the CCO and the subordinate credit team largely deferred to it.*

> *For his part, the CCO acknowledges that he was aware of the liquidity and DRAM pricing risks . . . and also of a reluctance by foreign lenders (other than Citibank) to participate in the proposed syndication. He also acknowledges that this information should have given him pause. But he deferred to the CEO and so acknowledges.*

This illustrated a cultural norm that was prevalent in Korea—one that Malcolm Gladwell wrote about in his book *Outliers*. He describes a 1997 plane crash to explain the dangers of this phenomenon. Korean Air flight 801 crashed into a hillside in the U.S. territory of Guam, killing 228 people. Gladwell attributes the crash to an element in Korean culture, that of juniors or subordinates deferring to their superiors, even when the risks of doing so are high. This deference prevented the first officer and the flight engineer from pointing out that the captain was on a crash course.

I don't believe that any flight crew, Korean or otherwise, would keep quiet in the face of clear, life-threatening danger. It was more likely, as the official investigation concluded, that the first officer and flight engineer had been so deferential to the captain that they failed to monitor and cross-check the approach he chose. In any case, nobody can possibly know if the two subordinates or the captain were aware of the danger, or what went through their heads, because they did not live to be interviewed.

At KFB, however, our chief credit officer was very much alive. He and his credit team confirmed to the investigators that they went along with the loan despite their reservations, in deference to the CEO. Nobody was killed, but the bank lost about $200 million, which almost wiped out all the profits the bank had made in the previous year. This aspect of the Korean culture had obviously interfered with the kind of credit culture we were trying to build at KFB. It hadn't occurred to us that our management team could be so strongly influenced by the Korean culture because Horie was an American and Lee was trained at Bank of America.

WCP's report concluded that the extent of the CEO's involvement in Hynix decisions was "inconsistent with reasonable expectations of the Board." He had deviated from the bank's mission to shift from *chaebol* lending to consumer banking, breached the board's risk management guidelines, and erred by becoming personally involved in credit decisions. Clearly, the chief executive officer was responsible for the losses. WCP also found the CCO's acquiescence, despite believing the Hynix loan to be a bad decision, was "inconsistent with the Board's reasonable expectation of his assigned role." It made us wonder how big a problem we had.

The report wrapped up by stating

WCP also believes it appropriate to acknowledge that, however large and egregious, Hynix is an exception rather than the rule. Both the CEO and the chief credit officer believe that the management has been effective in reducing KFB's overall exposures to most other major corporate clients. KFB had eight borrowers, other than Hynix, that exceeded the "House Limits" in February 2001. The chief credit officer reports that this number is now down to four. In addition, he reports that KFB has decreased its exposure to each of these borrowers.

The findings by WCP spoke for themselves. The CEO took full responsibility and resigned. The board accepted his resignation. The CCO shared responsibility for not having provided a check on the CEO's preferences. But the board, recognizing that SH Lee had done a good job controlling credit quality when given full credit authority, did not feel that he should be held too harshly accountable for the breakdown of our risk management system. Lee was reprimanded but kept in his position. We felt quite sure he had learned a good and hard lesson.

Chapter 15

Change Agent

A change of CEO always brings a huge amount of uncertainty to an organization. We needed someone with experience and a reputation for integrity, whom the board could immediately trust, and who was willing to relocate to Seoul. Importantly, it would have to be someone who could win the respect of our partner, the Korean government, and of KFB's employees. No matter how much experience a new leader arrives with, it remains a question whether he or she will be effective in a new environment, new culture, and new market. KFB, especially, was shifting course and implementing big internal changes, so the new CEO had to be a change agent and turnaround specialist. The task of finding the right person was urgent and daunting.

Immediately after the board meeting on September 13, we began our search. I was talking with Paul Chen that evening after dinner at the Shilla Hotel. "We have to find someone who is an experienced banker with proven leadership quality, who can be trusted by the board, and who is willing to take the job. That is very tough," I said.

After a pause, Chen turned to me and said, "How about Robert Cohen?"

It was a classic cartoon moment: I felt like a light switch in my head turned on and my eyes lit up. "Paul, that is a good idea," I said. "Why, it's a perfect idea!"

We all knew Cohen well by now. Robert (pronounced Rho-BEHR) Cohen had been invited to join the KFB board by Bonderman, who had known him for a long time. Medium height and bespectacled, Cohen wore a beard and an easy smile. He came with impeccable credentials as a veteran banking leader. He had been vice chairman of the Republic National Bank of New York before he retired. Before that he had been CEO of Crédit Lyonnais USA, with responsibility for the whole of the Americas. Cohen was also a scholar. With a PhD in finance from the Université Paris Dauphine, he had taught economics and finance in elite French schools for 16 years. With this rare combination of an academic background and a practitioner's experience, Robert Cohen not only knew banking inside and out, he also had experience running a large banking operation in a culture different from his own.

Cohen seemed the most suitable candidate for the CEO position, especially at that particular moment in time. Thinking over his participation on the board, we all saw him as one of our most diligent members. He invariably put in the hours to read every page of the meeting materials. He seemed to know every subject and every number by heart. He had made contributions to board discussions since the day he joined. His comments and suggestions were considered and thought provoking; he often offered new ideas and perspectives. For example, from early on, he advocated for lengthening the duration of KFB's assets, in anticipation of falling interest rates. (A fall in interest rates will increase the value of longer-dated interest-bearing assets more than shorter-dated ones). He would prove to be completely correct. The bank would have been more profitable if the management followed his advice on the asset mix.

We also knew that Cohen and his wife had taken a strong interest in Korean culture since they first visited for our board meeting. (See Exhibits 14, 15, and 16.) However, Korea at the time was generally not a popular posting for Western businesspeople, and the expatriate community in Seoul was relatively small. It was difficult to get around speaking English (and even harder speaking French, Cohen's mother tongue). The working language of KFB was predominantly Korean, which Cohen did not speak.

We had no idea if he would be interested in the challenges of such a difficult job or in moving his family to Seoul.

I called Cohen in his room and invited him out for a walk in the hills behind the Shilla Hotel.

"We have a problem . . . ," I began.

I was about to get into my prepared speech about the challenges we faced, searching for a new CEO, to start as soon as possible, whose credentials would pass muster with multiple constituencies, including the board, the Korean government, employees, customers, and, of course, the media. But before I could continue, Cohen interrupted me: "Do you think I am the solution to your problem?" "Why, yes. Of course, that is if you are interested to consider it." I said.

"I am interested but I need to talk with my wife." Cohen said.

I needed to speak with my partners and with Barnum, chairman of the board. I was confident that all would be delighted if Cohen was willing to take the job.

They were. Bonderman, Blum, and Carroll all thought Cohen was a great choice, and they were pleasantly surprised to hear that, after speaking with his wife, Cohen had agreed to do it.

The biggest question we were now facing was: How would a French CEO fare in a Korean organization?

"Well," Blum said, "at least they have something in common. They don't speak each other's languages, but they all speak English as a foreign language."

Our confidence in Cohen aside, what he took on was indeed a great challenge, as he would soon discover.

We announced the appointment of Cohen as president and CEO of Korea First Bank on October 23, 2001, effective immediately. The transition was smooth. The departing CEO and the incoming CEO held a joint press conference. The change surprised the market, but Cohen was quickly accepted by the employees and the banking community in Seoul as an experienced banker and leader.

★ ★ ★

As the new CEO, Cohen had to quickly set his strategy, develop his long-term plan, and establish his own team. Soon after he took office, he announced his three-year targets, which would aim to carry the bank from 2002 to 2004. These were simple but ambitious. He wanted to grow the total assets of the bank from about 25 trillion won to 40 trillion won. Of the 25 trillion won in total assets at the end of 2001, client assets, such as loans to customers, were only 11 trillion won. The rest, including government notes and real estate, were not as profitable. Because of the need to shed its nonperforming loans in the wake of the financial crisis, KFB had lost a large number of clients. Cohen's predecessor's reorientation toward retail banking resulted in the further loss of corporate clients. Cohen wanted to more than double client assets, from 11 trillion won to 25 trillion won, in three years. That was an ambitious goal, and it was initially met with strong skepticism by the bank's employees.

As one of his first orders of business, Cohen followed through on his idea to increase the amount of longer-dated interest-bearing assets, in anticipation of further drops in interest rates. The bank began to acquire long-term, fixed-interest-rate assets as soon as he became CEO. By then, the interest rate was already falling. He was able to acquire a few trillion won's worth of long-term, fixed-interest-rate assets, but the bank would have made more money if it had followed his advice much sooner.

He also found the accounting system that was prevalent in South Korea at that time to be woefully inadequate. For example, accounting was done on a cash basis, rather than the accrual basis that was standard in the West. Under the cash basis method, if the bank borrowed money at a 6 percent interest rate to be paid at the end of the year, no interest expenses were recorded by the bank until the money was actually paid. If accounting was done on an accrual basis, the bank would have recorded half of the interest accrued by the middle of the year even though the payment would not be made until the end of the year. Similarly, if the bank made a loan with a similar interest-payment structure, it would not record interest income until cash was received, whereas accounting on an accrual basis would allow some of the anticipated income from the loan to be booked before cash was received.

Needless to say, cash accounting did not give the management an adequate picture of the actual financial performance of the bank. Cohen worked with Ranvir Dewan, the former Citibanker and KFB's CFO, to quickly rectify these problems.

Cohen was a great communicator, despite his strongly accented English—and no Korean. For example, he pronounced "Seoul" as "sei woo," with an emphasis on "woo." He had to talk with his Korean executives and employees through an interpreter. He was undaunted, however, as he thought that getting his message across to all employees was critically important and that if the employees bought into his strategic targets, they would be able to help him achieve them. His method was to make his targets simple to understand—40 trillion won in total assets and 25 trillion in client assets in three years—and to explain it in meeting after meeting with both executives and employees, for hundreds of hours, until everyone was on board with his objectives.

The fact that he was a very experienced banker and could logically explain why his goals were achievable and could relate to his own experiences elsewhere allowed him to speak with clarity, authority, and credibility. He did more than convince his staff; he *excited* them. Every banker knew that the prestige of a bank and the respect its employees receive were often tied to the size of the bank, measured by its total assets. The employees were excited that, with this plan, they were restoring KFB to its former glory of being, once again, first in Korea.

To achieve these targets, Cohen had to change the mix of corporate and retail banking yet again. In 2000 and 2001, KFB had gradually moved away from corporate banking in favor of building retail assets. However, growing retail loans would take a long time because each retail loan, by definition, was small. It would be faster to build assets by growing corporate loans, which were typically much larger but, of course, riskier. Cohen's strategy was to reengage with corporate customers while continuing to grow the retail business.

As he was formulating his targets, Cohen also reorganized the management team. He did it in a way completely foreign to Korea, where a system of hierarchy by seniority was strictly observed. Unlike in the West, there was neither a performance evaluation system nor even personnel records of performance evaluations by superiors or peers. Cohen wanted the most capable, not necessarily the most senior, executives in key positions. He personally interviewed 50 candidates for one and a half hours each over a six-week period to find a new head of retail banking. He chose Seung-yeol Yang, who did not speak English (or French) yet commanded respect among the rank and file.

The biggest challenge in aggressively growing client assets for a bank was risk control, especially for loans made to corporate customers. Without a sound risk control system, loans made to customers with weak credit could become bad loans, as KFB painfully had experienced before its failure. How to rapidly grow client assets without taking too much risk was literally a science. In this regard, KFB under Cohen's leadership did something that no other Korean bank was doing.

Under a program dubbed *Pro-Branch*, KFB's entire network of more than 400 branches was completely restructured and reorganized. The concept was recommended by Bain & Company, which we engaged to help us with strategic analysis and recommendations, and was adopted by Cohen after the board had approved it. Pro-Branch was going to require a lot of capital investment, as the branches would be revamped and renovated, but the board concurred with Cohen that the investment was essential for the long-term growth of the bank.

In Korea, as in much of Asia at that time, the manager of a bank branch had a great deal of power, as he was the decision maker for approving or denying loans. But putting all that power in the hands of the branch manager created two problems. The first was that credit decisions were not based on a single set of criteria but on the personal judgment of an individual. Consequently, loan quality varied from branch to branch. The second problem was that it would be difficult for a branch manager to turn down a loan request from an acquaintance, especially if the acquaintance was senior to the manager in age, as Korean culture obliged younger people to be deferential to older people.

The Pro-Branch Program took corporate banking away from most of the branches and concentrated the corporate lending business at KFB headquarters and some major regional corporate banking centers. Branch managers and their bankers would be responsible for generating loan applications but not for making credit decisions or approving loans. Whether the loan would be approved or not was a decision made at headquarters. For corporate loans generated in certain large branches, the decision to lend would be made by the credit committee, headed by our chief credit officer, SH Lee. With the Hynix debacle behind him, Lee turned out to be a great gatekeeper.

For retail loans, the decision-making power was also taken away from branches and moved to the newly formed Decision Science Department, headed by Keith Shachat, an American whose prior experience included working at American Express and Associates First Capital, both leaders in consumer finance. His department was responsible for retail risk analysis and control as a basis to underwrite, meaning approve or reject, retail loans.

This department was called *Decision Science* because the team used sophisticated statistical tools, algorithms based on probability theory, and a large amount of historical data to score loan applicants based on the individual data they provided. The scores indicated the probability the applicant would be able to pay back a loan. Those whose scores were above a certain cut-off point would be approved, and those below would be rejected. The analytics were fully computerized. An operator only needed to know what personalized data went in and what results came out, without any knowledge of how the computation was done. The technologies and data were fine-tuned on an ongoing basis to make sure the calculated probabilities approximated reality as closely as possible. It was all so complex that we sometimes called it the *Rocket Science Department*. Today it would be called *artificial intelligence*.

Shachat and his family had to relocate from the United States to Seoul for the job, but there was one complication. He was attached to his dog, and for some reason—maybe because of its size, or maybe because they could not bear to be separated from each other during a long flight—he could not get any commercial airline to take the dog to Korea. But Shachat was firm that he would not come to Seoul without his dog. The next thing I knew, Bonderman flew to Seoul for a board meeting in his private jet with a guest passenger who was critically important for the future of KFB's growth: Shachat's dog. Not only were we able to get Shachat on board, we now knew we could keep him in his job in Seoul indefinitely, as there was no easy way to get his dog out.

Shachat built his department into a powerhouse, with more than 40 young decision scientists and technicians. The department created its own credit bureau, which housed data on the credit records of hundreds of thousands, if not millions, of consumers, pulled from different sources. Its capabilities allowed KFB to offer mortgage loans, secured against the properties of the borrowers, as well as unsecured consumer loans without taking undue risks.

The centralized and computerized decision-making process worked seamlessly. The branch banker would input the loan applicant's personal data into his or her computer with the customer sitting across the desk, and, within one minute, the results from headquarters would be returned. The banker would be able to tell the customer if the loan was approved, at what amount, and at what interest rate. To the customer, it looked like the branch officer was making the decision in real time. Most had no idea that it was actually being made in a black box developed by our rocket scientists. After the credit was approved, KFB was able to process a fully documented loan within three days—an efficiency that was previously unheard of in Korean banking.

The centralized loan approval process was efficient and accurate. It freed up branch bankers to increase production volume. KFB's management pushed out new products, such as 30-year mortgages with a few years of fixed interest followed by adjustable rates, similar to those found in the U.S. market. The Korean mortgage market had previously been limited to three-year loans with adjustable interest rates. The combination of rapid approval time, strong sales by the branches, and new products helped catapult KFB's market share in mortgages from less than 1 percent at the end of 2001 to 9 percent by 2003 and 11 percent by 2004. Even with this rapid growth, KFB's loan quality remained excellent, and its credit loss ratio was practically nil.

On the corporate loan side, the credit committee, led by SH Lee, was similarly impressive, growing the loan book while maintaining the best loan quality in Korea's entire banking system. KFB's nonperforming loan ratio, or the percentage of bad loans to total loans on its books, hovered around 1 percent—far below the 2 to 3 percent ratio experienced by other Korean banks.

Cohen was able to build a strong relationship with employees and their morale was high, but he had inherited a difficult situation with the labor union. The previous CEO had wanted to outsource KFB's IT services, because the old system was antiquated and had suffered years of neglect following KFB's failure and nationalization. While the board approved the decision, management had failed to discuss it with the union, even though shutting down the internal IT department meant loss of jobs. The decision was met with such strong resistance from the union that KFB's loan production nearly came to a halt.

Cohen's predecessor had eventually capitulated to the union's pressure. He agreed to cancel the outsourcing and also agreed to a three-year salary increase for all employees benchmarked against the largest Korean bank, Kookmin, even though KFB's productivity, measured by the dollar value of assets per employee, was less than half of the industry average at that time.

Cohen's strategy was to be completely transparent with his employees and with the union. He openly broadcast his plans, repeatedly and to everyone. There was no hidden agenda. A major challenge for the bank was overcapacity. Over the course of its failure and nationalization during the economic crisis, KFB was reduced to a shadow of its former self in terms of the size of its total assets, but the size of its workforce had not decreased correspondingly. KFB really needed only about half its existing staff, given its reduced asset size.

This redundancy was compounded by the Pro-Branch Program, which eliminated loan decision making at the branches. If KFB reduced its staff over an extended period of time, it would have two major unwanted side effects. It would create a big morale issue, as staff would be worried about job security and nobody would know when the next wave of layoffs would hit. And it would cost the bank, on average, about three years' salary to retire an employee, which was an expensive proposition.

The CEO's decision, which was approved by the board, was to go through with a limited payroll reduction, achieved over a limited period of time with generous early retirement packages. And it was clearly communicated to all employees that there would be no more staff reduction after this one-time cut. How would we address the issue of staff redundancy? Cohen's plan was that instead of cutting the oversized clothes to fit the body, he would grow the body into the clothes. Until there was a better fit between the size of the bank's total assets and its infrastructure, defined to a large extent by the number of the staff, there would be redundancy and inefficiency. Measured in terms of assets per employee, KFB would lag behind other banks on employee productivity. But it would have an abundant workforce to produce loans and rapidly grow its asset base to meet Cohen's objectives.

Cohen's strategy of growing assets to fit the infrastructure, as opposed to cutting payroll to fit the asset size, resulted in rapid asset growth, as expected, but profitability still lagged because of high staff costs. At the board level, we fretted about the slow growth in profitability and debated whether further staff reduction was a more advisable strategy. Some of our peers also noticed our bank was overstaffed. Seung-Yu Kim, CEO of Hana Bank, another major bank in South Korea, approached me and suggested that we consider merging the two banks, provided KFB cut its payroll by 1,000 people first. We did not accept his proposal, but as owners we worried about the issue. We eventually supported Cohen's strategy because his rationale was compelling. We were also happy we were able to keep so many jobs.

Cohen developed a respectable working relationship with KFB's labor union, although it got off to a rocky start. Soon after he became CEO, the union staged a showdown with him, probably for the purpose of warning him not to repeat the mistake of his predecessor, who decided to outsource IT services without consulting with the union first. As Cohen recalled in his memoir, *Turning Around a Bank in Korea*, "I fully expected this test, but it was brutal. The union asked management to step back on a minor decision (I even forgot what it was). I refused, and the big demonstration began." About 50 union members loudly and noisily demonstrated outside of his office on the executive floor, beating drums, shouting slogans, and blocking his exit until late at night.

At the first board meeting after Cohen's appointment, the demonstrating union members positioned themselves directly outside the boardroom. They wore black shirts and red headbands with slogans written in white. The slogans were written in Korean, so we had no idea what they said, but maybe that was for the best. They sat cross-legged, chanting and beating large Korean folk drums, which were incredibly loud. They raised their fists when they shouted slogans, which punctuated their chants. The directors walking into the meeting room were more amused than intimidated, as the demonstration, although noisy, was peaceful and presented an unusual sight. If the union members had not been punching air with their fists, the board members probably would have wanted their pictures taken with them.

Blum walked over to one of the protesters, shook his hand, and then gave him a bear hug. This happened in silence as neither spoke the other's language. Blum was about twice the age of the man he held in his arms and one full head taller. Blum hugged him so tightly and for so long it was as if he were holding a long-lost son. Everyone applauded. Another union member stepped forward and put a headband on Blum's head, which I suppose made him an honorary member of the union.

Cohen was eventually able to resolve his differences with the union and over time won members' trust and support. For the next few years, the management had a good and respectful relationship with the union and held a number of events at the suggestion of the union leaders, including the celebration of the 74th and 75th anniversaries of KFB's founding. The harmonious relationship helped boost employee morale and instilled a sense of common purpose in everyone's mind.

My view is that there is nothing that cannot be worked out if management treats the union and its employees with respect and with an open mind. Ultimately, employees are generally reasonable and unions are generally responsible. Everyone at KFB wants the bank to be a source of pride. About a decade after we'd sold KFB to a new owner, the company experienced the longest and most crippling labor strike in the history of Korean banking. Not surprisingly, financial performance deteriorated sharply. I found it hard to understand what differences between the bank's management and its employees could be so irreconcilable as to justify putting the whole business at risk.

★ ★ ★

By the end of 2002, Cohen's first full year at the helm, all the major international rating agencies, including Moody's, Standard & Poor's, and Fitch, had raised KFB's credit rating from junk to investment grade. Total assets grew from less than 27 trillion won at the end of 2001 to more than 32 trillion won—a 19 percent increase in one year—exceeding the original budget by 30 percent.

Cohen was determined that the bank required more capital to fund its growth. He proposed that it raise capital by issuing what was known as *tier-one hybrid subordinated debt.* This debt was subordinated to, or ranked below, all the other debt of the bank. In the event the bank went bust, holders of this debt would get paid last, making the debt more like equity capital. The *hybrid* label indicated that it was a cross between debt and equity. As such, regulators treated it as tier-one capital for the purpose of calculating the bank's capital adequacy ratio. International investors eagerly snapped up the hybrids, allowing KFB to quickly raise the additional capital to support its growth. It was a resounding endorsement by investors of KFB's success and prospects.

★ ★ ★

By 2002, South Korea was experiencing a boom in consumer credit. As mentioned, at the beginning of 2000, the country was largely a cash society, with limited credit card use. The government decided to promote the use of credit cards for two purposes. One was to increase private consumption to propel economic growth. The other was to prevent abuse and fraud relating to business expenses; credit card receipts were harder to falsify than cash transactions were. The government provided incentives like tax rebates for purchases using credit cards instead of cash. Not surprisingly, this triggered a boom in the issuance of credit cards. Some card issuers were bank subsidiaries, such as the credit card subsidiary of Korea Exchange Bank. Others were independent credit card companies affiliated with large *chaebols*, such as LG Card and Samsung Card.

At the peak of the credit card boom, card companies were literally giving out cards on the streets to anyone who cared to take one, without any meaningful credit approval process. In 2002, the total number of credit cards issued in South Korea reached 105 million. This was in a country with a population of 38 million people over the age of 14. On average, every adult in Korea had three cards. In urban centers like Seoul, the average was closer to four or five.

Why did people need so many cards? Credit cards were used not only for purchases but also for cash advances, which represented more than 60 percent of card billings in 2002. Credit card issuers allowed cardholders to pay off their credit card debt with other credit cards. Consumers were playing a Ponzi scheme against themselves, continuously obtaining and borrowing from a new card to pay back another. If one card issuer could not lend any more, the whole scheme would collapse, which was exactly what happened in 2003. The market was jolted by the news that LG Card, the largest credit card company in South Korea, was on the verge of bankruptcy, causing a credit card crisis.

KFB had been looking for ways to grow its assets and was a large provider of bulk lending, or large-size loans, to credit card companies. These loans were secured by the card receivables or obligations of cardholders to pay. In 2002, KFB's total lending to credit card companies amounted to about 5 trillion won, or about five times the bank's total equity capital. Cohen and his management team were concerned about the risks of the bank's exposure to credit card companies and began a program to cut it drastically. By the time the credit card crisis hit, KFB was completely out of the bulk lending business with, surprisingly, zero exposure to credit card companies. If management had not moved quickly and wisely, KFB would have failed again, many times over, in 2003. Under Cohen and his team, KFB not only dodged a huge bullet but stood out as the only bank without any exposure to credit card companies. Sixteen other banks were deeply mired in the LG Card fiasco alone.

Was KFB simply lucky to have gotten out just before the crisis hit? No. I would argue that management's awareness of peripheral risks had improved considerably. In May 2003, SK Global, the trading company subsidiary of SK Group, the third largest *chaebol* in South Korea, went into receivership. KFB was the lead bank for SK Group. But the management, led by Cohen, had grown increasingly jittery about SK Global and had begun to aggressively cut the bank's exposure to the subsidiary. SK Group threatened to terminate its relationship with KFB. Losing such a major account would be a big deal for any bank, but our management decided that SK Global had become too much of a risk. KFB did lose the SK Group account, but when SK Global flopped, KFB was unscathed, whereas many other banks got into trouble.

★ ★ ★

Many people think that private equity investors buy a business on the cheap, dress it up, and sell it for a higher price. That certainly was not and is not what we do. Sometimes we get lucky with the timing and market conditions. More often, success requires judgment, difficult decisions, and a lot of hard work. We create value by turning around troubled businesses and by improving their operations. It involves much pain, sacrifice, investment, and strategic trade-offs. Unlike public companies, we do not have to worry about profitability from quarter to quarter, and we can focus on improving the long-term value of an institution. Our ability to take the long-term view allows us to make strategic and fundamental changes and to build and grow the businesses we acquire. Cohen testified to this in his memoir. "I do not believe in a quick paint job on a crumbling building. Cosmetic changes just do not work," he wrote. "We totally rebuilt the bank from the foundation up like we thought it should have been, without shortcuts." Then he said, "I remember vividly a discussion at the board of directors on a large investment commitment and David Bonderman, the senior partner of TPG, saying, 'If it is needed for the long-term good of the bank, we must do it.'"

The successful turnaround of KFB was certainly not an accident. It represented private equity at its best. In a few years, we had transformed a once-failed, wobbly bank into the healthiest institution in Korea. And on this strong foundation it was growing rapidly, shattering industry records year after year.

★　★　★

By 2004, KFB had achieved the number one position in many categories. It was the best-capitalized bank in the country and had the lowest nonperforming loan ratio by far. It had the lowest credit card delinquency ratio. Its client assets (i.e., loans made to clients) per employee had tripled in three years, whereas no other bank came close to doubling. Cohen's initial plan was to reach 33.5 trillion won in total assets by the end of 2004. In fact, KFB achieved 43.5 trillion won in total assets, with almost all the increase coming from client assets, which had tripled in three years. KFB was fundamentally transformed. It was a sound, strong bank with the best governance structure, best risk management, and the best asset quality in the market. It truly became the first in Korea.

I recalled a *Wall Street Journal* editorial from January of 1999, when Newbridge was still struggling through negotiations with the FSC: "To those wailing about Seoul giving away the 'crown jewels' here: Listen, Korea First Bank ain't no jewel. But now it has a chance to become one."

Through so much effort and over so many years, we had seized that chance and achieved what we had set out to do. Korea First Bank had once again become the shining crown jewel of Korea.

Chapter 16

Lion's Chase

"**S**han, how have you been lately? Can I invite you to a coffe to catch up?"

The familiar voice betrayed a hint of an Indian accent. It was Chan dra from HSBC. The call came on September 17, 2004. I had not spo ken with him for almost a year. At that time, he had approached me t express HSBC's interest in acquiring KFB, but HSBC called off the talks a couple of months later as abruptly as it had approached us. What now?

Chandra, or K. B. Chandraseka, was responsible for corporate strategy and development at HSBC. Indian by origin, he was a 26-year veteran of HSBC, which he had joined at the age of 25. He had led the negotia- tions for a number of the bank's strategic investments, including those in China's Bank of Communications and PingAn Insurance Group, both of which were great successes. He was experienced and shrewd, and his deals had worked out very well for his bank over the years.

Chandra did not leave me in suspense for long.

"Shan, we want to talk with you again about buying Korea First Bank. We are seriously interested."

I needed to be sure. "I thought John Bond wasn't interested," I told him. Sir John was chairman of HSBC. "Do you have the authorization to speak with us?"

When Chandra had reached out to me the year before, I met with him and the new CEO of HSBC in Asia, Mike Smith, to hear them out. Mike had just been transferred from HSBC Argentina. He asked, rhetorically, "Why couldn't we have done a similar deal to buy this bank back in 2000?" Smith had a strong interest in KFB. He recognized that we had done a good job turning around the bank and that it was now a very different institution from the one we first bought.

I had spent about two months discussing a deal with Smith and Chandra back in 2003. But when my partner Blum called John Bond to confirm the bank's interest, the HSBC chairman said, to our surprise, "If you want to sell KFB, we aren't a buyer." Apparently, he had no idea that his people had approached us and that we weren't actively looking to sell. In any case, the discussions were scuttled.

This time, Chandra assured me that he was fully authorized to reach out to me, and HSBC was seriously interested in acquiring KFB. He wanted to meet to present us with a proposal.

KFB's successful turnaround had gotten noticed. Back in 1998, HSBC had been interested in buying it, but Newbridge had beaten it to the punch. Its bid for Seoul Bank had also broken down. Now that the Korean economy had recovered, its banks were tempting targets. Citibank had just acquired Korea's KorAm Bank. A few months earlier, Standard Chartered's CFO, Peter Sands, and its head of strategy and corporate development, David Stileman, had invited me to lunch to inquire about KFB, although they did not express an explicit interest in buying the bank.

By the time Chandra called me the second time, we had owned KFB for almost five years and had successfully transformed it. We would be interested in selling KFB for the right price. However, we were a patient investor and were in no hurry to sell. We knew the bank had further growth potential, but I was willing to engage with HSBC based on Chandra's assurance that, this time around, Bond had blessed their interest.

In every acquisition, valuation is always the most difficult issue. Once the parties agree to the price, the rest, even though complicated, usually can be worked out. There was, however, not much to negotiate on KFB's valuation, at least from our point of view, because Citibank's purchase of KorAm had already set a benchmark. Citi had bought KorAm at about

twice its net asset or book value. Any interested buyer knew they could not buy KFB for less than that multiple of book value.

But there remained the question of how to determine the bank's book value. This might seem like an odd question because the book value of the bank was an audited figure, which KFB published annually. As a nonpublic company, normally KFB would not have to publish its annual reports. But at the request of Chairman Lee of the FSC, it had retained its status as a publicly listed company, even though there were no public shareholders and the shares were no longer traded. Since the bank had been nationalized using taxpayers' money, the FSC wanted to make sure that we maintained full transparency. We had been happy to oblige.

But the reported book value (or net asset value) is not what a buyer of a bank always accepts as the basis for valuation. Buyers generally want to know if the reported book value correctly reflects the true value of the bank's equity capital. Reported book value may not be "clean" because of inadequate provisions for bad loans, and it may include intangible assets, such as goodwill. For example, if a bank pays $100 for an asset whose net asset value is $75, the bank typically books the full purchase price of $100 as the value of the asset, although the asset's tangible value is only $75. The other $25 is recorded as goodwill, which is considered an intangible asset. A buyer may not accept goodwill or other intangible assets as having real value.

Additionally, if a bank does not correctly classify its problem loans and does not fully provision or reserve for possible loan losses and other potential impairments, the buyer may want to adjust the book value downward. A savvy buyer would want to determine the adjusted tangible book value of a bank, to see if there is a meaningful discrepancy between the reported and the adjusted book values.

Classification of a loan is often a subjective process, especially under the forward-looking methodology specified by the Bank for International Settlements. Using this methodology, a bank was supposed to classify a loan as impaired if it thought the customer might have difficulty paying off the loan in the future, even if the customer was still making payments now. By definition, "forward-looking" implied a subjective judgment. No two people would come to the same conclusion as to the amount of provision required for a particular loan—or even if a provision is required. This might present a problem, because a buyer might be more conservative than a seller. So, whose standard should the transacting parties accept? How would they resolve their differences?

That was exactly what we faced with HSBC. I made a proposal, which Chandra readily accepted, that we would jointly engage a third party from among the Big Four accounting firms to do the valuation. Whatever result was would be accepted by both sides. The Big Four include KPMG, Deloitte, PwC, and E&Y. KPMG was HSBC's own auditor and E&Y was KFB's, so they were excluded. The remaining two were well qualified, so we didn't have any preference. We knew that KFB's loan book was clean and our management was conservative, so we did not worry about anyone questioning whether management had correctly classified loans and made appropriate provisions. We had strong confidence in KFB's reported book value.

The board of directors of KFB held four regular meetings a year, alternating the venue between somewhere in Korea and San Francisco. On September 23, 2004, we were in San Francisco for a KFB board meeting. The occasion provided the Newbridge team with a good opportunity to discuss HSBC's interest. In the end, the partners of Newbridge decided to move forward with HSBC.

Bonderman suggested engaging an investment bank to advise us on the sale. I did not think it necessary. I thought we were fully capable of managing a sale by ourselves, and it would be easier to preserve confidentiality by keeping the matter within a small, tight circle. Coincidentally, I received an email from Chandra while in San Francisco. He proposed doing the deal through a fast process, which was much to our liking.

Two weeks later, on October 6, HSBC came back with a verbal indication of $3 billion for KFB. This came as a surprise. Until this point, we had only been referring to a sale based on a multiple of book value. Based on the previous agreement, we'd assumed the parties would eventually agree to a precise multiple and precise book value, and use those to derive the purchase price. But HSBC decided simply to give us a number, without bothering to include any basis for the valuation.

When I next saw Chandra, I asked him how HSBC had come up with $3 billion. He just shrugged. I could only guess, and I suspected that HSBC wished to lock in the price in U.S. dollars because the Korean won was strengthening, raising the value of KFB's assets and book value with it.

After several weeks of discussion, HSBC still had not communicated its intentions or presented its $3 billion offer to us in writing. Presumably, it wanted to reserve maximum flexibility to make changes.

I did not terribly mind HSBC's approach, as I knew its offer was not binding anyhow. It only amounted to an indication. As such, we weren't obliged to respond, one way or the other, as to whether we felt the offer was acceptable. But we thought the indication formed a basis for further discussion and were willing to allow HSBC to proceed with due diligence on KFB.

We were concerned about any premature leak or rumors of a possible sale, which could disturb our operations, especially if the sale did not go through. Given the high profile of KFB in Korea, any rumors about it were sensitive. HSBC was similarly concerned about leaks, because at this stage a deal might or might not happen. We agreed, therefore, to bring the management team of KFB to Hong Kong, to be interviewed by the HSBC team as part of the latter's due diligence process. We would also ship most, if not all, relevant data from Seoul to Hong Kong for HSBC to review. We thought we could minimize the chances of a leak if we stayed far away from Korea, even though bringing people and data to Hong Kong was quite a costly and involved process.

HSBC requested a month of exclusivity to come to terms with us for a deal. Starting from October 6, 2004, we would deal only with HSBC and would not talk with any other parties interested in buying KFB or entertain any potential offers from any third parties. Sellers usually do not want to give exclusivity to someone before knowing that there was a high probability of a deal, because doing so would shut the door on other potential suitors. We could end up with no buyers if HSBC decided to walk. But we agreed in good faith because we thought their interest was genuine and serious.

At this point, HSBC still had not given us anything in writing, not even a letter of intent. All its indications were verbal. Nonetheless, we had, as always, every intention to honor our commitment. Prior to this date, we had received some expressions of interest from a few other parties, but we stopped talking with them after we granted HSBC exclusivity, even though that was not written down either.

The understanding between the parties was that after the due diligence process was completed, HSBC would provide us with a firm and binding offer. Of course, it also had the right to not make an offer if it did not like what it saw. We ran the risk of KFB being perceived as damaged goods if HSBC walked away after due diligence, which was one more reason for us to keep the discussion strictly confidential.

But, almost immediately, HSBC wanted to change the rules of engagement. It wanted to specify PwC as the appraiser and auditor, even though we had agreed earlier to a joint and random selection process. Nonetheless, I acquiesced. All these firms were professional, and it shouldn't make too much of a difference which one did the work, even though I knew too well that service providers tend to be biased, within a defensible range, in favor of their clients, as we had seen repeatedly in the negotiation process for acquiring KFB.

When we met the PwC team with HSBC's team on October 21, it was clear that HSBC wanted to influence PwC's work. I did not like that, but I still did not think it would make too much of a difference. We were confident in the quality of KFB's assets and its book value. So we agreed with HSBC to jointly appoint PwC as the independent auditor, even though the company was their choice.

To our great surprise, Chandra came back a few days later to say HSBC no longer felt comfortable with both parties jointly appointing the auditor and accepting the results. Rather, HSBC wanted to appoint its own auditor. I thought this was like proposing to hire your own judge in a court case or bringing your own referee to a ball game. I told him that was different from what we had agreed, but, nevertheless, if HSBC insisted, we would let them.

At this point, HSBC had indicated a price to us without regard to KFB's book value. My thinking was that if they withdrew the offer after their own due diligence, by their own auditor, there was nothing we could do about it since there was nothing binding between us. But I was confident that the quality of the bank and its assets would stand up to stringent scrutiny by the most discerning auditor. I decided to let HSBC go ahead. I thought they probably would fall more deeply in love with our bank after checking it out.

I also suspected HSBC was hoping to adjust down the indicated price after their audit. At any rate, I knew they would not volunteer to adjust the price up. I made it clear to Chandra that we would agree to HSBC engaging its own auditor but we would reserve the right not to do a deal if they came up with a book value number that deviated materially from the reported book value, say by more than 5 percent. We did not have to explicitly state that, of course; without a binding agreement, we did not have to do anything if we did not like the price. But I wanted to be up front with our counterparties and draw a line in the sand, lest they have unrealistic expectations about how far we could be pushed.

HSBC was a leading global bank. In my experience, persuading such an organization to accept a different position is often hard. Decision making at such organizations is an involved, multi-layered, and time-consuming process. Once a decision is made, changing it is difficult. Each employee, no matter how senior, has limited authority.

We tried to be understanding and reasonable, but we were not quite sure if the other side appreciated our willingness to accommodate. From the start of the process, we had met every deadline, for everything, including arriving punctually for all appointments and meetings.

The lawyers on both sides were charged with producing a draft sales and purchase agreement or the final contract for the sale. Understandably, their lawyers wanted to shift all the transaction-related risks to our side. Our counsel did not accept this, considering it not reasonable or a deviation from accepted market practice. One of the issues was severance payment for members of the management team who would be terminated by the buyer upon a change of control, as HSBC wanted to install its own management. Naturally, the buyer or the bank itself should make such payments, but HSBC initially insisted the selling shareholders should pay.

I pointed out to Chandra and others that in the month that had elapsed since they verbally indicated HSBC's offer price for KFB, the Korean won had appreciated so much that if we concluded the transaction based on the $3 billion price, HSBC would have gained more than $100 million from the appreciation of the Korean currency alone. I showed them the calculation and told them there was really no point for them to nickel-and-dime us, as these minor issues were insignificant in the context of this multi-billion-dollar transaction.

Based on our verbal agreement, if, after its month of exclusivity, HSBC wished to proceed with a transaction, it was supposed to provide us with a binding offer in writing. During the exclusivity period, we at Newbridge and the management team at KFB, led by Cohen, cooperated with the HSBC team and worked closely with them, ensuring HSBC got everything it wanted. The work was done in absolute secrecy. We took every precaution possible to keep everything under wraps.

On November 11, I received a call from Robert Cohen. "I have bad news to report," he told me. "There is a leak. A Korean newspaper, *Economic Daily*, just printed a story about the sale of KFB to HSBC. All hell is breaking loose in Seoul."

Sure enough, no sooner had Cohen hung up than my phone rang again. It was JT Kim of the KDIC, demanding to know what was going on. I gave him a full update on our talks with HSBC and explained that we had not signed anything.

Under the terms of our deal for KFB, Newbridge controlled 100 percent of the voting rights and had the right to sell 100 percent of KFB's shares including those owned by the government by exercising our drag-along right, meaning the government would be obligated to sell when we did. Of course, I intended to inform the government side if a sale was imminent. Even though we were working with HSBC, we had had enough experience to know that there was no deal until there was a deal. I offered to go to Seoul to meet JT Kim and the president of the KDIC to update them.

I also called Chandra to tell him of this development in the press. He said HSBC would always take the position of "no comment on rumors" with no denial and no confirmation, if asked by the press. I told him that would be our position as well.

KFB was probably the most written-about Korean bank by the Western media. Leading publications like the *Financial Times* and the *Wall Street Journal* picked up the *Economic Daily* story, even without confirmation from either HSBC or Newbridge. To our relief, the international press coverage strongly endorsed the rumored deal, considering HSBC to have smartly "stolen a march on its rivals." It soon became clear that HSBC's main rivals had noticed.

★ ★ ★

In spite of HSBC missing the deadlines and changing what we had agreed, Chandra told me, to our great comfort, that the HSBC team liked what they saw. Their review did not discover any significant problems. They thought we had negotiated a good deal with the Korean government and that KFB's management was also very good. However, HSBC had not completed its due diligence by the end of the exclusivity period (November 5), which he requested that we extend.

Furthermore, HSBC wanted a written agreement between us, by which we would accept their verbal offer, even though it would still be subject to due diligence. Basically, they wanted us to commit to selling the bank to them at the price they had indicated, but they might or might not buy it or honor the price. That was unfair, I thought, so I said no.

Now that HSBC had failed to give us a binding offer at the end of the exclusivity period, there was no telling if the bank would eventually confirm a deal with us or at what price. We ran the risk of no deal—again.

When refusing to extend the exclusivity, my calculation was that HSBC would not walk away at this point, because it had done a lot of work, was impressed with the quality of KFB, and was genuinely interested in the bank.

I made two proposals to Chandra. One was that HSBC and Newbridge would sign a mutually binding agreement, but the price could still be adjusted by a third-party adjudicator if HSBC discovered material discrepancies between the numbers we provided and HSBC's own due diligence. Alternatively, we would let them continue to do the work without exclusivity, but either party would have the right to walk away.

On Friday, November 12, the day after the news of our deal broke in the *Economic Daily*, Chandra called to request that I meet with him and Mike Smith, HSBC's Asia CEO. He warned me that Smith was not comfortable with the idea of an independent adjudicator. Neither would HSBC be willing to have a binding agreement prior to further due diligence. Since Newbridge was not willing to give HSBC further exclusivity, he asked me repeatedly, "Are you going to run a limited auction?"

Instead of answering his question I said, "Chandra, we would prefer to have one bird in hand, which is the certainty we have been talking about. But if this bird refuses to be in our hand, we would not shoo away all the birds in bushes."

I did not know what HSBC wanted to do. I thought if it should decide to walk away at this point, it would mean either they never took this transaction seriously, which was unlikely, or they were too proud to concede anything, which was more likely. Given this uncertainty, and the fact that we had already gone this far down the path toward a sale, there was no turning back, and we had to keep our door open for any third-party bidders.

I met with Smith and Chandra as scheduled, on the morning of Monday, November 15, at HSBC's headquarters in Hong Kong's Central district.

The HSBC building was iconic: A broad, square tower, 44 stories tall, it looked like a futuristic factory made out of glass-and-steel LEGOs, without using any reinforced concrete in its inner core. Designed by Norman Foster, it was reputed to be the most expensive building ever built when it opened in 1985; its massive prefabricated components had to be made in the United Kingdom and shipped in. The bank sits just across a narrow lane from the Old Bank of China building, and about 220 yards (200 meters) diagonally from the 72-floor Bank of China Tower designed by I. M. Pei.

On the roof of the HSBC building are two maintenance cranes that look like big cannons pointing directly at the Bank of China Tower. Their alleged purpose, apocryphal or not, is to fend off the negative energy or whatever ill winds blow from that bank, in accordance with *feng shui*, a type of Chinese superstition, in my view, that connects one's fortune with one's surroundings.

I do not know if the decision makers of the British bank truly believed in their own magical powers or in those of the Bank of China, but they probably figured it was better to be safe than sorry. The nearby Citibank building is shaped like a shield, which is rumored to have the same protective effect against the potential dark energy emanating from the Bank of China. Citi obviously did not know, while HSBC apparently did, that the best defense is offense, and a cannon should be more effective than a shield. No wonder HSBC was the largest and seemingly most successful bank in Hong Kong.

I was ushered into Smith's spacious office, where he and Chandra were already waiting. After we sat down, Smith declared himself to be very disappointed and upset. He accused Newbridge of having acted in bad faith.

"My lawyers tell me that your markups on the SPA [sales and purchase agreement] are mean," he said, "This is a fully priced deal. If you run an auction now, we will bid, but at a much lower price."

"Mike, we have acted in good faith," I responded. "If we have had some reservations about the tactics used by your team, we have not wished to complain. If there are differences between our markups, we should meet to work them out. But we would not characterize your side as being 'mean.' We considered your bank to be the most logical buyer, and we still think so. For a week we have asked for a meeting between both parties, plus lawyers, but your team refused. We met every deadline agreed on, but your team missed them all."

Upon hearing that, he calmed down. But staring at me sternly, he asked, "Do you trust Robert?" Clearly, he suspected that KFB's CEO, Robert Cohen, had leaked the news of the deal to the press.

"I trust him absolutely," I said. "The leak would do far greater damage to us than to you."

The discussion shifted to the issue of tax withholding. HSBC wanted to withhold any estimated taxes Newbridge might be liable to pay on the sale, but our lawyers would not agree. "Tax is your problem," Smith said emphatically.

I explained to him that yes, taxes were our problem. But there was no reason for HSBC to withhold taxes on our behalf. Tax authorities in Korea had never gone to the buyer for taxes owed by the seller, and because of the tax treaties between South Korea and many jurisdictions in which our investors resided, we would have to work with tax authorities to determine the liabilities. We could not allow HSBC to withhold, and pay, an arbitrary amount on our behalf.

"If you did so," I told Smith and Chandra, "it would be unprecedented in the history of Korea." I pointed out a few precedents, including Citibank's recent purchase of KorAm, in which there had been absolutely no issue on this point. The risk of tax authorities going after the buyer was almost nil.

"If we allow you to withhold, we would have to pay you a far greater amount than the risk of your being found liable," I said. "The risk is hugely asymmetrical in HSBC's favor. Besides, you have already gained $120 million on currency appreciation, by my last count," I said.

Smith knew that the potential tax liability was only a fraction of that amount. In fact, the won had appreciated more than I'd realized. HSBC's currency gain on its $3 billion offer, made about a month ago, was up to $170 million by then. And HSBC's stock price had risen 3 percent or so in the past two sessions of trading, partially due to the leaked KFB story. That added nearly $6 billion to the company's market capitalization. It was really not necessary for them to pinch pennies, in the scheme of things.

After I finished talking, I gave Smith a copy of a tax opinion issued by Kim & Chang, our Korean counsel. He mumbled something about "bloody Kim & Chang, telling us one thing and them another," which presumably meant they had gotten some advice on some other deals from the same law firm. But he seemed to understand the issue and our position.

On due diligence, he did not know what the issue was, and began by asking if we had anything to hide. I said we were perfectly willing to let them do whatever they considered necessary within the agreed time frame. But we would like to have some objectivity in the process, as both parties had earlier agreed to use an independent auditor, so we would both be bound by the results.

"Or," I said, "you do whatever you want for three weeks and then tell us what you wish to do, but it should not be unilaterally binding. If you make an offer, we have the right to accept it or not."

"That is fair," Smith said.

Then Chandra explained why they had changed their minds about using an independent third-party auditor. Earlier I had suggested that both parties should accept the results of the independent auditor and could not walk from the deal unless there was a *material* discrepancy between what we presented and what the auditor found. According to Chandra, HSBC's lawyers would not agree to the concept of materiality, claiming that they had never heard of such a concept before.

Materiality is a well-known concept in contracts. I thought that if HSBC's lawyers had not heard of the concept, then they were grossly incompetent and should be fired. But I held my tongue. We both knew they were using their lawyers as a scapegoat here.

Regarding next steps, Chandra said that they needed seven to 10 days more than the three additional weeks Newbridge had agreed to give them to prepare a due diligence report. I reminded him we had both agreed to another three weeks, but not more than that. Now Smith turned to Chandra: "Why can't you do due diligence in two and a half weeks and use three days to prepare a report?"

It seemed to me that Smith was relaxed about not getting further exclusivity from us. The risk to HSBC of working without exclusivity was, of course, that we would be free to entertain other potential bids. But they probably calculated that they had gotten a one-month head start on any competition and that nobody else would be able to catch up quickly enough to compete with them in another month. I was not sure there would be anyone stepping forward at this stage either.

★ ★ ★

I left for Seoul at two that afternoon, November 15, 2004. I had promised to visit the KDIC to provide it with a full download of the work we were doing with potential buyers for the bank. I wrote a memo to my partners on the flight, summarizing my meeting with Smith and Chandra.

"It seems quite clear to me that Mike Smith is rather reasonable and fair minded," I reported, after noting he had held a biased view of how Newbridge had conducted the sale process. "Today's meeting at least allows Smith to hear our side of the story. Smith said that he would need to think about my proposal and get back to me tonight."

I also noted in the memo that the Korean won had appreciated considerably. A month ago, the $3 billion price tag indicated by HSBC would translate into 1.92 times KFB's net asset value; but now it was only 1.82 times, or about $170 million cheaper for HSBC. I thought this might cause a problem for the KDIC because the multiple was significantly lower than that for KorAm. But, of course, we had never agreed to either the currency in which the price should be denominated or the amount of HSBC's verbal indication.

While Hong Kong was still warm, at about 77 degrees Fahrenheit (25 degrees Celsius) in mid-November, Seoul was chilly. The morning after I arrived, November 16, the highest temperature for the day was only about 45 degrees Fahrenheit (7 degrees Celsius).

I got a call from Chandra after my morning run. He had a message from Smith. HSBC was willing to table the question of tax withholding for the time being. Assuming there were no surprises when their due diligence was completed, and the estimated tax obligation was not going to shift much from their estimates, HSBC would not let the deal fall apart over that.

HSBC also assumed that Newbridge would now want to run an auction (or a bidding process) for the bank sale, which they would be willing to participate in. Chandra agreed to send us an indication of interest in writing. It would not contain a stated offer price, but HSBC was willing to negotiate in good faith.

Chandra assured me the due diligence process would be completed in three weeks, although HSBC would need four more days to submit a binding bid. He also wanted to have the lawyers keep working simultaneously on the sale and purchase agreement, which would be submitted together with their bid.

That evening, I received HSBC's draft letter of interest.

"This in fact is the only thing in writing we have ever received from them," I wrote to my colleagues, updating them on the development.

We had codenamed HSBC *Lion* in our internal communications, after the two bronze lion statues that guarded the entrance to its Hong Kong headquarters on Des Voeux Road.

"Lion wishes to sign the letter with us as soon as possible and make an announcement immediately after," I continued. This was partly because Smith and Chandra did not think they would be able to keep the negotiations secret for long. They also wanted to be able to have conversations with the KDIC and with KFB's union, which would widen the circle of people who knew about the deal and make it virtually impossible to keep quiet. "I think we cannot do it until probably Monday next week. Meanwhile, I have asked Robert to begin to prepare for the on-site due diligence." So far, HSBC's due diligence had been offsite, away from Korea and in Hong Kong. It would be almost impossible for us to keep things under wraps if they began due diligence on KFB premises.

* * *

The next day, November 16, I met with both the KDIC and the FSC to update them. My visit was kept secret, so as not to make Lion or anyone else nervous. Nor did I go anywhere near KFB, to avoid being seen.

I met with the KDIC's new chairman, In-Won Lee, in his office. JT Kim and another senior executive were also present. I informed them that we had at least one party interested in buying KFB and that Newbridge would shortly decide whether to run a limited auction. It would take between four to six weeks to complete. Lee said the KDIC had a slight preference for HSBC over any other potential bidders, because it was a large bank and already had an office in Korea; but it would be happy with any buyer that was a financial institution.

We discussed Newbridge's drag-along right, which gave us the right to sell the government's shares along with ours by issuing a formal notice. I proposed that we should simply have Newbridge and the KDIC sign the same sales and purchase agreement, instead of having the KDIC get dragged into the deal by a notice. I thought it would be much better optics, because being dragged might be perceived as being forced. The KDIC readily agreed.

Another encouraging piece of news was that though the sale of KDIC's stake would be subject to approval by the Public Fund Oversight Commission, of which, incidentally, the former FSC chairman Hun-jai Lee was a co-chair, the KDIC did not think the Korean government had a choice, given the binding nature of our drag-along right. The KDIC saw no apparent obstacles to the sale.

After the KDIC, I went to the FSC to meet with the officials there. The FSC team listened to my description of the situation and informed me that its approval process for a sale of this nature typically took three months. The FSC officials echoed the KDIC's comments on the sale and concurred in their opinion regarding HSBC. They said that the bar would be very high for potential bidders that were nonbank financial institutions, but any bank would be great from the government's viewpoint.

I knew that under the banking rules of Korea, a private equity firm like Newbridge would not be permitted to acquire control of a bank; we had been able to do so only because KFB was distressed during the Asian Financial Crisis. Now times had changed, and the opportunity we had had was unlikely to be repeated.

That evening, I went to Robert Cohen's home in Seoul for dinner, as invited by Robert and his wife, Annie. Their home was decorated with traditional Korean furniture and artwork, in addition to some furniture shipped over from their home in New York City. In the living room, there was a painting of a large persimmon tree, its branches loaded with bright red-orange-colored fruit. Persimmon was a popular fruit in Korea and it was in season. I thought the painting captured what we were going through at the moment. Our effort had borne fruit; KFB had been transformed into a sound and healthy bank. Now it was harvest-time, and it looked like we would have a bumper crop.

I immensely enjoyed the exquisite French cuisine that Annie cooked in a setting that blended Korean and Western cultures. The dinner had a celebratory air even though no deal had officially been agreed. Cohen was happy that things seemed to be moving in the right direction. We had all worried about what impact the press leak might have had on the process. Happily for us all, the episode seemed to have blown over. I was sure it was not lost on the Cohens that if we completed the sale, they would have accomplished their mission and would soon be going home in New York.

★ ★ ★

Newbridge's offices were located in Hong Kong's International Financial Center, a massive complex right next to Victoria Harbour. We had moved from our old office on Queen's Road Central into One IFC, an ultra-modern, 37-story tower shortly after it opened in 1999 at the tail end of the Asian Financial Crisis. Four years later we moved again, to Two IFC, an 88-story tower that at the time was the tallest building in Hong Kong. My 57th-floor window looked out over the harbor, bustling with boat and ship traffic, and at the high-rises of Kowloon across the water.

On Monday, November 22, 2004, I spent 10 minutes walking from our office at Two IFC to the HSBC building. Many buildings in Central were connected by a network of walkways and passageways, over roads and through buildings, which allowed people to get from one part of the district to another without getting wet, even in one of Hong Kong's legendary typhoons.

Arriving at HSBC, I went again to Smith's office. This time, he was in a good mood. At about noon, he and I signed HSBC's "letter of expression of interest" in his office. The signing was more symbolic than substantive because there was no mention of price, but it did represent the bank's expression of serious interest in acquiring KFB, with the exact terms remaining to be negotiated and agreed upon by the parties.

After the signing, we chatted for a while. I mentioned that I had heard a story about him being chased by gunmen during his time as HSBC's head in Argentina. It was indeed a true story, he told me. He had exposed a kickback scheme, and those involved had chased and shot at him in his car in an act of retribution. Smith opened his drawer and pulled out some photographs of the damaged car, riddled with bullet holes and stained with blood on his seat. He had been shot in the thigh.

I thought this was quite horrible and that he was lucky to be alive. I had never thought of banking as a life-threatening occupation. Smith was animated and cheerful when he told me the story, as if he were describing an exciting James Bond movie. Only the bloodstained upholstery of the car in the photo reminded me of how close he had come to being killed.

Chapter 17

It's a Race

O n November 10, 2004, I received an unexpected phone call from Rodney Ward. The tall, silver-haired Englishman was the Asia Pacific chairman of UBS, the Swiss banking giant. We had known each other for years, and I considered him a friend.

Ward quickly came to the point. He was calling on behalf of Standard Chartered Bank to express interest in acquiring KFB.

StanChart, as Standard Chartered was sometimes known, had made an overture to us months earlier but had not been able to move forward. Its renewed interest was timely, as HSBC's exclusivity period had just expired five days ago and we were at liberty to speak with other suitors. I was hoping StanChart would step forward because we needed to keep our options open in case HSBC's offer did not come through.

I was a little surprised that the call had come from Ward, though. I knew both Peter Sands, StanChart's CFO, and David Stileman, its chief of strategy and business development. They could have easily reached out directly. Yet it was not unusual for a prospective buyer to use an intermediary to facilitate serious discussions. The more I thought about it, the more I considered it to be a good sign. StanChart must have been serious if it had engaged UBS to advise it on a potential deal.

But I was soon disappointed. When I asked Ward how serious StanChart's interest was, he said, "I think it is highly unlikely that StanChart will come through with a confirmation of interest and an offer."

This was quite odd. It was like saying "We are interested, but our interest is unlikely to be real." Why would anyone deliver such a mixed message? What was the point? Then I realized that UBS was probably StanChart's long-term and regular advisor in matters like this. As such, UBS would be obliged to make a phone call when asked to by someone senior at StanChart, but in Ward's honest opinion, his client was unlikely to be a serious buyer. He probably wanted to be up front with me as a friend, lest he got my hopes up for nothing.

The subtext of our conversation, though, was that StanChart did have an interest in buying KFB and had tasked UBS to look into it, but Ward thought StanChart wouldn't be able to pull off such a big acquisition. Whether he thought StanChart could not afford it or its board would not give its approval, he did not say.

Nonetheless, we were willing to work with StanChart to see how its interest might develop.

We had moved boxes of files and KFB data to Hong Kong for HSBC's due diligence needs. We agreed to share the material with StanChart, after signing a confidentiality agreement, to enable it to develop a proposal. I reported to my partners in a memo on November 16, 2004, about this new potential buyer:

Re: Project Daisy

Meanwhile, the advisor to another potential buyer (code-named Project Daisy) has indicated that it will provide us with a proposal by the end of this week. They know the price guideline is Citi/KorAm benchmark and their proposal will have had the benefit of no less data than what Lion has received to date.

David Stileman, StanChart's chief of strategy and business development, was a tall and impeccably mannered British gentleman. I found his upper-crust accent pleasing, as it reminded me of the Lingua-phone language courses on cassette, which I'd used when I first began to study English in college. Stileman also had a good sense of humor, which I appreciated. He reported to Peter Sands, the bank's CFO, who would take over as CEO in 2006. Where Sands was uptight and circumspect, Stileman was relaxed and direct.

StanChart's headquarters in Hong Kong is a narrow, sand-colored tower that stands shoulder-to-shoulder with HSBC's broader edifice, facing Hong Kong's Des Voeux Road. Completed a few years after the HSBC building, StanChart's was more modest in appearance—a sloop to HSBC's battleship. It did, however, have a long flight of stone stairs one had to climb to reach its heavy front door, giving it the feel of an old, distinguished bank.

On Monday, November 22, my colleague Daniel Poon and I met with Sands, Stileman, and Nancy Wong, Stileman's deputy, in a small conference room in the corner of the building, with windows looking out onto a busy street. The StanChart executives were prepared to give us a proposal.

We all knew what we were here for, but Sands did not immediately come to the point. Instead, he danced around with small questions about this and that for more than half an hour. He finally gave us the proposal after I said that we were not interested in continuing to discuss a deal in abstract terms.

When I told them that KFB would announce later that afternoon that Newbridge was in preliminary discussions with potential buyers, Sands promptly asked for the proposal back. Daniel Poon had already left with StanChart's proposal and was heading back to the office. Sands must have thought the announcement indicated we were close to a deal with HSBC and was disturbed that we might be using StanChart as a stalking horse. I explained to him that KFB had no choice but to make an announcement because the sale had been leaked to the press and we would not be able to keep it a secret anyhow because due diligence work by prospective buyers at KFB headquarters would involve many KFB employees. I tried to reassure him that we always dealt with people in good faith. But I could tell he remained deeply skeptical.

Meanwhile, I had to intercept Poon en route to the office to hand the proposal back to Sands.

★ ★ ★

Thursday, November 25 was Thanksgiving Day. Even though it was not officially observed in Hong Kong, my family never missed a turkey meal together. In the middle of dinner, I received a phone call from Ward at UBS. Without being prompted, he spoke somewhat apologetically about the "eccentric behavior" of StanChart, his client for taking back its proposal. Nonetheless, he reiterated his view that it would be difficult for StanChart to buy KFB.

Shortly after I got off the phone with Ward, Stileman called. There had been a debate among StanChart executive directors, he told me, about pursuing the KFB deal. Some of them continued to worry that we might be using them as a stalking horse against HSBC, he said, but earlier that day one of their advisors had received a phone call from a senior executive at HSBC who said that StanChart would be "ill-advised" to go after Korea First Bank. That warning shot had apparently backfired. Stileman was calling to tell me that Standard Chartered wanted to move forward.

How ironic, I thought. There was no better way for someone to shoot himself in the foot than by ordering his rival to stand down. It produced exactly the opposite effect by galvanizing the competitor to rise up to the challenge.

However, Stileman and his CEO, Mervyn Davies, needed to meet with their own chairman to get him to "check the box." Stileman said he would get back to me overnight as to whether or not they had received the chairman's go-ahead.

I appreciated Stileman's candor. To further encourage StanChart, I told him that we would prepare the data room for their immediate use and that we could give them a draft sales and purchase agreement by the following Monday. StanChart had to tell us how fast it could move, and we would do everything we could to accommodate their dates. I was quite happy about this communication and hoped that StanChart would indeed come through. A real competitive process would make the KFB sale much more foolproof.

I was enjoying a second turkey dinner at a Thanksgiving party the next evening when Stileman called back at about 9 pm. He told me the good news that StanChart's chairman had given the potential deal his blessing and that the StanChart team would begin due diligence on KFB on Monday. In fact, the StanChart team had already geared up; Poon had heard from them earlier in the day. Stileman made no mention of StanChart's earlier proposal or any further details. I was encouraged nonetheless and hoped once StanChart was drawn into the process, its people would build a strong conviction about our bank. At a minimum, we would have a viable alternative to HSBC. And in an ideal situation, the two-horse race would allow us to get a better price.

★ ★ ★

Hong Kong was unusually warm in the winter of 2004. It was already December 12, but the temperature was a tropical 87 degrees Fahrenheit (31 degrees Celsius).

StanChart proposed a conversation between its CEO, Mervyn Davies, and Newbridge's co-chairman, David Bonderman. I wrote a memo that evening to prep Bonderman for the meeting. In it, I advised that we manage StanChart and HSBC differently. StanChart was unsure of itself, afraid it might be used as a stalking horse and therefore reluctant to step forward, whereas HSBC was the opposite. It was so confident, in fact, that it did not consider the possibility of any viable competition. Therefore, our strategy should be to encourage StanChart and to draw it deep into the process.

One telling sign of HSBC's confidence and StanChart's reluctance was the number of people each sent to conduct due diligence in Seoul on the first day we opened data rooms for them. "HSBC showed up with an army, probably 20 people from different departments and even more people from their advisors, all headed by the head of its audit department," reported Poon. In contrast, "StanChart showed up with only three people."

Our other co-chairman, Dick Blum, called me on the morning of Saturday, December 18, to tell me that he had had a conversation with John Bond. Blum and Bond knew each other well, and I was somewhat wary of that. We had a competitive process going and I did not want it to be preempted. That would not be fair to StanChart, to which I already had given assurances, as had Bonderman, that we would treat them equally with other bidders. Blum told me that Bond had reiterated the offer HSBC had indicated from the start: HSBC would buy KFB for $3 billion.

Later that day, I went to the China Club to have lunch with Chandra. The club was located on the top three floors of the Old Bank of China, a dignified 1950s-era, 17-story stone building that now looked somewhat quaint nestled between the HSBC building and the new Bank of China tower across the street. The club was founded by TT Tsui, a well-known socialite and antique collector in Hong Kong. Styled after a Shanghai tea house circa 1930, its walls are covered with contemporary and classical works of Chinese art. Curated by Johnson Chang of Hanart TZ Gallery, the eye-popping collection features the work of artists who have become staples of the contemporary art scene. Many of the works were humorous, satirical, or mocking in nature. For example, there was a dark oil painting, in the style of a classical group portrait, of some Manchurian officials in traditional imperial costumes. But if you looked closely, among the mandarins were Chris Patten, the last British governor of Hong Kong, in a tall hat, tailcoat, and bow tie, and Tsui himself dressed as a Qing dynasty official.

Chandra arrived late. He apologized and told me that on Bond's orders he had worked the whole night to give us an offer letter by lunchtime. I had no idea what had prompted Bond to do so, other than that the conversation he had with Blum must have given him the idea HSBC could preempt the auction process. The letter confirmed the purchase price of $3 billion for KFB. Chandra told me they wanted us to take or leave the offer by noon on Monday, which I considered unreasonable. Nevertheless, we had a pleasant lunch. Chandra repeated how impressed HSBC was by KFB under our management.

That afternoon, I talked with Stileman by phone. He was in England and was about to go out to shoot pheasants, which the English considered a sport. Earlier, he had given us a valuation range for KFB, and now he said that Standard Chartered would bid at or above the high end. I thought he was testing me, but I did not have a chance to tell him that his number was not good enough before he signed off.

At about 11:30 pm, I reached Bonderman, who was on his plane, en route to his home in Aspen, Colorado. I told him of my conversations with both HSBC and StanChart. Now that HSBC had made a bid, we needed a bid from StanChart as soon as possible. I asked Bonderman to call Bryan Sanderson, Standard Chartered's chairman, to prompt him to give us a bid.

Early the next morning, I went for my usual early morning run on Bowen Road. Tree-lined and cool, the street was blocked to traffic for most of its length, making it a popular place for people to exercise.

As I ran, I thought over our negotiations with both HSBC and StanChart. I had yet to hear back from Bonderman about his conversation with Sanderson. After I finished my run, I called Bonderman. He told me that Sanderson had suggested that StanChart would bid at the top end of its indicated range, which was 3.1 trillion won, or just shy of $3 billion, but the price was in Korean won, which was appreciating in value.

It was a Sunday and I was mindful of Chandra's request for us to get back to HSBC no later than noon on Monday. The indication from StanChart, coming from its highest level, provided me with enough confidence not to accept HSBC's offer, and I thought I didn't have to wait until Monday to let them know. I called Chandra and informed him that HSBC's offer was not good enough. He did not seem surprised. HSBC knew someone else was looking, which was probably the reason HSBC wanted to preempt the process. I think he was only surprised that the competition had been able to move fast enough to make a bid. It had taken HSBC more than two months to get to that point.

At 5 pm, Stileman called and told me that StanChart would offer no less than 3.25 trillion won, up from 3.1 trillion. I thought about Bonderman's call with Sanderson and realized the StanChart chairman must have sensed that 3.1 trillion won was not good enough, as Bonderman must have seemed far from overjoyed to hear it. The new offer of 3.25 trillion won would translate into $3.08 billion at the exchange rate of the day, so StanChart's offer was already about $80 million better than HSBC's. This was a relief. I now knew a two-horse race had begun.

Stileman emphasized that StanChart would give us a real offer after Bonderman spoke again with Sanderson and with the CEO, Mervyn Davies, later that day. I did not understand why they would stretch it out like this, with Stileman calling me to give an indication and senior leadership calling Bonderman to give us a "real offer." But I supposed they wanted us to take their offer seriously by making it in a formal way, chairman to chairman.

I immediately wrote Bonderman to inform him of what had transpired on both HSBC's and StanChart's sides and to prepare him for his call with the StanChart people.

The next morning, Monday, December 20, I learned that Bonderman had spoken with Mervyn Davies. Even better than what Stileman had told me, StanChart's CEO communicated their bid to Bonderman at 3.3 trillion won, which was about $128 million better than HSBC's at that day's exchange rate. Davies also told Bonderman that StanChart's written offer would come in by 5 pm London time that day.

I was scheduled to meet with Chandra at 11 am. But that morning, I received an email from him, saying that HSBC had kept its word with its offer and that they expected us to sign the offer letter by noon today or it would expire. I also received an email from Smith saying the same thing. These messages implied we had given them our word, which they now expected us to keep, when in truth we had never given them our word nor accepted their offered price. Having willingly entered into what they referred to as a "mini-auction" process, they wanted to preempt that process by pushing us to accept their offer. Apart from that, their offer was not even binding without a fully negotiated sales and purchase agreement. There were still many contractual and legal issues outstanding. HSBC simply wanted to pressure us into accepting its offer by threatening to go away otherwise.

I was more amused than threatened, however. I had already informed Chandra that we would not be able to make a decision by the proposed deadline of noon today. We certainly did not want to lose HSBC as a bidder, but I knew a bluff when I saw it. HSBC was already too invested in this process, and their pressure on us, I felt, simply betrayed the team's anxiety.

I also knew that even if HSBC walked, there was a better offer on the table from Standard Chartered. Even though it was also lacking in detail, I was not too worried. I imagined it was quite solid, as it was communicated directly to Bonderman by StanChart's CEO. So, I let HSBC's deadline pass while discussing with Chandra, face-to-face, a number of issues in the offer letter in his office. I also informed Chandra we had a better offer.

I then told Chandra that we needed an offer in Korean won, not in U.S. dollars. There were two reasons. The Korean won was appreciating, which meant the value of KFB was appreciating in U.S. dollar terms. If we had fixed the price in U.S. dollars, we would not be able to capture the appreciation in value from a stronger won. More importantly, our partner and fellow shareholder in KFB was the Korean government, and it would need to be paid in won.

I had thought that as a global bank, HSBC would have no problem offering the price in Korean won, as it could easily hedge its own currency risks. But for some reasons, HSBC simply would not agree to offer a price in Korean currency. My only explanation for this was that it wanted to profit from the weakening of the dollar against the won, even though it could have achieved the same effect by buying forward won contracts, which would allow it to essentially lock in any future currency appreciation. I tried to impress upon Chandra how imperative it was to receive a price in won. But it seemed impossible for HSBC to accept. We finished the meeting at 12:30 pm, 30 minutes after HSBC's self-imposed deadline.

StanChart had engaged Allen & Overy, a London law firm with a large practice in Hong Kong, for the proposed transaction. Its offices were in Two IFC as well. That afternoon, I went to Allen & Overy to meet with a representative of StanChart and a few lawyers. Poon and another colleague, Scott Chen, joined me for the meeting as well. There were only a few key issues arising from our draft sales and purchase agreement. I led the discussion on our side. We had to adjourn several times for our side to caucus among ourselves.

We were mindful of the fact that the stickiest issue with HSBC was its insistence on withholding taxes on our behalf. We were relieved that StanChart did not raise the issue at all, as it was indeed not market practice for the buyer to withhold taxes on behalf of the seller. But our Korean counsel, Kim & Chang, insisted that we raise the issue ourselves and get StanChart to explicitly agree not to withhold taxes on our behalf. I was not enthusiastic about this plan. If it was not an issue for them, why did we have to bring it up? If we brought it up, would we practically invite them to insist on being able to withhold taxes?

The Kim & Chang lawyers thought there was a risk for us if we did not to spell out the withholding issue because of a legal concept called "unjust enrichment." In this case, the buyer might be able to come back to us for recovery if there was ever a withholding tax imposed on the buyer, unless the buyer had specifically agreed to accept the risk. I always thought lawyers would imagine the most remote possibilities in preparing a legal document, which was the reason why these documents were so long.

Poon and Yong Lee, one of our lawyers from Cleary Gottlieb, suggested that we include some specific "tax gross up" language, which basically would require the buyer to accept the risk of potential liability. I thought suggesting such language would be risky because it could raise a new issue that the other side might not agree with. Eventually, I suggested that we revise the "no-claim" language, which basically said that the buyer would have absolutely no claim against the seller after closing, excluding fraud and willful misconduct. Both our lawyers and theirs agreed to the proposed language, which would eliminate the risk of StanChart ever coming back to us for not having withheld taxes on our behalf.

Another issue that HSBC had sensitized us to was management compensation. HSBC wanted the seller to pay for the severance of any management personnel it decided not to keep. We wanted to make sure StanChart would accept that any severance pay would be the responsibility of the bank after the sale. StanChart lawyers initially were concerned whether there might be "illegality" under Korean regulations on management compensation if the bank accepted that responsibility. Eventually, we agreed that StanChart would have the right to restructure the compensation after closing, to minimize any risk of sensitivities caused by the possibility of large severance packages for senior management people. That resolved a major concern of ours, and by the close of the meeting we reached agreement on all the key issues.

Bonderman called me at about 7:20 pm. I gave him an update and told him that I was still waiting to receive the promised offer letter from Stileman. As I was on the conference call, Blum called a couple of times. He was worried about StanChart's offer. He wanted to talk with Bond of HSBC and cut a deal with him quickly because of their relationship. I was concerned about this plan, because that would be unfair to StanChart and to us. Blum asked me if I would agree to his asking Bond to accept a deal for $3.1 billion and giving him two hours to decide. I did not like the idea because we would not give StanChart an opportunity to counter, and StanChart might not even send us the promised written offer. I was mindful of having given my word to StanChart to provide it with a fair chance.

However, while StanChart's offer was better, we all knew there was more uncertainty with it. Standard Chartered did not have enough cash on hand to consummate the transaction and would need to raise capital.

HSBC had more than enough cash on its balance sheet to close the deal. At the current exchange rate, StanChart's offer was worth about $3.128 billion. Reasoning that $3.1 billion with certainty was better than $3.128 billion without it, I advised Blum that if he could get Bond to make that offer, we should take it.

I woke up on the morning of December 21, 2004, to a big surprise. Dan Carroll called me to say that Blum had cut a deal with Bond overnight to sell the bank to HSBC for $3.05 billion. This obviously was not as good as I would have liked, but I could understand Blum's desire to help Bond and his institution. StanChart's offer letter came through the previous night as well. Unfortunately, the fax machine in my office had run out of paper, so we did not see the offer until StanChart followed up with an email. The email confirmed the offer price of 3.3 trillion won, but there were a number of conditions attached.

The main condition, of course, was that StanChart's offer was subject to its being able to raise the needed capital. Another condition was that if its stock price fell below 900 pence per share on the London stock exchange, it would have the right to walk away. StanChart also wanted a right to back out of the transaction by paying a $50 million penalty, or breakup fee. Furthermore, the offer was subject to approval by StanChart's shareholders both in Hong Kong, where StanChart was also listed, and in London. I did not think any of the conditions were acceptable. Even though the offer was better in terms of price, the uncertainty associated with it made it almost impossible for us to consider.

I called JT Kim of the KDIC before 8 am to inform him there were two competing offers. He asked me a number of questions. After mulling things over, he agreed HSBC's offer with certainty was better.

Blum, Bonderman, Carroll, and I, along with a few others, jumped on an internal conference call to discuss. Blum was somewhat upset that I had even checked with the KDIC regarding the two bids, because he did not want us to risk being told no. He felt we should sell KFB to HSBC regardless of what StanChart came back with, because he had already cut a deal with Bond at $3.05 billion. Even though we thought StanChart might improve its offer, we all agreed a deal was a deal if struck by Blum. We would proceed with HSBC.

However, although we had completed most of the work on our documentation with StanChart in our meeting at Allen & Overy, there were still a number of outstanding issues with the sales and purchase agreement with HSBC. The problem was that HSBC was never in a hurry. It just did not have a sense of urgency. We could not afford to lose the StanChart offer and also fail to conclude a deal with HSBC because of the failure to reach agreement on outstanding issues in the document. Bonderman told me that the deal with HSBC had only 24 hours' exclusivity. If HSBC did not complete the transaction with us in that time, we would be free to accept a better bid.

I called Chandra at about 9 am to tell him what had transpired overnight between Blum and Bond. Chandra was incredulous and said he had not heard anything. I requested to meet with him as soon as possible and also asked his banking colleagues to meet with Cohen to work out the transition agreement, which still contained many issues Cohen had not agreed to. But Chandra later called Poon to say he could meet with me only at 4 pm, because he needed confirmation from London regarding the agreement between Bond and Blum. I was surprised that Bond had not communicated with his own team. At this rate, I very much doubted if HSBC would be able to conclude the final agreement in 24 hours.

At about 3 pm, Stileman reached me on my mobile. It was only 6 am in London, where he was. I told him that we could not accept the uncertainty in StanChart's offer. He replied that they were working on removing all the conditions in the offer, but I remained skeptical that they would be able make it fully unconditional. I spoke with a couple investment bankers, including Mike O'Hanlon of Lehman, to see if they thought StanChart could get a bank to "hard, firm, and unconditionally" underwrite its stock offering to finance this deal. A "hard, firm, and unconditional" underwriting was an obligation by the underwriter to either raise the capital from the market or provide the capital itself. Everyone I spoke with thought the odds of Standard Chartered arranging such a deal were long. I thought that even if HSBC missed the 24-hour deadline, there was little chance of StanChart following through on what Stileman was offering.

When I met with Chandra at 4 pm, he said he had received a one-line email from Douglas Flint, HSBC's Group Finance Director, to confirm that $3.050 billion "is consistent with our understanding." Chandra came with his lawyers from Freshfields Bruckhaus Deringer, a London-based law firm with a big practice in Hong Kong. The team of lawyers included Teresa Ko, a senior partner and capable lawyer whom I knew well. The meeting was reasonably smooth. I reminded Chandra that the deal with them would be valid for 24 hours, although by then they had spent almost a whole day waiting for London's confirmation. Furthermore, the HSBC team would only be able to meet with Cohen in Seoul the next day, adding another day to the clock. Based on my experience working with HSBC, I thought it unlikely that they would be able to get there in 48 hours, let alone 24. At this pace, HSBC would certainly miss the window, but its team betrayed no urgency.

Later that day, I got a call from Stan Chow, a lawyer at Allen & Overy, who told me StanChart had just received a waiver from the Hong Kong stock exchange, exempting it from the need for shareholders' approval for the deal. This removed a huge uncertainty from StanChart's offer, but it still had to find an investment bank to hard underwrite its stock offering. It seemed that while HSBC was still taking its time, StanChart was rushing and making every effort to remove all conditions from its offer.

I sent the following email to Stileman before going to bed, laying out what it would take for us to seriously consider StanChart's offer:

David,

I may have gone to bed by the time your 2:30 pm meeting is over. I am very appreciative of the fact that you are making such an effort. As I mentioned, your price is slightly better than your competition but, candidly, does not justify the risk we will have to take. My own view is that there are probably two ways, either of which will get us there. I know that neither is easy. The first, needless to say, is to give us complete certainty, e.g., if some bank hard underwrites the offering. In the absence of such certainty, it probably will require a combination of substantial reduction of risks, as you are trying to do, and an improvement in price, which I think Mervyn spoke with Bonderman about. Please note that I am not trying to negotiate at all. I just wish to give you my candid view from where I stand and hope it helps. I know that Mervyn will speak with David Bonderman again today. I sincerely hope that they can work something out between themselves before I wake up! I spoke with David just now and he is most up to date. He says that he will be going into town but is reachable by his mobile phone. As you must have gathered, he is very straightforward. Please work with him.

Shan

I called Bonderman as soon as I got up on Wednesday, December 22. He said that StanChart was working hard to get someone to unconditionally underwrite its stock offering, which would remove a significant element of uncertainty in its offer. At about 7:45 am Hong Kong time, I called Stileman in London but apparently woke him up. He sounded annoyed and grouchy, even though he had sent me an email overnight asking me to call him at any time. He mumbled that they would give us certainty and I let him go back to sleep.

According to Bonderman, StanChart was working with UBS to see if UBS could unconditionally underwrite StanChart's stock offering. Later in the day, Stileman sent me an email explaining that he had only six hours of sleep since Saturday, four days ago. He had been working extremely hard and the StanChart team was really making a great effort. He also sent me a new draft offer letter. There were a number of changes. Whereas the previous letter included a press release to be sent out once we accepted the offer, the new one required confidentiality and silence, probably because of the regulatory requirement ahead of a stock offering. Whereas the previous letter would give StanChart the right to walk if its stock price fell below 900 pence per share, that reference was removed, pending confirmation that UBS would hard underwrite the offering.

I thought we had to bring this process to a close by imposing a deadline on both bidders. I informed both HSBC and StanChart that we had to sign the final documents by 5 pm the next day, December 23, which would be the fifth anniversary of signing of our definitive agreements for the KFB purchase. I wanted both of them to have completed the documentation and provided us with a firm and binding offer by then.

As December 22 ticked by, StanChart kept working hard to improve its offer. We received a number of drafts of its offer letter, each one removing more conditions. By the end of the day, practically all the conditions in StanChart's offer were removed. I faxed a copy of the last draft offer letter from StanChart to Bonderman and told him to anticipate a call from Mervyn Davies.

Blum was getting anxious about HSBC, which was still taking its time. He was concerned we would not be able to finalize a deal with it. He asked me to tell Chandra to hurry up so we could close the door before anyone else could come in.

HSBC remained uncompromising on a number of issues in the document, and it had let the deadline pass without giving us a binding deal.
At one point, Chandra had sent me an email in which he indicated HSBC
was prepared to give us an offer in terms of Korean won, but someone at
the bank subsequently changed their mind and the offer was rescinded.
Nevertheless, Chandra kept repeating that HSBC had kept its side of the
bargain, even as it continued to let deadlines lapse.

"We believe we have kept our word on the Purchase Price and have
given you a deal which has certainty of completion," he concluded in
an email I received on the morning of December 20. "As our deal does
not contain any surprises and is therefore in a form which can readily be
accepted by you, we are unable to extend the acceptance deadline unless
you can offer us exclusivity."

His "acceptance deadline" had passed while we were meeting later
that day. Now I had to tell him to hurry. I had to make it clear that the
window was fast closing and it would be their own fault if they could not
come through within the allotted time. Further, I could not let stand his
insinuation that HSBC had kept its word but we did not keep ours. I said
in my response:

> *Referring to the last paragraph of your email, I also wish to assure*
> *you that we have kept our word on all the understandings between us,*
> *including keeping to each of the deadlines agreed between us. As you*
> *recall, we agreed to a price and we granted you an exclusivity period at*
> *the end of which we were supposed to give certainty to each other of a*
> *transaction at the price agreed. As you were not in a position to give us*
> *certainty of a deal as we had mutually envisioned when your exclusiv-*
> *ity expired, we agreed that that we would begin a competitive process in*
> *which you would participate. In other words, the deal that we had origi-*
> *nally agreed to was off at that point by mutual understanding. Once we*
> *are through a competitive process, not only do we have a fiduciary duty*
> *to our limited partners, but also to our Korean Government shareholders,*
> *to take the best offer. We have kept and will always keep our word.*

Hong Kong had been caught up in the holiday spirit for weeks. As a
Chinese city, Hong Kong celebrates all the Chinese traditional holidays,
such as Chinese New Year, the Mid-Autumn Festival, and Buddha's

Birthday. But as a former British colony, it also celebrates major Western holidays, including Christmas and New Year's. It used to celebrate the queen's birthday, a holiday that was shifted back a few weeks to become Hong Kong Special Administrative Region Establishment Day after the return of Hong Kong's sovereignty to China in 1997.

Immediately after Thanksgiving, all the tall buildings facing Victoria Harbour put up decorative neon lights, with giant images of Santa Claus, reindeer, and shining stars running their entire height. At night, the colorful lights on both sides of the harbor lit up the entire waterfront, their reflections dancing on the waves as if there were a fairytale world under the water. But by Thursday, December 23, with Christmas only two days away, Central was a lot quieter than usual. Many people, especially foreign expatriates, had already left for holidays elsewhere. We were still working hard, however.

I woke up before 5 am to find that StanChart had come through overnight with a firm and unconditional underwriting by its banker, UBS, for a stock offering of some $2 billion. Combined with the cash on its balance sheet, this would give it enough money to do the deal and removed yet another element of uncertainty from its offer.

I sent to my colleagues a copy of the drag-along language from our agreement with the Korean government, to remind them that we had a duty to our shareholders. I remembered the terms we had agonized over during our negotiations, whether to say the drag-along was to "enable" or "allow" the maximization of shareholder value. Either way, now that the time was upon us, our duty was clear. We had to inform both bidders that we were under a contractual obligation with the Korean government to take the best offer, lest they have any illusions we might play favorites. Of course, we would value certainty even above price because we could not afford for the sale to fall through, certainly not after the sale process had become public knowledge.

I finished my run at about 8:30 am, just when our conference call was scheduled to start. I did not have time to get home and dialed in from my car parked at the entrance of the running trail. Blum, Bonderman, Carroll, and Poon were on the call, as was BM Park from Kim & Chang. We went over the two offers in detail. StanChart's bid stood at 3.3 trillion won, or $3.128 billion. HSBC's offer was at $3.05 billion. We debated for over an hour among ourselves which way to go.

StanChart's offer was higher, but it required us to sign the definitive documents during the week of January 10, three weeks away and into the new year. StanChart wanted to sign and announce the deal and do the stock offering to finance it at the same time. It thought that making an announcement today would require it to consolidate KFB's financial results into its own for this year, which would significantly and unnecessarily complicate its regulatory filings.

Blum favored the HSBC deal regardless, based on his handshake with Bond, even though HSBC was not able to close the deal in the agreed 24-hour window. Bonderman also thought we should go with HSBC, calling the $78 million difference in price "a rounding error" that did not justify the risk. I agreed. Certainty around closing the deal was more important. I knew that the KDIC would not object, because the Korean government had expressed a preference for HSBC and considered it a bigger bank globally. The KDIC probably would also agree that certainty would trump the "rounding error" in price.

But StanChart's price was higher and it had been working extremely hard and expediently to remove uncertainty. It would be unfair not to give it a chance to remove the remaining conditions from its offer. If StanChart was able to match HSBC's offer on certainty, its bid would be better, although only marginally so in the grand scheme of things. If we allowed StanChart a chance to make its offer unconditional, we should also give HSBC an equal chance to put its best foot forward. We concluded that it would be fair if we requested both parties to put their best bids on the table. We would make a final decision the next day.

I set up a meeting with Chandra for 2 pm at the office of Freshfields, which was the law firm advising HSBC. I arrived there at 1:50.

As I was parking my car, I received a call from Stileman, who had just woken up in London. I told him what we had decided this morning. He was disappointed. I told him that his team's offer was better, but by a "rounding error," in Bonderman's words. I also told him that when HSBC first made us an offer, it was a higher price in Korean won terms (approximately 3,480 billion won by the exchange rate at that time), but the movement in the exchange rate meant its offer was actually lower than StanChart's today.

Stileman speculated that HSBC's offer was 3,200 billion won. I knew he was fishing for any hint as to what HSBC's number was, but I did not take the bait. In my mind, we needed to be fair to both parties, and it would not be fair to HSBC if I shopped, or disclosed, its actual bid to a competitor. I just said "absolutely not" without giving him any further indication.

Stileman was not going to give up on Standard Chartered's bid and said he was going to speak with his CEO. I offered that they should speak with Bonderman as well.

When we were gathered in the Freshfields office at 2:20 pm, I asked all the lawyers to leave the room, as I wanted to have a private moment with Chandra.

I said to him that HSBC's price was lower and that it was denominated in the wrong currency (dollars as opposed to won), even though just a few days ago he had said HSBC could price it in Korean won. I also told him that we would like to do a deal with HSBC, because of the certainty it would bring, but that as HSBC dragged the negotiations on, its competition had largely removed the uncertainties in its competing offer.

After this conversation, Chandra droppped two unresolved issues related to the severance payments to management and the reference to the possible need for approval from the Public Fund Oversight Committee. But he still insisted HSBC's offer be priced in dollars, not in won. The meeting was adjourned at about 3 pm.

A couple of hours later, Stileman called me. Mervyn Davies wanted to talk with Bonderman to give him a better offer, but he would need an instantaneous response. I sent him an email later to tell him that I thought it was unlikely Bonderman would be able to provide an instantaneous answer unless the offer either gave us complete certainty or was overwhelmingly better than the competition. I also laid out a number of issues that remained open between us. I wrote a memo to Blum and Bonderman to report my meeting with Chandra that afternoon. By the time I got home, it was late, and Bin and the children had already finished dinner.

Bonderman called me that night at about 9:45 pm. I told him about my discussion with Stileman and we got on a conference call with the StanChart people an hour later. On the call Davies said StanChart was prepared to give us a new offer but asked what process we had in mind. Bonderman responded that we would need to make a decision tomorrow, but they could wait for a day to give us the offer. This was to give assurance to StanChart we would not shop its bid. I suggested that we speak again at 10 am Hong Kong time the next day, which would be 2 am London time. It appeared clear that StanChart was prepared to up the ante. This was getting more interesting, I thought, as I went to bed that night.

On Christmas Eve, I got up before 5 am to review the final documents for HSBC. Then I spoke with Bonderman by phone. He was back in Aspen. As it happened, Blum was there for Christmas as well, as was Bond, who also had a home there and had already arrived from London. Blum and Bonderman had set up a meeting with Bond for later that day.

I left for the office at about 7:30 am to attend a KFB board meeting via video conference. The purpose of the meeting was to approve the transition agreements with HSBC and StanChart respectively. We did not know which of the two bidders would win out, so we needed the board to approve both of them. The transition agreements laid out a set of rules to govern how KFB would be managed during the transition period between the signing of final agreements and the formal closing, at which time we would receive payment and no longer have any involvement with the bank. It was uncertain how long that period would be, because any sale of a bank required regulatory approvals, which would take time. However, we expected there would not be any problems obtaining them in view of the qualifications of HSBC and StanChart, both of which were large international financial institutions.

There was one nay vote and one abstention among the directors representing the government. I assumed the reason was to save the need to go back to their respective institutions to ask for approval, since the board meeting was called on short notice. They also knew their votes would not affect the result. Otherwise, the transition agreements were approved, as the rest of the board all voted aye.

Blum and Bonderman called to say that they had met with Bond at his Aspen home. Blum had arrived first, about half an hour earlier than Bonderman, and handed Bond the memo I had written recording my meeting with Chandra and his team the day before. The memo set the record straight that we had honored the exclusivity agreement with HSBC. According to Bonderman, Bond was somewhat unhappy and a little snappy. Even though our co-chairmen extended a goodwill gesture with a personal visit and invited HSBC to give us the best offer it could, they were met with a cold shoulder. Even the cheery Christmas atmosphere in snowy Aspen was not enough to produce a pleasant meeting.

At 10 am, Bonderman and I got on a scheduled conference call with the Standard Chartered team. Those on the call represented the top brass of StanChart: Davies, Sands, and Stileman, plus their board director, Gareth Bullock, and their financial advisors. Bryan Sanderson, StanChart's chairman, was also personally involved in the process, having spoken with Bonderman multiple times, even though he was not on the call. The call began at 2 am in London, where the StanChart people were. I was impressed by their willingness to do the call so early in the morning on Christmas Eve, or so late at night, depending how you look at it.

It seemed that StanChart was pulling out all the stops to win this deal. This stood in sharp contrast with the approach of HSBC, which lacked internal coordination between Bond and his team, not to mention flexibility, and sense of urgency even in the face of an agreed deadline and a fast-moving competitive situation.

Davies started the call by asking how long it would take us to get back to them if they gave us a new offer. Bonderman said two hours, then he offered to let them delay the call for another hour. Bonderman was again signaling that we would not shop their bid. What he wanted to do was to spend the next hour getting HSBC's best offer, so that when StanChart executives gave us theirs, we could do a quick comparison and make a decision. So we agreed to schedule another call with Standard Chartered at 11:25 am, or 3:25 am London time.

At the same time, Blum spoke with Bond again by phone. Bond increased the price by $25 million to $3.075 million, which was not enough to move the needle. In fact, in Korean won terms, it was literally nothing, because one day's appreciation in the won's exchange rate would wipe out this gain entirely.

HSBC had been trying to buy a bank in Korea since 1998. Its team had spent months working on this transaction. Now HSBC was in a preferred position to win. Its team members knew that this was their last chance. Yet they were willing to risk losing the deal at the last minute for less than a rounding error. I was amazed and began to understand why HSBC had not been successful in its acquisition attempts in Korea. It seemed that it was only suited to win if it was the only buyer, with a desperate seller.

The 11:25 am call was brief. Davies requested postponement for another hour, to 1 pm (5 am London time). However, Stileman called back half an hour later to say they were ready. My 21-year-old son, Bo, was home for Christmas. He was studying economics at the University of Chicago and was always interested in investments. I invited him to listen in on the call. I knew this was it—show time—and Bo would probably get a kick out of listening to some top business leaders conclude a multi-billion-dollar deal.

I did not know what StanChart would come up with at this final moment, but I expected it to step up. At such a critical point on such a big deal, nobody was going to throw out a number that did not make a meaningful difference, unless he did not care to win. It appeared that StanChart cared enough.

Standard Chartered, Davies said, would offer 3.4 trillion won for KFB and would remove all remaining conditions to provide certainty that the deal would close. This new offer was about $100 million more than StanChart's last one. We said we would get back to them in an hour and adjourned the meeting.

Bonderman, Blum, and I spoke with Matthew Ginsburg and Jason Shin of Morgan Stanley to debrief them on the offers we had received. Morgan Stanley was still the financial advisor to the Korean government, as it had been at the beginning of our encounter with KFB in 1998. Even though we did not need the government's approval to make a decision, we wanted to consult with them as a matter of courtesy. Jason felt that pricing in Korean won was helpful, and the gap was sufficiently large to tilt the balance in favor of StanChart. However, the government would support the deal either way, as we'd expected.

At about 12:40 pm, I called Stileman to ask him to send me StanChart's draft final offer letter for review, to see if there were any issues we could not agree to. Once it arrived, I reviewed it word by word. Everything seemed to be in order, with the price still blank. When we resumed the call at 1 pm, Bonderman said, "Gentlemen, congratulations. You have won the bid."

Then he complimented them for having "played so skillfully that you didn't leave a penny on the table."

Indeed, if StanChart had not improved its offer in such a meaningful way on our last call, the deal might very well have gone the other way. HSBC had been the preferred bidder all along, from Newbridge's perspective, especially in view of Blum's relationship with Bond. It was preferred by the Korean government as well. StanChart just made us an offer we could not refuse.

Stileman faxed me the executed offer letter. It took me almost 15 minutes and three tries, dialing numbers he had given me, to fax my executed copy back to him. At this point in the deal process, everyone was anxious to see a signature on the dotted line, so the delay was unnerving. I imagined Stileman staring at his fax machine waiting for my document to arrive. Finally, I got through and watched as the last signed page slid through the fax machine. Now I imagined it spooling out the other end, into Stileman's eager hands.

The deal was done. The difference between StanChart's price of 3.4 trillion won and HSBC's price of $3.075 billion was about $175 million at the day's exchange rate. We had gained about $250 million since we began the auction process and stood to gain more if the Korean won continued to strengthen. A competitive process, even a limited one, does wonders for a seller.

If I had been HSBC, I would have done everything possible to deliver an agreement as promised at the expiration of exclusivity, without risking getting into an auction. It would have secured KFB for $250 million less than what we wound up selling for. But HSBC's bureaucracy prevented it from moving quickly and decisively, even though all members of its team were top-rate professionals.

The sale process, however, had been extremely exhausting. Poon, who once again supported me with a careful review of all the legal papers as he had done when we bought the bank, probably slept less than one night in five days. He was so meticulous, and so capable, that I knew he would not miss the slightest error in any of the voluminous documents—even on hardly any sleep.

We held one more conference call, this time with Cohen, the KFB CEO, and Duncan Parker, his COO. Bonderman, Blum, Poon, and I informed Cohen and Parker of what had transpired and that StanChart had won the bid to acquire our bank. I also issued a gag order on the call for all, in deference to StanChart's wishes, until StanChart was ready to announce it.

We had signed the definitive agreement to acquire KFB on December 23, 1999. We signed the legally binding letter to sell it on Christmas

Eve, December 24, 2004, five years and one day later. The concluded deals, buying or selling, were big Christmas gifts for all of us.

★ ★ ★

KFB was a successful investment for Newbridge Capital and its investors. Together, the Korean government and Newbridge had invested 1 trillion won, or less than $900 million, five years earlier. Because the sale was priced in Korean won, which continued its ascent while we were waiting for regulatory approvals, we received about $3.3 billion when the transaction with Standard Chartered Bank finally closed. To show our appreciation of the Korean government and society, after the deal closed, we made a donation of $20 million to charitable organizations in the country (Exhibit 17 and 18).

The only investor that did not make money was SoftBank. It had decided to sell its stake in KFB two years into the investment, possibly because it had not anticipated how long it would take to turn around a bank and did not have the patience or the confidence to wait. SoftBank's stake was bought by Cerberus Capital, another private equity firm, for less than SoftBank had paid. As a result, Cerberus made more money than other investors in the deal or more than SoftBank would have made if SoftBank had stayed in. But that was good for Newbridge Capital, because we received a percentage of an investor's capital gain as our fee, so the more money Cerberus made, the better off we were.

The bank we handed over to StanChart was healthy and strong. We had doubled its assets and made it very profitable. The StanChart team told me that our risk management system at KFB was better than its own. Both the seller and the buyer were happy with the transaction. StanChart eventually changed the name of the bank to Standard Chartered First Bank, relegating the name and the story of Korea First Bank to history.

Epilogue

T he sale on Christmas Eve brought the story of KFB to a happy ending, but it brought little respite to my worries on that day. In fact, the sale of KFB was far from the only project that had kept me busy. We had been working on another major bank deal, with an even higher profile—this time in China, where no private investor, domestic or foreign, had ever controlled a nationwide commercial bank, as we were about to do.

I had received a phone call the previous day, December 23, from Liu Mingkang (Liu being his family name), chairman of the China Banking Regulatory Commission, or CBRC. The subject was Shenzhen Development Bank (SDB), a nationwide commercial bank in China. We had been fighting for the control of this bank for the past 30 months, but we were scheduled to close the deal in about a week.

Liu told me, "We noted the problems you have identified for Shenzhen Development Bank and we have sent a report of these problems to the State Council." The State Council is China's cabinet, headed by the prime minister. The bank's problems were severe enough to warrant attention at the highest levels of government. Then he said, switching to English from Chinese, "Tell your partners that in case of any emergency, like a bank run, the PBOC and CBRC will be on standby, to provide liquidity support."

The PBOC, or the People's Bank of China, is the country's central bank. Liu spoke in English to make sure I would convey his exact message to my American partners. He was trying to give us confidence that China's central bank and the banking regulator would not let SDB fail.

The call was extraordinary. Chairman Liu would not have said this about SDB had he not thought such a risk was real. In 2004, the bank's reported bad loan ratio was 11.4 percent, although the true number, our analysis indicated, was probably about double what was reported. Its capital adequacy ratio stood at 2.3 percent, way below the regulatory minimum of 8 percent. The real capital ratio would have been negative if all the bad loans had been properly provisioned. Technically, the bank was insolvent. If the public became aware of just how weak it was, a run on SDB was not impossible.

But we were planning to take over control of that technically insolvent bank before year-end. Now that we had turned the page on KFB, we had to immediately focus our attention on another troubled bank. SDB was in much worse shape than KFB had been when we had first taken it over. But the market potential in China was so much greater.

Appendix

A Primer
on Commercial Banking

To follow the story of this book, it is useful to be familiar with the basics of commercial banking, or how banks operate. This primer covers the major concepts and terminology of commercial banking. A reader can flip back to this primer as a reference for some key banking concepts and terminologies discussed in the book. For the convenience of the reader, I use italics to highlight the key terms below.

By *banks* mentioned in this primer and elsewhere in the book, I am generally referring to commercial banks, whose business is mainly to collect deposits and make loans. Investment banks are a different type; they generally function, for a fee, as intermediaries between sources and uses of capital, such as when they arrange for a company to sell its stocks or bonds in the public market.

Some banks do both investment and commercial banking; others specialize in one or the other. In the United States, banks used to be able to do both, but they were required to choose one or the other by the Glass-Steagall Act, a law passed in 1933 in the wake of the Great Depression during which thousands of banks had failed. The act prohibited commercial banks from engaging in the investment banking business. For example, the old and venerated JP Morgan, also known as the House of Morgan, was separated into JP Morgan, which became a commercial bank, and Morgan Stanley, which operated as an investment bank. By the time I went to work for JP Morgan in 1993, these laws had been significantly loosened.

The Glass-Steagall Act was largely repealed by 1999, allowing large American banks such as JP Morgan and Citibank to engage in both commercial and investment banking businesses, although traditional investment banks, such as Morgan Stanley and Goldman Sachs, still focus mostly on investment banking. Those that do both commercial and investment banking are often referred to as *universal banks*. In Europe, banks have always been allowed to operate as universal banks, although large institutions, such as HSBC and Standard Chartered Bank, are predominantly commercial banks.

A *commercial bank* receives funding by collecting deposits from customers and by borrowing from the market or from other banks. It has money of its own, which is its *equity capital*, or the money invested in the bank by its shareholders. Some liabilities do not bear interest. Those that do, such as deposits, bonds issued by the bank, or borrowings from other banks, are called *interest-bearing liabilities*.

The average costs a bank pays for the funds it receives are referred to as its *funding costs*, which are usually expressed in percentage terms to compare with the average interest rate of its loans. For example, we can say that a bank's funding cost is 3 percent.

The bank's *assets* include loans made by the bank to its customers, securities it has invested in, and any properties it owns, such as its headquarters or branch offices. The bank generates *income* by charging interest on the loans it makes, receiving fees for services it provides, collecting coupons from the bonds it has bought, and so on. Some assets, such as a branch building or a computer system, do not generate an income in and of themselves. Those assets that do produce an income are referred to as *earning assets*. A stream of income from an asset, such as the interest on a loan, is also referred to as the *yield*. And those earning assets that earn a yield are also known as *yielding assets*.

A bank makes money mostly from the *spread*, which is the difference in interest rates between its lending and its borrowing. For example, a bank may pay 3 percent interest for deposits and charge 5 percent for a loan. The 2 percent difference is the spread, which compensates the bank for the risk it takes by lending money: The bank is obligated to pay back all of its deposits, regardless of whether it is able to collect on all its loans.

A bank incurs *operating costs* by paying its staff, rent, and utility bills. A bank can make money only if its operating income, consisting mostly of interest income and fees minus interest expenses, is greater than its operating costs. The ratio between operating costs and operating income is known as the *cost/income ratio*, which needs to be less than 1 (i.e., costs need to be less than income in order for the bank to earn a profit). If the cost/income ratio is greater than 1, the bank loses money as its operating income does not cover its operating costs.

A bank's net profit divided by its equity capital is its *return on equity*, or *ROE*. The net profit of a bank divided by its total assets is its *return on assets*, or *ROA*. Both ROE and ROA are important measures of a bank's profitability.

A bank cannot make money from a loan if it fails to collect the interest and principal of the loan. If a borrower makes regular interest and principal payments, the loan is considered a *performing loan*. If a customer stops making payments, the loan becomes a *nonperforming loan* or *NPL*. Such a loan is also called a *bad loan*.

A bank classifies its loans on its own books into various categories depending on how confident the bank is that it will be able to recoup its money. These categories have names such as *normal*, *special mention* (or *precautionary*, or *questionable*), *substandard*, *doubtful*, or *loss*. A performing loan is not always classified as normal; a bank may change a loan's classification if it determines that the borrower's ability to repay is impaired (i.e., that there is a risk that the borrower may not be able to pay back all the interest and the principal). In general, banks consider loans classified as substandard or below as impaired. Impaired loans are also called *classified loans* or, more colloquially, *bad loans*.

Normally, a bank lends only to a customer whom it judges to be *creditworthy* or to have the ability to pay back the loan, including its interest and principal, by each of the due dates and by the loan's *maturity*, which is the final date for repayment. There is, of course, always a risk that a loan cannot be recovered, such as when a corporate customer goes bankrupt or when the bank simply misjudges the credit of the borrower. To compensate for such risks or potential losses, the bank typically charges a higher interest rate for riskier customers. Charging different interest rates in accordance with the risk profile of the customer is known as *risk pricing*.

The interest rate that the bank charges its best, or prime, corporate customers is referred to as the *prime rate*. The difference between the interest charged to a customer and the prime rate is the *risk premium*.

Since there is always a risk that some loans will go bad, the bank needs to set aside some money to offset such potential losses. The money put aside is referred to as *provisions* or *reserves*. Larger provisions or reserves are required for riskier loans. For example, the provisioning for a loan classified as substandard may be 20 percent of its principal amount, whereas for a doubtful loan, the provisioning can be 50 percent or more. A loan's remaining unpaid principal amount is referred to as its *book value*, since it refers to how the loan is recorded on the accounting books of the bank. The actual value of a loan may be less than its book value if it is impaired.

The total amount of nonperforming loans divided by the total loan portfolio of the bank is known as the bank's *nonperforming loan ratio*, or *NPL ratio*.

A bank has an obligation to pay back its depositors, no matter if it makes or loses money. Therefore, it must have adequate equity capital in case its assets are not sufficient to cover its borrowings, such as when its NPL ratio is too high or too many of its assets are impaired or written off. The bank's capital as a percentage of its risk-weighted total assets is called its *capital ratio* or *capital adequacy ratio*. There is an international norm for what capital ratio is considered adequate or required for a bank; this capital adequacy requirement is set by the Bank for International Settlements (BIS) in Basel, Switzerland. Therefore, the capital adequacy ratio is also referred to as the *BIS ratio*.

The bank's equity capital is also referred to as its *net asset value (NAV)* or *book value*. The reported book value or reported NAV may or may not reflect how much equity the bank actually has, because the book value may include intangibles. If a bank buys an asset and pays a price higher than the net asset value, then the difference is recorded on the bank's book as *goodwill*, which is an intangible asset. The book value without intangibles is the *tangible book value* or the *tangible net asset value*.

Sometimes a bank under-provisions against its bad loans. In such a case, if the bank is fully provisioned for potential losses, the bank's book value will need to be adjusted down. A buyer of a bank typically wants to make its own determination as to whether there is under-provision, and, if so, the buyer would want to adjust its book value. This new book value becomes the *adjusted book value*. In fact, a buyer also tends to look only at the tangible book value, which, once adjusted, becomes *adjusted tangible book value*, which is the most conservative assessment of the bank's real net asset value.

When a bank's NPL ratio is higher than its capital ratio, it is in danger of going bankrupt: It does not have enough money to pay back all its liabilities. In a financial crisis, when many companies cannot repay their loans, the NPL ratio can shoot up suddenly, causing the bank to fail. This is what was happening to many banks in South Korea during the 1997–1998 Asian Financial Crisis and in America and Europe during the 2008–2009 Global Economic Crisis.

A bank can fail even if it has enough capital but it does not have enough *liquidity*, or cash on hand, to meet demand—such as when customers need to withdraw unexpected amounts of cash, or when the bank needs to pay back its own borrowings. When a large number of depositors rush to withdraw their deposits in a panic because they are worried that the bank may fail, the phenomenon is called a *bank run*. A bank run can drain a bank's available cash, causing it to fail.

In most developed countries, there is a national deposit insurance system to prevent such bank runs: Deposits up to a certain limit are insured by a government-owned insurance company so that even if a bank fails, retail depositors can still get their money back, up to a certain limit, from the government-owned deposit insurance company. Examples include the Federal Deposit Insurance Corporation (FDIC) in the United States and the Korea Deposit Insurance Corporation (KDIC) in Korea. If the deposit insurance company does not have enough funds to pay back the depositors, the government will often use taxpayers' money to make the depositors whole or to bail out the bank, as the government of South Korea did in 1998–1999 and as the U.S. government did in 2008–2009.

Index

317